DEI C.R.E.D.E.N.T.I.A.L

The Top 10 Global DEI Focus Areas for Promoting Progress and Sustaining Systemic Solutions

Jarvis W. Sam III

"DEI is not a feel-good buzzword, it's allyship, it's advocacy, it's activism illuminated. A proverbial battle cry demanding corrective action against systemic barriers that continue to deny us rights, access, and equality. We will not be silenced or settle for crumbs of partial representation while others enjoy delicacies of fullness and complete authority in leadership roles. We will shatter ALL ceilings and cliffs—glass, bamboo, rainbow, or otherwise! We will tear down the walls of discrimination and bigotry to rise up not just as A force, but THE force for change and equity."—Jarvis Sam

Acknowledgments

To my mother Theresia Spearman, who instilled in me the values of equity, justice, freedom, peace, and liberty from an early age. Thank you for showing me the importance of standing up for what is right and for being a constant source of support and guidance throughout my life.

To my siblings Meagan Bradford, Mesuron 'Shawn' Spearman, and Jarvis Sam Jr., thank you for being my constant sources of love, support, and inspiration. Your unwavering support of my work has been a driving force behind my achievements, and I am grateful for the strong bond we share.

To the many teachers and professors who have shaped my education and my worldview, from Foster Elementary, Grady Middle School, Carnegie Vanguard High School, Rice University, Brown University, and IE School of Business - thank you for your dedication to your craft and for imparting your knowledge onto me. Your teachings have been invaluable to my personal and professional growth.

To my colleagues, friends, and professional partners who have inspired and motivated me throughout the years - I am forever grateful for your support and encouragement. Your insights and perspectives have enriched my work and challenged me to strive for excellence.

To all the marginalized, underrepresented, and voiceless individuals, this book is dedicated to YOU. May the words within these pages provide inspiration, hope, and empowerment and help leaders to create a better space for us all. You are not alone, and your voice matters. Together, let us continue to strive for a more just and equitable world!

This book, DEI C.R.E.D.E.N.T.I.A.L, is a testament to the values and principles that I have learned from every one of you. Thank you for your contributions and for helping me to become the person I am today.

Table of Contents

Trigger Warning: This novel contains discussions on race, gender, sexual orientation, disability, nationality, age, and religion. The contents featured therein maybe triggering for some who experience the impact of trauma surrounding various -isms and -phobias tied to these identities on a daily basis.

Introduction

Diversity requires commitment. Achieving the superior performance diversity can produce needs further action—most notably, a commitment to develop a culture of inclusion. People do not just need to be different; they need to be fully involved and feel their voices are heard. –Alain Dehaze

From the #MeToo movement calling out sexual abuse and harassment in workplaces and the #BlackLivesMatter movement striving for social equity and racial justice to the COVID-19 pandemic that upended all spheres of our lives, we have experienced much global social unrest in recent years. The socio-political, economic, and cultural trauma has taken a toll on humans across the globe, but especially on those who are subjected to systemic barriers and discrimination often. Racial and ethnic minorities, women, those living in poverty, LGBTQIA2+ individuals, disabled people, religious minorities, and immigrants around the world have been disproportionately and adversely affected by recent events.

We have observed the impact of underfunded schools, lack of access to adequate healthcare, and rising unemployment rates hindering our socio-economic mobility, equitable access and opportunities, and our sense of belonging and community within and beyond the workplace. As marginalized communities try to heal from the ongoing trauma of social inequality, we continue to witness watershed moments: The overturning of Roe v. Wade and limited access to reproductive rights; the overturning of affirmative action policies and practices in college and university admissions; increasingly graphic instances of police brutality; the rising popularity of white nationalism and supremacy; and political threats to the livelihoods of LGBTQIA2+ individuals, to name only a few examples (Peterson, 2022). The need to empower our communities, dismantle systemic power imbalances, and confront social atrocities tied to discrimination and prejudice in all their forms has been brought to the forefront of social justice conversations.

The landscapes of our households, classrooms, workplaces, and social spaces are changing at a speed we can barely match. But it is imperative that we advocate for the importance of diversity, equity, and inclusion in these spaces to rebuild our communities, educate our youth, and care for the well-being of our people. During the early years of my career, I noticed that there was a lack of Black and/or queer men who resembled me in positions of power and authority. I wasn't alone in this observation: Being Black in America means seldom seeing ourselves reflected in leadership and senior management positions. I spent extensive amounts of energy as well as social and intellectual capital believing the narrative that the only way to succeed was to assimilate into a system that excluded people like me.

As my career progressed, I witnessed something similar in many other individuals from marginalized communities, and I often questioned whether I could amplify and celebrate my Blackness and queerness in the workplace authentically. I've since spent over a decade leading DEI work at major tech, retail, and sports companies, like Snapchat and Nike, as well as being on DEI and strategy teams with Google and Deloitte and throughout of my career, I arrived at the following realization: *Assimilation is a tool of the oppressor to erase the richness of identity and ideology, culture and character, history and heritage of individuals and communities they deem as powerless.* I abjectly refused to assimilate and instead committed to using my positional authority and political capital in these elevated roles to give voice to underrepresented communities around the world and a voice to the issues most relevant to them and their experiences. I became the Black, queer leader my younger self so desperately wanted to see in the world.

Organizations seem to have finally recognized the importance of turning the values of diversity, equity, and inclusion (DEI) into action to incite meaningful change. When we hear the words "diversity," "equity," and "inclusion", our first thought may be about hiring people from a wider array of backgrounds. This is a key aspect of DEI, but there is so much more to it: An organization can only truly thrive if we focus on systemic change and if we integrate and embed DEI into the fabric of the organization. In doing so, the organization will effectively build a diverse workforce and foster a culture of belonging and inclusion, which, in turn, will enable it to create congruent experiences in the marketplace with consumers, business partners, and other organizations. In today's highly competitive and global marketplace, DEI practices and processes play a pivotal role in ensuring the organization's prosperity, external reputation, and long-term sustainability.

As a framework that advocates for the fair and equitable treatment and full participation of all individuals in the workplace, DEI acknowledges the array of differences that exist in the human population. By recognizing the diverse backgrounds and experiences of people, organizations can provide personalized approaches based on needs. When an organization includes DEI in its structure and culture, it also ensures a healthy and productive work environment in which its leaders and employees can perform at optimal levels, experience professional growth and greater job satisfaction, and be further motivated to reach the organization's goals or objectives. Whether you are a CEO, people manager, retail or distribution center employee, or individual contributor, *DEI C.R.E.D.E.N.T.I.A.L* will explore the complexities of DEI frameworks and provide a practical, intersectional lens with which to advance DEI efforts in your workplace or organization.

These components include:

1. **C**ulture of Community and Belonging

2. **R**epresentation and the Contours of Diversity

3. **E**mpathy through Education

4. **D**ecolonization of the Mind and Organization

5. **E**quity as a Means to Achieve Equality

6. **N**eurodiversity and the Practical Benefits

7. **T**eam and Talent Strategies that Work

8. **I**nclusion and Implicit and Unconscious Bias

9. **A**ccountability Driven Through Authenticity

10. **L**ead and Leverage with a Growth Mindset

Each chapter explores the nuances of the C.R.E.D.E.N.T.I.A.L. framework aiming to spark open conversations on DEI and highlight the numerous opportunities DEI can (and will) bring to organizations and their employees. DEI is everybody's job! Yes, DEI begins with the leaders of organizations, but it is an ongoing, highly adaptable process that serves and empowers *all* employees so that they have the resources and opportunities to succeed—regardless of their race or ethnicity, gender, sexuality, gender identity, religion, ability, or age.

Defining Diversity, Equity, and Inclusion

The Four Types of Diversity in the Workplace

In the context of organizations or workplaces, diversity refers to the intentional employment, advancement, and development of a workforce that is composed of individuals with a variety of characteristics, backgrounds, and perspectives, such as race, gender, religion, ethnicity, age, nationality, sexual orientation, and education, to name a few of the countless attributes. There are four types of diversity that are present in workplaces: internal diversity, external diversity, organizational diversity, and worldview diversity. Internal diversity refers to what a person is born into, such as race, ethnicity, national origin, sexual orientation, or physical ability, amongst a host of other characteristics. Many of these factors are included in the Universal Declaration of Human Rights, and as such employers around the world are often obliged to ensure protection from discrimination, prejudice, or bias based on these factors.

External diversity is related to a person's experiences and influences and specifically includes factors that a person is not born into but that impact them, including education level, religion or spirituality, income or socio-economic status, citizenship status, and marital and family status. These factors can change throughout a person's life: For example, an employee can get married, have children, or further their studies while working. An inclusive workplace or organization needs to therefore take these external diversities into account, as an employee may need to take a day off to celebrate a religious holiday or may prefer a remote or virtual working type of employment if they live in a remote area.

Organizational diversity is related to how a diverse workplace can contribute positively to the entire company or organization, and this includes union affiliations, employee benefits, the ability to progress in an organization, department or function, work location, tenure, and management/leadership. For instance, if a certain racial group dominates the senior leadership positions while a marginalized racial group dominates the lower echelons of a company (with minimal chance of upward mobility), the organization or company will lack organizational diversity.

The fourth type of diversity, worldview diversity, refers to how diverse backgrounds and past experiences can inform or shape the worldviews, opinions, and thoughts of employees and leaders in an organization. People's worldviews are often influenced by their lifestyles, cultures and traditions, political beliefs, attitudes, and outlooks on life and work, to name a couple of examples.

Equity vs. Equality

Equity in the workplace goes together with these four types of diversity. Defined as "fair treatment, access, and advancement for each person in an organization," equity also considers the historical and socio-economic factors that impact an individual's experiences and access to opportunities (Pendell, 2022). As such, equity in the workplace focuses on the systems, policies, and processes that help meet the unique needs of employees (and leaders) without providing certain employees with unfair advantages over others. This often includes fairness when it comes to compensation, advancement opportunities, and daily operations or experiences in the organization. Let us look at an example of the importance of equity working together with diversity measures. An organization may have successfully implemented diversity measures and, as a result, have a diverse workforce. Because the organization lacks adequate equity measures and continues to use traditional forms of workplace advancement selection criteria, historically marginalized employees may struggle to be promoted to higher positions.

Over time, the organization may experience a disproportionate congregation of historically marginalized employees in the lower levels of the organization and historically privileged employees occupying the higher echelons of the organization—in turn, undermining the diversity efforts of the organization. Moreover, as evidenced in the example above, an organization's diversity challenges and opportunity areas may actually be an equity issue. Indeed, having a diverse workforce is fantastic, but organizations must ensure that this diversity occurs at all levels of the organization so that the needs and concerns of historically marginalized groups are also represented in senior decision-making positions. Whether the organization makes use of leadership workshops or mentoring sessions, equity policies and measures can strengthen diversity and inclusion in an organization.

The terms "equity" and "equality" are often used interchangeably, but they are two different concepts and philosophies. While "equality" refers to treating everyone the same, "equity" describes the allocation of resources based on need and circumstance. For example, an organization that wants to expand its workforce starts the job recruitment process. The job posting allows anyone to apply, and the candidates are assured that they will be judged on their merits. This is considered equality, as every candidate is treated the same. However, judging candidates based on their perceived merits can pose a few problems. Sure, candidates with a college or university education are considered more qualified than those without, but we also know that college or university admissions decisions and processes can be quite exclusionary, and your organization may inherit the impact of the same biased practices from that space. Or perhaps a candidate has 10 to 20 consecutive years of industry experience and is therefore deemed better qualified for a senior job position. Yet, this type of thinking discounts candidates who have "gaps" in their career—perhaps due to medical issues, maternity, or paternity leave, becoming a stay-at-home parent, or any other personal reasons.

Discrimination often begins long before the selection process and can intentionally or unintentionally inform the parameters of merit. From the schools and colleges the candidates attended to the formal jobs they have worked, or the informal, usually unpaid labor of childcare or eldercare, candidates' merits depend on a myriad of factors that, in many cases, are out of their control. Nonetheless, these factors continue to play a significant role in the hiring practices of countless organizations and can hinder DEI strategies or policies. Simply put, equal access does not necessarily denote an equal playing field, and organizations must work toward transforming their talent practices if they want a diverse workforce and an inclusive, productive organizational culture. A key part of this type of organizational culture is the organization's inclusion policies and approaches.

The Importance of Inclusion

Inclusion in an organization refers to a workplace environment and culture in which its employees feel comfortable around their coworkers and feel confident in their skills and abilities. Here, an inclusive workplace has employees whose needs are being met, whose professional goals are being achieved, and whose skills and abilities are being developed at a comfortable yet realistic pace so that the employees are satisfied with their jobs and are motivated to reach the organization's goals or objectives. Organizations with an inclusive workplace culture can help empower their existing workforce as well as attract and retain a more diverse talent pool. But inclusion goes beyond having a comfortable workplace environment; an inclusive workplace can foster greater engagement (among employees or between the organization and clients) and innovation. For instance, an organization with a diverse workforce and an inclusive culture promotes the sharing of different perspectives and experiences, and, in turn, its employees are more likely to develop new ideas or products.

As stated by Carter-Rogers et al. (2022), in an inclusive workplace culture, "[d]ifferences among individuals are not just identified; they are celebrated and integrated into daily work life... [and they] are also woven into the organization's culture through policies, climate, leadership, and practices." As such, a workplace can only truly be inclusive if diversity, equity, and inclusion are etched into its structures to combat systemic issues and discrimination and to ensure that at all levels, the employees of an organization feel valued, have a sense of belonging, and can work effectively with coworkers who have different experiences, beliefs, values, and perceptions. Here, it is important to note that the organization's leaders (CEOs, managers, supervisors, etc.) are the driving force behind inclusion in the workplace. This is because the organizations have the power and authority to establish and maintain an inclusive workplace culture, adapt to changing workplace norms and cultures, create opportunities for open discussions and conversations on DEI and other workplace matters, and encourage others to be accepting of those with different beliefs or opinions.

DEI in the Modern Workplace

Changing times call for changing workplace practices, norms, and cultures, and DEI strategies and practices are a fantastic place to start. Having or hiring employees from an array of cultures, backgrounds, or nationalities brings new perspectives and fresh talent into the organization, which can lead to better productivity or more efficient problem-solving and decision-making processes. Recent research reveals that diverse work teams experience a 60% improvement in decision-making skills (Lee, 2022). Moreover, diversity policies and commitments in the workplace can lead to a wider talent pool as the most diverse generations in history, the millennial, and Gen Z generations, often look for progressive organizations for which to work. According to a 2020 Glassdoor study, 76% of job seekers claim that a diverse workforce is an important factor when evaluating job offers and organizations. Diverse workplaces also translate into increased profits, and a McKinsey report (Hunt et al., 2015) that covered 366 public companies reveals that the companies in the top quartile for racial and ethnic diversity in management positions were 35% more likely to achieve financial returns higher than their industry average.

Inclusive practices, such as all-inclusive structures, languages, and policies, also have several benefits for organizations, as such practices help foster greater professional relationships among employees, leaders, customers or clients, and business partners, as well as increase individual and organizational performance. Inclusive work environments also boost team morale and can positively influence the personal lives of the employees. Indeed, employees feel more satisfied and loyal to an organization when they perceive their leaders (and the organization as a whole) are interested in their perspectives, thoughts, and ideas. Therefore, inclusion has strategic value, as employees who feel valued, fulfilled, and respected at their jobs are more likely to advocate for their organization or company. For instance, inclusion and a sense of belonging in the workplace allow workers to create meaningful connections with others and improve their self-worth and self-confidence; this sense of belonging is all the more important in our increasingly connected, globalized, and multicultural societies.

Chapter 1:

Culture of Community and

Belonging

It is not our differences that divide us. It is our inability to recognize, accept, and celebrate those differences. –Audre Lorde

Creating a sense of belonging and a culture of community in the workplace plays a vital role in promoting DEI policies, strategies, and initiatives there. For DEI efforts to work systemically and sustainably, we must integrate DEI into our workplace cultures rather than treating it as an afterthought, or a legal & compliance requirement. That is, DEI must be directly linked, aligned, and integrated with company culture, as well as the corporate and HR strategies. Hiring a diverse workforce and including more women leaders and/or leaders of color are steps in the right direction, but this does not automatically lead to greater inclusivity. In fact, hiring underrepresented employees and leaders without structural and cultural change in an organization can end up backfiring, as these employees and leaders may be forced to enter a workplace environment that is hostile toward them or completely ignorant of their perspectives and experiences.

The Impact of DEI on Corporate Culture

Covert racism, microaggressions, and unconscious biases often plague an organization for years or even decades, so it would be wise to avoid not onboarding newly hired employees and leaders, and not acknowledging the adverse effects these forms of discrimination may have on them. Similarly, DEI programs and systemic progress does not just happen overnight but rather must be planned, developed, executed, and managed should an organization aspire to change its culture. These efforts must also be open to new ideas, trends, and methods, as we cannot usher in progressive working norms and environments without considering all of the options available to us. Besides, the DEI tools and methods of the past may be unsuitable for the needs of the present and future. In today's workplaces, employees need more than token gestures of support or emails and LinkedIn messages affirming solidarity or expressing sympathy during periods of tragedy and trauma; they need to see tangible, structural change at all levels of the organization. Here, it is important to remember that not all employees experience the workplace in the same way, and recent Gallup studies reveal that employees of different genders, races, and sexual orientations have significantly different experiences in the workplace.

For example, a recent study by the Gallup Center on Black Voices (Lloyd, 2021) finds that around one in four African American (24%) and Hispanic (24%) employees have reported being discriminated against throughout 2020. The study analyzes data from over 8,000 respondents and reveals that 27% of African American men and 23% of African American women have similar experiences of workplace discrimination. Moreover, younger African American employees (under the age of 40) are twice as likely to report experiences of discrimination in comparison to older African American employees. Similarly, younger Hispanic employees (31%) are twice as likely as their older counterparts to report discrimination in the workplace. The follow-up questions in this study also show that 75% of the African American employees indicated that their experiences of discrimination are based on their race or ethnicity.

These findings further support another poll (Lloyd, 2020) on microaggressions in the workplace. The poll reveals that one in three African American adults (32%) experience other people acting superior to them, while one in four (25%) state that other people have questioned or insulted their intelligence. In some cases, African Americans have reported being treated with less courtesy and respect than others. In addition, many reported coworkers and teammates fearing or acting afraid of them. There is also a gendered aspect to this data, as the Gallup poll also reveals that African American men (27%)

are over twice as likely to have people fear them as African American women (11%). Of course, these various experiences of discrimination and mistreatment are worrisome, but when we contextualize them within the historical background of the US and current national conversations on racism, the findings of these polls are appalling. As evidenced by the numerous police killings of unarmed African Americans, being feared can be a life-or-death situation for Black people in the United States and around the world.

Be it microaggressions or more overt forms of racism, young African American employees who are just starting their careers are more likely to report experiences of workplace discrimination. These experiences not only demonstrate the need for structural change in countless organizations, but they may also have a significant, and perhaps long-term, influence on the trajectories of young African Americans' careers. Young professionals around the world want and need jobs, and we know that organizations are looking to diversify their workforces, but herein lies a disconnect: Organizations must integrate DEI into the fabric of their being if they want to avoid creating a workplace environment where discrimination is the norm. While racism continues to persist in many workplace cultures, many other -isms and -phobias impact cultural amplification for many organizations as well. Many LGBTQIA2+ employees in the US have stated that they do not feel heard, seen, or valued at their workplaces, and as a result, these employees are less likely to perform at optimal levels. Organizations that do little to make their work environments welcoming for LGBTQIA2+ employees suffer in terms of productivity, staff retention, and innovation and force their LGBTQIA2+ employees to constantly filter their language, opinions, and ideas. This is exhausting for organizations and their employees alike.

Recent research into DEI implementation in the workplace has yielded significant results. For example, 78% of employees want to work for organizations that value DEI, as such programs link directly to their sense of job satisfaction and happiness (Wronski, 2021). When employees feel a sense of belonging at their workplace, they are far more productive, efficient and more likely to be retained by the company. This, of course, drives innovation, and organizations with diverse management teams report a total innovation revenue of 45%, while organizations that score low on the diversity scale report a total innovation revenue of only 26% (Lorenzo et al., 2020). These are only a few of the many benefits of developing, implementing, and monitoring DEI at an organization, but for an organization's DEI strategy to be successful, we need to consider the attitudes, perspectives, and opinions of all employees to truly capture the employee experience at all levels of the organization. Besides, it is through the employee experience that organizations can establish an inclusive culture and a sense of community in the workplace.

Strategies for Fostering a Culture of Belonging

Strategy One: Understand the Psychological Impacts of Belonging at Work

Belonging at work has become an increasingly popular topic of discussion among business leaders, HR professionals, and organizations, with it being ranked a top topic on Deloitte's 2020 Global Human Capital Trends survey. Here, 79% of organizations state that they consider a sense of belonging in the workplace as an important part of the organization's success (Achievers Workforce Institute, 2021). Belonging refers to a sense or experience of security, community, and connection in a particular place, and in the context of a workplace, employees who feel a deep sense of belonging at work usually experience higher levels of job satisfaction, better mental health, greater productivity, and lower levels of exhaustion. As such, a sense of belonging in a workplace is not just a "nice-to-have" but rather essential for the well-being of an organization's employees. A sense of belonging is developed due to a myriad of factors, such as being welcomed into organizational culture and community, being understood and celebrated as an individual, feeling included and supported, and being able to develop and maintain healthy workplace relationships with coworkers and leaders.

A sense of belonging not only helps to boost an individual's self-esteem, but it also can improve the individual's sense of self-worth and self-confidence. Many theorists argue that belonging is part of human nature and can be considered a human need. From making friends on the playground and joining social clubs at high school to hosting parties and catching up with friends and family, we see this need for belonging at all stages of an individual's life. Conversely, those who feel like an outsider or pariahs often use their cognitive energy to analyze existing or potential discrimination or obstacles. This leaves very little resources or energy for other important activities, such as learning or social engagement. The social ties that form part of a sense of belonging can help us manage stress, anxiety, and other behavioral issues. For example, someone who is supported and knows that they are not alone is more likely to be resilient and tends to have better-coping mechanisms than those who feel isolated or disconnected. In fact, anxiety, depression, and suicide are mental health conditions that are often associated with a lack of a sense of belonging, as these conditions can hinder an individual's ability to connect with others, creating a cycle that further weakens the individual's sense of belonging.

Claude Steele, a social psychologist, performed the following experiment: In cases where Black college students' race was highlighted, the students performed worse on standardized tests in comparison to white college students, but when their race was not mentioned, they performed on par with or outperformed their white counterparts. This experiment (along with others) demonstrated the negative and harmful effects of an individual being aware that they are being seen through the lens of a stereotype. Here, the possibility of confirming a stereotype can cause anxiety and psychological distress, and as a result, an individual's performance is impaired. This is just one of the many reasons why a sense of belonging must go together with DEI commitments. Indeed, creating a sense of belonging in the workplace is important for all employees, but it is especially relevant for employees who are part of a marginalized population.

When employees feel as though they do not belong at their workplace, they may also feel insecure about their work or their value to the organization, and subsequently, they may underperform or be less willing to collaborate with or engage with others. On the other hand, employees who feel a sense of belonging at their work often look forward to going to work, are more likely to remain at their organization for years and are more willing to collaborate with others. So, how can an organization tell if someone belongs in the workplace? Firstly, organizations must have access to reliable, qualitative, and quantitative employee experience data and feedback. This data can be gathered through surveys, individual check-in sessions, team meetings, or anonymous communication channels. Confidential communication channels and/or surveys often ensure that employees are honest and open in their feedback. Secondly, organizations must ensure that their leaders understand the importance of belonging in the workplace, as, in many cases, the onus is on them to maintain a healthy and productive work environment.

Thirdly, and most significantly, organizations must establish a workplace environment that encourages the formation of social bonds. For instance, having designated break rooms or spaces where employees can take a break from their screens and chat with their coworkers can increase a sense of belonging among the employees. In another example, office spaces or working stations can be transformed or restructured to promote social interactions, or remote teams can have regular in-person meetings to create or strengthen social bonds. Even something as simple as asking for input or ideas via a shared document or hosting brainstorming sessions where each employee has the chance to share their ideas can help foster social bonding and, therefore, a sense of belonging. A sense of belonging is important in any organization, but it must also be supported by DEI commitments and progressive programs to ensure that those who have been marginalized (as a result of their race, gender, nationality, or sexuality), too, feel welcome and safe at their jobs.

Why "Cultural Fit" Is Not the Solution

A significant barrier to a sense of belonging in the workplace is the prioritization of cultural 'fit' over cultural diversity and cultural enhancement. Cultural fit refers to "the concept of screening potential candidates to determine what type of cultural impact they would have on the organization," and it is based on "the alignment of values, beliefs, and behaviors between the employee and employer" (Lee, 2022). The idea of "cultural fit" dates to the 1980s, and it highlights the importance of organizations hiring individuals whose personalities mesh well with the organization's strategy and goals. However, cultural fit also implies that the candidates must conform to the organization's workplace norms and culture to have a better chance of being hired and promoted. If the candidates-turned-employees are pressured to assimilate into the existing corporate culture and to think and work in a similar way to their coworkers and leaders, then the organization is not truly diversifying its workforce and will not have much room for innovation. Employees should feel a sense of belonging in the workplace, and this should not come at the expense of the employees' unique ideas, perspectives, and experiences.

Hiring based on cultural fit achieves only surface-level diversity and can encourage implicit or unconscious bias and groupthink. Miles (2022) explains that having a team that gets along well is having a "team that doesn't question its assumptions or bring in challenging perspectives," and including cultural fit in the hiring process can cause team members to "become invested in their fit, encouraging conformity and consensus." The recruiters and hiring managers enter the process with a preconceived idea of what the "ideal candidate" should be, and this may cloud their judgment and sway their opinions on certain candidates. Plus, there is no guarantee that such candidates will meet the organization's expectations once they have been hired. Hiring managers may select candidates based on their personalities rather than their skills, work ethic, and experience, and some candidates (who know that they are not a cultural 'fit') may even change their behavior, values, and goals during the interview process to portray themselves as a cultural fit for the organization. Moreover, employees who are not a cultural fit may struggle to 'fit in' or assimilate into organizations where almost all employees think and work the same. Without a sense of belonging and community, these employees are likely to leave the organization, hindering employee retention and performance in the organization, which can come at an estimated replacement cost ranging from 90%-200% according to SHRM.

This is particularly important for small to mid-size companies and startup organizations who may still be actively defining certain elements of the values and culture of the company. With each new hire class and even new leader in some cases, the culture of the org may shift.

Strategy Two: Obsess the Employee Experience at all Times

As the term suggests, the "employee experience" is the journey or trajectory an employee takes with a company or business and focuses on how the employee interacts, behaves, and engages their workplace and colleagues. This includes the daily operations of an organization, all of an employee's interactions with coworkers, leaders, and customers, major career milestones or achieving professional goals, the skills learned or gained in the workplace, and the physical work environment. As such, the employee experience is inextricably linked to how the employee feels about the company's purpose, brand, and overall culture and is a vital part of ensuring an inclusive culture and community within organizations. In essence, when an organization's employees feel valued, they are less likely to be absent from work, their productivity increases, and they are more likely to report greater job satisfaction. The employee experience also has a direct impact on the employee's decision to remain at their jobs and continually develop their skills and recommend the organization to other highly talented or skilled individuals. As a result, the organization can attract and acquire skilled workers to add to their workforce while also retaining employees who are eager to grow professionally. So, let us look at how organizations can improve their employee experience so that they may thrive in the global marketplace.

Connecting the Employee Experience to a Purpose

Creating and maintaining a healthy and productive work environment and culture is key, and this entails aligning the employee experience with the goals, purpose, or orientation of the organization. Whether the organization's goals are product-centric or customer-centric, every organization should have a few clearly outlined goals or objectives that they can link to the employee experience. That is, employees need to be motivated to work toward reaching the organization's goals, and this can only be achieved when such goals are realistic and clear. Connecting the employee experience to a higher purpose shows the employees that they are making a difference (be it in the organization or broader society), and consequently, the employees will be more open to trying new things, motivated to build on their expertise, and more committed to the organization.

Connect Employee Satisfaction to DEI Goals

While employees have a financial incentive to perform at optimal levels in the workplace, organizations need to acknowledge that there are alternative ways to ensure job satisfaction and, therefore, improve the employee experience. For example, organizations can implement flexible work environments and hours that allow their employees to determine their own schedules. This is especially important for employees who have children and for those with disabilities and/or chronic illnesses. Another way an organization can ensure employee satisfaction is by creating employee benefit programs that are linked to its DEI efforts. As the demographics of modern workplaces change, traditional employee benefits, too, need to change. Employee benefits programs need to become more equitable, as employees who face financial, social, or physical limitations may struggle to take advantage of such programs. As explained by Stille & Simon (2022), employee benefits "are most often underutilized by people who lack the education or time to participate, due to competing work-life demands or a lack of resources," and cultural differences and language barriers, too, can be disincentives.

For example, racial or gender bias in the healthcare system and a lack of access to quality healthcare can adversely affect an employee's well-being. According to the Stepping Up for Equality Report (Jeffries et al., 2022) by Mercer, most companies in the US are unaware of how their employee benefits impact their Black employees; for example, 85% of employers do not track the use of health benefits by race or ethnicity, while only 10% have implemented equity initiatives for their health-related employee benefits. The 2018 Census Bureau's American Community Survey (cited in Bittker, 2020) found that with employer-sponsored health insurance covering 66% of white employees, 46% of Black employees, 41% of Hispanic and Latino employees, and 36% of American Indian and Alaska Native employees, poor health is often directly linked to American employees' employment. Moreover, Black employees are 10% less likely to have employer-sponsored health insurance in comparison to their white counterparts—making the limited access to and disparities in health benefits for employees along racial and ethnic lines all the more insidious and dangerous.

Consequently, Black employees may choose short-term treatments that do not require follow-up appointments and may delay or completely avoid getting medical help in fear of future medical bills. These disparities along racial lines are exacerbated by the fact that there are correlations between ongoing acts of discrimination and increased rates of illness in the African American community. As stated by Bittker (2020), the "expectation of racist encounters, in addition to actual lived experiences, causes biological reactions—rapid heart rate and the increased flow of stress hormones—that resemble other stress reactions," and over time, "they accumulate and contribute to health problems that might otherwise have been less severe or completely avoided." However, employee benefits programs that are cognizant of such biases and lack of access to resources can bolster an organization's DEI efforts while also ensuring the health and well-being of its employees.

To approach employee benefits through a DEI lens, the leaders of an organization must ask the following questions:

- Why are certain benefits being underutilized, and how can the organization combat this?

- Where is the organization lacking in terms of its employee benefit programs?

- Is there a difference between scheduled work hours and actual work hours?

- What is the link between higher healthcare needs and employee absenteeism?

- What are the key reasons for the lack of productivity in the workplace?

- Are the organization's employee benefits truly beneficial for marginalized groups, including women, people of color, people with disabilities, and LGBTQIA2+ people, to name a few examples?

- What drives employee participation and work performance, and are these factors linked to employee benefits?

These are only a few of the many questions the leaders of an organization need to ask themselves as the lens of DEI helps inform the organization's employee benefits programs and strategies. These questions also help an organization determine why pre-existing employee benefits are being underutilized and identify the links between this underutilization and the demographics of the workforce.

Establish Open Communication in the Workplace

When a workplace environment encourages its employees to share their thoughts, ideas, perspectives, and even doubts, the employees will feel more connected to their professional goals and their organization's goals. A healthy workplace environment also helps foster more meaningful engagement and psychological safety among employees (and their leaders), and, in turn, employees may be more willing to communicate any workplace struggles with their manager or supervisor. This is all the more relevant in cases where employees report any form of discrimination or harassment in the workplace. According to a recent Forbes report (Schmidt, 2022), 55% of employees have experienced discrimination at their current workplace, yet of those who reported discrimination, just over half saw these issues being fully resolved. Organizations often rely on their employees to alert them to instances of discrimination or any issues that negatively affect employee experience, but employees also need their leaders to address discrimination or such issues. Should an organization lack adequate processes to address discrimination, and should the leaders refuse to take the initiative, employees will be less likely to report discrimination. This may eventually lead to employees leaving workplaces where their reports of discrimination are not addressed.

Whether an organization improves or streamlines its human resources processes, establishes chat forums, or runs monthly campaigns, internal communication must build trust, promote transparency, and foster collaboration in the workplace. Such initiatives can (and should) also involve the organization's employees, and, here, the organization's leaders can ask their employees for their feedback on the discrimination reporting processes, invite them to strategy and planning meetings, or create anonymous channels for communication. Recent research shows that employees provide honest feedback when there are confidential communication channels in the organization, and consequently, reports of discrimination can be collected, tracked, and resolved efficiently. This provides employees with the opportunity to discuss their concerns as well as demonstrates the organization's commitment to addressing discrimination.

A key aspect of reporting discrimination includes educating employees on what discrimination is and how to recognize it. In many cases, employees do not report instances of discrimination as they may believe that what they experienced was not "a big deal" or "not as bad" as other forms of discrimination. This is evident in cases of less overt discrimination, such as microaggressions and casual racism or sexism, as employees may try to minimize their experiences. Moreover, employees may not be aware of feedback or reporting processes, and it is the responsibility of the organization and its leaders to consistently mention the tools or processes available to employees should an issue arise. In doing so, employees will know how to communicate their feedback and report instances of discrimination without having to frantically search for resources.

Invest in Employee Well-Being and Growth

It is easy to get caught up in the nine-to-five normalcy, so it is all the more important to shine a light on employees' personal and professional well-being and growth. Recognizing milestones, great teamwork, and individual successes are some of the many ways to boost employee and team morale in an organization. Whether the organization and its leaders publicly celebrate employees' achievements, or they award promotions or new roles to hard-working employees, an organization must help their employees' career progress. Otherwise, employees may feel unsatisfied or stunted in their careers and may pursue their professional goals elsewhere. Investing in employee well-being and growth entails providing mentoring or coaching sessions, skills development workshops, one-on-one sessions between a leader and their employee, or casual check-ins with employees. Employee well-being, however, goes beyond such initiatives and may also entail changes in organizational cultures and working norms. For example, allowing hybrid or partially remote working options can help foster a healthy work-life balance among employees; hosting mental health sessions for employees can help an organization identify the causes of stress and burnout; and staff surveys and voluntary feedback sessions all help to strengthen the well-being of a workforce.

Understand How Employees and Candidates Perceive Corporate Culture

How which employees interact with each other can significantly affect the organization's "corporate culture"—a term that refers to the lasting and tangible impression an organization leaves on past, current, and future employees. Corporate culture is the emotional environment of the workplace and defines the professional relationships among leaders, employees, and clients or customers.

When we think about an organization's corporate culture, we need to ask ourselves the following questions:

- Are there any social cliques?

- Are gossip and miscommunication a norm in the organization?

- Do any employees express aggressive or passive-aggressive behavior toward others?

- Are the organization's leaders dictatorial in their leadership style?

- Do the leaders demonstrate biased behavior and employee favoritism?

- Is there an excess of employee complaints and/or absenteeism?

- Do the employees experience exhaustion and/or burnout?

- Do the employees experience and/or report overwhelming or unrealistic workloads and deadlines?

- What impression does the organization leave on its employees?

These are some of the salient questions that organizations and their leaders need to consistently reflect on to ensure that the company culture is healthy, transparent, and productive for all employees. Social cliques, idle chit-chat, and some tension is expected in any given workplace (and arguably, this type of behavior is part of human nature), but problems arise when these cliques, conversations, and tensions escalate and negatively affect the professional and/or personal well-being of an organization's employees. In this case, the organization and its leaders must address such escalations, hostilities, or issues in the workplace without further contributing to these concerns.

Strategy Three: Prioritize Community Over Competition

Here is the thing about competition in the workplace: It can sometimes be healthy and lead to high productivity, but it can also turn toxic if not kept in check. Some organizations create a cutthroat culture that pits employees against each other, while others focus more on creating a cooperative and collaborative workplace culture. So, what is the right way? Well, some believe that workplace competition can drive productivity and excellence and can even increase employee motivation and engagement. In addition, workplace competition can also ignite innovation and creativity among employees who struggle with self-doubt and self-confidence. For instance, an organization's leaders can split employees into teams and provide an incentive for the team that can create a new product, lead a successful marketing campaign, or increase their department's sales. Paradoxically, this healthy competition not only spurs innovation but can also boost teamwork efforts and morale as the employees are extra motivated to perform well. Besides, in many modern workplaces, employees often perform better when they feel challenged by their work.

Nevertheless, even healthy competition can have adverse effects on an organization's employees, as some may struggle to adapt to working in a team and, as a result, may become disengaged in the competition and/or their usual work. The impact of workplace competition, therefore, largely depends on the individual employees and their personalities; some rise to the challenge and see the competition as a fun way to do their jobs, while others may prefer to work alone and without the pressure of competition. If competition is the only or main form of employee motivation, the organization and its employees may suffer in the long run, as constant competition may create a toxic workplace environment, decrease teamwork efforts and morale, or reduce work performance and productivity. Albeit unintentionally, workplace competition may also bring employee differences to the surface. Perhaps newer hires will feel that they are at a disadvantage against more established employees, or some employees may not have the same qualifications or specific skills as others and, as a result, may feel that the competition is unfair.

Workplace competition also sets unrealistic expectations for employees, especially in organizations with a large workforce. It is easy to set goals among a workforce of 10 to twenty employees, but in a workforce of hundreds or thousands of employees, it may be near impossible for these goals to be realistic or reasonable. In some cases, this can even lead to cheating, which is especially relevant when the employees' livelihoods depend on reaching specific goals or targets. As explained by Dublino (2022), competition "creates a sense of fear that can derail your workplace—introducing a need for employees to hurt each other instead of fostering collaboration and joint problem-solving." Here, employees are extra motivated to "win" because their financial security is at risk, and some may resort to acting unethically, lying about results, or sabotaging others. In short order, this can turn a healthy workplace culture into one that is toxic and hostile.

Healthy workplace competition also requires a strong level of trust and fairness between leaders and their employees. Employees need to trust that their hard work will be rewarded and that they will not be unfairly compared to employees with vastly different levels of skills and experience. Ensuring fair and transparent competition is incredibly challenging in transnational organizations with a large workforce, so the leaders may be forced to work even harder to manage or supervise workplace competition. Workplace competition cannot be truly fair in a diverse workforce, as some employees, by their varying backgrounds, experiences, perspectives, and beliefs, may still have unfair advantages over others. If an organization wishes to strengthen the cooperation among employees, workplace competition may need to focus more on team building than on meeting specific goals or targets. If not, workplace competition can adversely affect the employees' sense of belonging in the organization and workplace environment.

Strategy Four: Invest in Gen Z as part of Future of Work Strategies

As the most diverse generation in the US, Generation Z (Gen Z), or Zoomers, have recently entered the workplace, and it is estimated that 60 million Gen Z members will follow suit. This influx of Gen Z employees into the workforce, however, comes with several terms and conditions. Gen Z (those who were born after 1996) is the first generation of digital natives, as they have been raised with smart devices, the internet, and social media platforms at their disposal. As such, they are generally considered to be tech-savvy, educated (their university and college enrollment rates are higher than those of previous generations), and more socially conscious (thanks to social media, which makes news and current affairs incredibly accessible). So how does this play out in the workplace? Since they are a far more diverse generation, Gen Z considers DEI programs and initiatives as a workplace necessity—to the extent that a lack of DEI in the workplace can be a dealbreaker when they apply for jobs or when it comes to retention.

A Tallo (2020) survey, for instance, reveals the following: One-third of the respondents will choose not to apply for a job because they fear discrimination, while 69% of the respondents state that they are more likely to apply for a job at a company whose marketing and branding reflect a more diverse workforce. For Gen Z, diversity extends beyond race and ethnicity to also encompass gender identity and fluidity of expression, and here, 88% of the Gen Z respondents stated that it is important for employers to ask them their gender pronouns. Moreover, Gen Z values authenticity, ethics, and activism in addition to financial security, and a 2018 poll by Deloitte and NEW reveals that 77% of the Gen Z respondents believe that it is important to work for a company or organization with values that are closely aligned with their own. Besides, Gen Z was raised in the digital information age and had a well-developed sense of whether a company or organization is being ethical, transparent, and authentic. And they also have the tools and confidence to call out the organizations they deem unethical or problematic.

Green (2021) explains that the digital world has "shaped Zoomers' ideas about access to key leaders, flattening hierarchies, and heightening communications expectations," and should organizations want to retain their younger employees, they should empower their Gen Z employees by motivating them to pursue their activism in addition to their professional careers. Whether this entails volunteer work or outreach programs, organizations must demonstrate their commitment to ethics and activism, as Gen Z employees often have a broader and more action-oriented view. Another key aspect of improving the employee experience for a Gen Z workforce is the organization's openness to new technology. Many Gen Zers consider the technology offered by an employer or organization to directly influence their job choices. This does not necessarily mean that all work communication and engagements must be online, but rather, organizations should have a hybrid approach to communication. Indeed, employees (no matter their generation) still value in-person communication and engagements to build trust with others. Green (2021) goes on to state that Gen Z's appetite for in-person engagement helps "forge bonds and understanding between team members across ages, especially if companies encourage the types of mentoring opportunities that Gen Z craves."

Generation Z also prioritizes a more flexible and balanced employee experience, and as seen during the COVID-19 pandemic, remote or hybrid work options can work wonders when it comes to employee health and well-being. Gone are the days when all employees must sit at their desks between 9 a.m. and 5 p.m., and nowadays, many employees still have the option to work from the comfort of their homes. However, as tech-savvy as they are, many Gen Zers still crave physical office spaces as long as they can find a balance between their work and the rest of their lives. The Zoomer generation is independent by nature and desires a more customized employee experience; therefore, they are more likely to choose jobs that allow them to maintain a good quality of life. Simply put, Gen Z employees want to excel at their jobs, but they also need the time to further their education, do volunteer work, care for their dependents (be it children or pets), socialize with friends, and enjoy what life has to offer.

Creating a culture of community in the workplace does not mean that all employees have to agree on certain ideas, issues, and projects, nor does it suggest that all employees think and behave in the same (or similar) way. Instead, "community" in the workplace describes increased collaborations, positive interactions, and meaningful connections among employees. Of course, there are business benefits to such a culture in the workplace, such as increasing innovation and profits and boosting employee well-being and job satisfaction. Indeed, the community is a pivotal part of DEI efforts as it enables all the leaders, employees, business partners, and other stakeholders to work toward achieving the organization's objectives and securing the organization's place in a global, competitive market.

Chapter 2:

Representation and the Contours

of Diversity

Representation is a crucial location of struggle for any exploited and oppressed people asserting subjectivity and decolonization of the mind. –bell Hooks

Many of us grew up watching films or TV series with characters that looked nothing like us. The protagonists that graced our screens usually had light hair and light skin, while the villainous characters often had the opposite—dark hair and, in many cases, dark skin. Even kid's movies such as Disney's *Aladdin* (1992) and *Peter Pan* (1953) have rather problematic, reductive depictions of their characters of color. These negative representations followed us into adulthood, with the white-savior trope in full force in films like *The Blind Side* (2009), *The Help (2011)*, and *Avatar* (2009) or the blatant misogyny and underdevelopment of female characters in so many of Hollywood's action and superhero films. This isn't to bash these films, but what I'm demonstrating is the normalization of a lack of representation or problematic misrepresentations that we are exposed to in the media. But these representation issues extend beyond the silver screen and are interwoven into the fabric of global society. From the histories left out of our school curricula to the lack of women—and more specifically, women of color—in senior leadership or decision-making roles in the corporate sector, we are surrounded by a lack of adequate representation and/or an overabundance of misrepresentation.

Sure, seeing more women, queer individuals, people with disabilities, and racial minorities in political, business, and community leadership is fantastic and a step in the right direction. We also need to look at the lack of adequate representation as a systemic issue that cannot be solved simply by a few marginalized people rising the ranks in their industries. Instead, we need to see the transformation at a structural level so that the representation of marginalized people in all types of leadership truly reflects our country's demographics. That is, the representation of marginalized people must be the norm rather than the exception to the rule. Representation does not only serve as a major tool of DEI programs, but it is also a means for minorities or marginalized people to find support and validation. Having Black women lead on screen and in the writer's room, as in the case of Issa Rae's *Insecure* (2015–2021) and Quinta Brunson's *Abbott Elementary* (2021-), or epitomizing Black excellence in sports and television, as in the case of Serena Williams, Gayle King, Sheryl Swoopes, Sheryl Lee Ralph, Viola Davis, and Sanya Richards-Ross, paves the way for Black girls and young adults to know that they, too, can aspire to greatness.

Why Representation Matters

Increased representation also has the potential to undermine negative stereotypes about people of color, women, people with disabilities, immigrants, and LGBTQIA2+ people. Some theorists and researchers argue that those who have increased exposure to or contact with people who are different from them are less likely to maintain their prejudice or continue believing in negative stereotypes. For example, positive media representation of LGBTQIA2+ people has helped change public opinion about this group, and data from the Pew Research Center (Poushter & Kent, 2020) supports this. In 2004, 60% of the American population opposed same-sex marriage, but in 2019, around 61% were reported to be in favor of same-sex marriage. Sarah Kate Ellis, and the incredible team at GLAAD, along with increased visibility by network and streaming services has greatly contributed to this progress. Of course, there are a myriad of factors that have contributed to this change in attitude and perspective, but we cannot deny the immense influence the media can have in shaping public opinion. Recent Asian American visibility in the media, such as in Crazy Rich Asians (2018), Mindy Kaling's Never Have I Ever (2020), Everything Everywhere All at Once (2022), and other amazing projects from production companies like Gold House also demonstrates the importance of creators of color writing their own storylines and, in turn, increasing the representation of communities of color.

However, increased positive representation is not the final goal but rather an important step toward equity, and as explained by Nadal (2021), being the "first" at anything "is pointless if there aren't efforts to address the systemic obstacles that prevent people from certain groups from succeeding in the first place." The representation must be intentional, and those in leadership positions should strive to reflect the demographics of their audiences or society in their organizations. Such conscious efforts strengthen the diversity of the workforce and remind others that we, as marginalized people, not only exist but are here to stay and prosper. Leaders, such as educators, community organizers, politicians, managers, and CEOs, must understand the importance of representation and know how to effectively implement practices, processes, and programs that aim to increase representation within the organization, within the consumer base or audience, and in marketing and advertising decisions.

Creating a dissonance between the advertising of your product and your consumer base is a surefire way to cause controversy. In 2017, for instance, skincare company Shea Moisture had to quickly deliver an apology for an advertising campaign that fell flat with its main consumer base. As part of their #EverybodyGetsLove campaign, Shea Moisture released a 60-second video that featured various women discussing how the company's products delivered them from their "hair hate." Shea Moisture is known for celebrating its major consumer base, Black women, so many were surprised to see only one Black woman model featured among the blonde and redhead models. At best, some audiences found this video to be awkward and confusing, but many viewed the campaign as an erasure of Shea Moisture's loyal consumer base. Indeed, Black women consumers have supported the company from the very beginning. The advertisement was not a simple oversight or misstep, but instead, it whitewashed the politics of Black hair, as Black women are disproportionately discriminated against as a result of Eurocentric beauty and hair standards in the US. The advertisement could have sparked important conversations on "hair hate" in a country where hair can get Black people fired from their jobs, but it ended up missing the mark and isolating many of its consumers.

Intersectionality in Practice

Before we look at representation in the workplace, we must first explore the concept of intersectionality. Coined by civil rights activist and feminist scholar Kimberlé Crenshaw in 1989, the term "intersectionality" refers to an analytical framework that seeks to understand how an individual's political and social identities combine or overlap to create different modes of advantage and disadvantage. That is, factors such as race, ethnicity, class, gender, religion, sexuality, and disability can intersect to empower or oppress individuals. Intersectionality is often used in the context of feminism as it seeks to include those who were left out of the first and second-wave feminist movements in the West. Indeed, the early feminist movements mainly focused on the experiences of white, middle-class, and cisgender women in the Western world and glossed over the fact that women can have different identities and experiences. For example, intersectionality takes into account that the experiences of white women will undoubtedly differ from the experiences of Black women, as the latter group is often subjected to both racist and sexist discrimination. If we take this example a step further, the experiences of queer Black women will also be different from those of heterosexual Black women and even from those of queer white women.

While the above examples focus on how individuals can be oppressed as a result of overlapping social and political identities, intersectionality also describes how such identities can also empower individuals. In patriarchal societies, men are placed at the apex of social hierarchies, but owing to systemic racism, white men occupy this position while men of color remain below them (yet still above women of color). This is not to say that there are rigid hierarchies when it comes to oppression (disadvantage) and privilege (advantage), but rather, individuals can experience oppression and privilege depending on their socio-political identities. So, how does intersectionality translate to workplace contexts? Well, employees who belong to two or more marginalized or underrepresented identities experience workplace discrimination and a lack of opportunities in unique ways. If we take the wage gap in the US as an example, white women earn 81 cents for every dollar a white man earns, while women of color, including Black

(58% of what non-Hispanic white men earn), Native American (51% of what non-Hispanic white men earn), and Hispanic women (54% of what non-Hispanic white men earn). As such, women of color in the US do not experience only a gender pay gap but also a race pay gap (Bagalini, 2020).

Moreover, intersectionality also affects hiring practices and professional development. For instance, people with disabilities (and especially those from other marginalized groups) are disproportionately represented when it comes to employment. In the US, 28.6% of disabled African Americans were employed in comparison to 73.7% of employed, able-bodied African Americans (Tapp, 2019). In terms of professional development, Black women have fewer opportunities to advance in their professional careers in comparison to white women. Recent research demonstrates that Black women employees have less access to training and skills development sessions, and they receive less sponsorship and mentorship. Another consequence of overlapping marginalized identities can be seen in sexual harassment cases in the workplace. Queer women with disabilities have reported higher levels of sexual harassment in the workplace, and Black women, too, are more likely to be subjected to workplace sexual harassment in comparison to their white counterparts (Cassino & Besen-Cassino, 2019).

With this in mind, it is essential that organizations view DEI through an intersectional lens. As stated by Bagalini (2020), organizations must "collect and analyze data on pay and employee engagement, separating variables of race, gender, sexual orientation, or physical ability" to ensure that no one is excluded, and that unconscious bias can be eradicated in the workplace. Indeed, organizations can employ a gender-diverse workforce, but if they exclude people with disabilities or LGBTQIA2+ people from this workforce, their DEI efforts need of evaluation and, hopefully, transformation. In addition, intersectionality needs to be addressed from the top: CEOs, senior executives, and other leaders must recognize and remedy their unconscious (or conscious) biases to ensure that the organization's DEI efforts truly benefit the employees.

How Representation Moves Societies Forward

The Impact of Representation on Child Development

For many of us, our first taste of the lack of adequate diversity, equity, and inclusion was in the classroom, and, disappointingly but not surprisingly, not much has changed. In 2021, it was reported that around half of the students in K–12 public schools are of color, yet only one in five school principals identify as people of color. Moreover, 11% of school principals are Black, and a mere 9% are Hispanic, and this reveals that school leaders (teachers and principals alike) do not actually reflect the racial and cultural diversity of their classrooms, schools, and broader communities (National Center for Education Statistics, 2022). This has been termed the "representation gap" in school leadership, but it also exists across institutions and industries. Because students of color are fueled by representation (that is, seeing themselves in their teachers and other leaders), a lack of adequate DEI in education tells young students that leaders do not look like them. Instead, it tells them that they should place their aspirations elsewhere or change their view of success.

Recent research shows that students of color thrive when they are taught and led by teachers and principals of color. For instance, a study by Grissom et al. (2017) at Vanderbilt University reveals that Black and Hispanic students have increased representation in gifted programs when they attend schools that are led by principals who share the same racial identity as them. Principals of color, too, establish more sustainable and supportive school cultures for their teachers, and this type of leadership has also been found to be beneficial for white students. While the majority of public school teachers are women (76%), only 20% are people of color, and in terms of intersections between race and gender, only 2% of public school teachers are Black and male (Whitfield, 2019). Such statistics are worrisome, as research shows that Black elementary school teachers can have a lasting influence on their students; their Black students are less likely to drop out of high school and are more likely to attend college or university. A study by John Hopkins University found that Black students are 13%

more likely to attend college if they had at least one Black teacher in elementary school. If the students had at least two Black teachers, they were 32% more likely to attend college.

Here, the students see themselves as their role models and witness their teachers and principals challenge stereotypes and create a culture of inclusivity and respect in the school environment. Such an environment is all the more important for students of color and those from lower-income households. While representation alone may not challenge the larger systemic inequities in education, it can help all students thrive in the classroom. Indeed, with greater representation of teachers of color, schools can create and maintain an inclusive environment for staff, parents, and students, provide their students with culturally relevant curricula, equitably distribute resources, and uplift teachers and students from historically marginalized groups. The lack of adequate DEI strategy and structure in public schools is also seen in other sectors of American society, including the business or corporate sector. While the corporate sector operates differently from school institutions, we need to place greater importance on learning and education in our organizations so that we may be better informed about not just the world around us but also how history, sociology, and anthropology inform our organizations.

Representation in the Workplace

Representation in the workplace refers to having employees and leaders of various races, genders, ages, religions, ethnicities, nationalities, and sexualities, and it is especially important in senior leadership and decision-making positions where marginalized groups are severely underrepresented (or even non-existent). By having greater representation in their higher echelons, organizations demonstrate that they value diversity and inclusion.

But representation is still lagging in C-suite positions, and current data on the Fortune 500 and S&P 500 companies reveals the following (Kurt, 2021):

- While the representation of women in CEO and CFO positions is at its highest level in history, only 6.9% of companies have women CEOs, and 15.1% have women CFOs.

- Women run 41 companies on the Fortune 500 list, yet there are only two Black women among this group.

- 73 CFO positions (11%) are held by people of color, but the number of Hispanic and Latino CEOs decreased from 23 to 20 over the course of a year (from 2020 to 2021).

- In 2021, 40 CEOs were Asian American, while six were Black. Interestingly, the number of Asian American and Hispanic and Latino CEOs has significantly increased since 2004, yet the number of Black CEOs has remained between four and seven for the past 18 years.

In terms of boardroom diversity and representation, a 2021 report by leadership consulting firm Spencer Stuart focuses on 493 companies of the S&P 500:

- 21% of directors from all S&P 500 companies were from the following racial and ethnic groups: Black, Hispanic and Latino, Native American, Asian American, multiracial, or Alaska Native.

- 30% of directors and 43% of new directors were women.

- 47% of new directors are from historically marginalized racial or ethnic groups, with 33% of new independent directors being Black.

So, what do all of these statistics mean? Firstly, the rise of the Black Lives Matter movement urged organizations to boost their DEI investments, yet racial and ethnic minorities and women are still underrepresented in leadership positions. There have been several attempts across all industries to increase representation, and while some racial and ethnic minorities and women were appointed to higher positions, most organizations lack a strong enough pipeline to deliver these groups to executive and leadership positions. Or this underrepresentation may be a result of biased hiring and promotion practices, organizations struggling to retain marginalized employees and leaders, and discrimination in the workplace.

Increased representation of marginalized groups allows organizations to gain an array of perspectives, experiences, and ideas, which can drive innovation and creativity, boost employee productivity, and increase profits. This starts in the recruitment process, where hiring candidates from diverse backgrounds provides organizations with access to a larger talent pool. Besides, a larger talent pool can lead to organizations finding highly skilled candidates who may otherwise be overlooked because of their race, gender, sexuality, etc. A diverse workforce can also lead to a significant improvement in problem-solving and decision-making processes as employees bring their unique perspectives and skills to the table. Another key benefit of having greater representation in the workplace is that a diverse workforce most likely reflects the organization's diverse customer base. If an organization has a large national (or even international) client or consumer base, chances are that these clients or consumers come from a variety of cultures, ethnicities, nationalities, and experiences, so it makes sense that organizations diversify their workforce to truly cater to the needs of their consumers and/or clients. Moreover, the organization's underrepresented employees will be able to find common ground with clients or consumers who share a similar identity to them, and this can build greater trust between organizations and their clients or consumers.

Increased diversity and representation in the workforce have the potential to boost employee growth and personal development as employees are exposed to multiple perspectives, ideas, and opinions. Outside of innovation, greater representation of employees from a variety of backgrounds allows an organization's workforce to adapt to different circumstances and work with or around each other's differences in cultures, perspectives, and backgrounds. Consequently, cross-cultural learning and understanding in the workplace helps to dispel negative stereotypes and prejudices and can foster cross-cultural unity and social bonding. In addition, greater representation promotes corporate attractiveness and appeals to Gen Z job seekers and potential business partners and collaborators. Organizations that hire and retain employees from diverse cultures and backgrounds are often portrayed positively in national and international media platforms, and this can provide such organizations with access to wider talent pools. Besides, which job seeker wouldn't want to work for an organization that has shown itself to be progressive, inclusive, employee-focused, and welcoming?

As echoed by Cletus et al. (2018), "In the era of scarcity of talent and skilled employees, attracting the best talent can further enhance the profitability, survival, and future of companies." A McKinsey report also demonstrates that diversity and representation in the workplace not only boost employee satisfaction but also help keep professional relationships among employees healthy and conflict-free. With this people-centric or employee-centric approach, organizations can better understand their client or consumer base—especially if this base transcends cultures and countries. When it comes to gender, organizations with gender-diverse teams and leaders report higher profits compared to those with a male-dominated workforce, but there are several other advantages to having more women in the workplace. For instance, in workplaces with high percentages of female leaders and employees, there are higher rates of organizational dedication, job satisfaction, and employee benefits, and fewer reports of burnout.

Several studies show that women outperform men in senior leadership positions as they tend to champion diversity, equity, and inclusion programs and commitments, prioritize sustainability and eco-conscious operations, invest more in innovation, and are usually more qualified than male leaders. Indeed, women outnumber and outperform men in colleges and universities. Moreover, women leaders often adopt a transformational leadership style that values cooperation and teamwork over authority and individualism. According to a survey by the Pew Research Center's Social and Demographic Trends (2008), women leaders are seen as more honest, smarter, compassionate, and creative than their male counterparts. In general, women leaders also tend to value open communication, are more likely to create mentorship and coaching sessions, and find ways to close the gender pay gap in their organizations.

The Scope of Representation in the Workplace

While diversity and greater representation in the workplace have proven to increase profits, employee retention, and corporate attractiveness, we can be remiss of the various challenges that may come with this. The concept of "diversity" is constantly undergoing social and cultural transformation across industries and countries. This is because diversity is a multi-faceted concept that can be even more complex in practice, and diversity strategies and the requisite goals must be able to adapt to changing working environments and population demographics. As such, it is all the more important to address the (potential) challenges of diversity and representation in workplaces to prevent current and future DEI programs from failing. Indeed, we must plan for any challenges and obstacles to ensure that they are adequately addressed or remedied before they impact an organization's leaders and employees.

Avoiding Tokenism at All Costs

There are many forms of diversity that can exist in the workplace, but organizations must also be weary of tokenism. This term refers to an organization's symbolic effort to hire or promote a small group of underrepresented or marginalized people to avoid public scrutiny and give the impression that the organization is diverse and inclusive. Tokenism in the workplace has adverse consequences for employees from marginalized groups as they may deal with imposter syndrome and/or face overwhelming pressure to "represent" their group. Of course, this leads to increased anxiety as any of their missteps or failures are hypervisible in the workplace, or they may feel isolated or lonely in the workplace. In some cases, the "tokenized" employees may be pressured to conform to stereotypes or assumptions usually associated with them or to exaggerate how they are different from their stereotypes. As such, organizations should not expect their tokenized employees to be the "spokespeople" for their groups or communities, nor should these employees be used as photo opportunities to increase company attractiveness. Besides, organizations may appoint individuals from marginalized groups to positions of power to check the diversity box, but without the necessary support, these individuals are set up for failure. Ideally, organizations should make an effort to have a diverse workforce, but they should also view their employees outside of their marginalized or underrepresented identities.

Implementing DEI strategies in the workplace can bring organizations positive publicity and help them garner praise among Millennial and Gen Z consumers; consequently, many organizations, knowingly or unknowingly, tokenize their employees from underrepresented or marginalized groups. Tokenizing employees can occur in several ways. Most noticeably, organizations lure consumers and potential employees by featuring marginalized individuals in their advertising, banners, brochures, and other forms of corporate branding. The corporate branding may not truly represent the organization's workforce demographics, and/or it forces the underrepresented employees to be paraded around as evidence of the organization's DEI efforts. Some organizations tokenize their employees by partaking in symbolic diversity, and here, the organizations appoint people from marginalized backgrounds to leadership positions to show that they take DEI seriously. While having diversity in senior leadership and decision-making positions is important, sometimes those appointed to these positions do not work toward uplifting their communities. As stated by Zora Neale Hurston, "all my skinfolk ain't kinfolk," and some organizations—no matter their intentions—appoint those from marginalized groups to positions of power simply to check a diversity box; this does not necessarily lead to progress within the organization.

Organizations (and their leaders) can take the following steps to avoid tokenism in the workplace:

- Align recruitment and hiring goals to DEI goals to avoid quota-based hiring.

- Ensure all interviewers and hiring managers are trained in DEI.

- Approach DEI through an intersectional lens to create a diverse workforce.

- Avoid pressuring diverse employees to be spokespeople for their communities.

- Hire diversity experts and professionals to educate employees instead of relying on marginalized employees to educate their peers and coworkers.

- Encourage cross-cultural interactions to foster a sense of belonging and community.

- Pay attention to advertising, branding, and marketing visuals to ensure they accurately represent the demographics of the organization's workforce.

Scope One: Embrace Multiple Gender Identities and Sexualities

Almost 6% of adults in the US identify as LGBTQIA2+, and while this is the highest recording in the history of the country, discrimination based on gender identity and sexual orientation remains rife in the workplace and broader global society. The workplace is considered a high-stakes space in which queer people's experiences with the fluidity of sexual orientation and gender identity often result in them having to negotiate their coming out (if they decide to come out). In the US, employment, and workplace discrimination on the basis of gender and sexual identity is prohibited, yet 36% of all LGBTQIA2+ people have reported some form of workplace discrimination, and 46% remain closeted at work (Gattuso, 2021). There are various reasons for almost half of LGBTQIA2+ people remaining closeted in their workplaces, such as stigmas surrounding queerness, microaggressions, and the fear that public knowledge of their gender and/or sexual identity may put their jobs at risk.

As Gattuso (2021) explains, most LGBTQIA2+ people carefully navigate the disclosure of their gender identity and sexuality:

> For those who can "pass" as heterosexual or cisgender, coming out can often mean choosing between paying a psychological price for the relative safety of invisibility, and paying a potential social and economic price for being open about one's identity. For others, especially

those who are gender nonconforming, being closeted at work isn't an option. This can have significant detrimental effects: people who are perceived as falling outside of conventional gender norms are at higher risk of career-disrupting workplace harassment and discrimination. (Paragraph 7)

LGBTQIA2+ employees often pay the price for defying society's traditional gender and sexual orientation norms, as they may have to deal with isolation, harassment, and ignorance in the workplace. For example, transgender individuals are twice as likely to be unemployed (compared to cisgender individuals), and even when they are employed, 90% of them have reported instances of workplace discrimination (Gattuso, 2020). Research from McKinsey & Company (Baboolall et al., 2021) reveals that regardless of education levels and credentials, cisgender employees earn 32% more than their transgender counterparts, and two-thirds of transgender employees remain in the closet in professional settings and interactions. These statistics are even more worrisome when we take into account that 22% of transgender adults and 32% of transgender adults of color do not have any form of health coverage, and an estimated 29% of transgender people live in poverty in the US (Baboolall et al., 2021).

Queerphobia is harmful to employees who identify as LGBTQIA2+ but is especially nefarious for those at the intersections of multiple forms of oppression, such as LGBTQIA2+ people of color who work in majority white and heterosexual workplaces. Moreover, coming out in the workplace is seldom a once-off event, as LGBTQIA2+ employees and leaders may have come out to new employees, colleagues, leaders, clients, or customers throughout their careers. To be inclusive of all gender identities and sexualities, organizations can embed various policies and practices in the fabric of their daily operations.

For instance, policies that are aligned with traditional or nuclear family structures can be transformed to be inclusive of those with all types of familial structures. Indeed, there are employees who are sole or primary caregivers to children and/or elderly family members or those with disabilities who may need paid leave or extra time from work, to name a few examples. In terms of tactical approaches, organizations should highlight the importance of using employees' pronouns and clearly communicate the consequences of deadnaming in the workplace. While these policies or systemic changes can be beneficial for closeted or out LGBTQIA2+ employees, employees' negative attitudes toward and opinions of LGBTQIA2+ people also need to change. As such, change needs to occur on a systemic and social level—an incredibly challenging feat!

Here are a few ways to boost the representation and inclusion of gender diversity and the spectrum of sexual orientations:

- Recognize that gender identity and sexual orientation are complex and intersectional.

- Allow every employee the option of whether they would like to disclose their gender identity and/or sexual orientation in the workplace.

- Conduct workshops and training sessions to ensure employees are educated on the gender and sexuality spectrums and are updated on the relevant terminology.

- Update policies or guidelines to make sure that the expected dress code is gender-neutral and inclusive of all gender expressions.

- Create gender-neutral or everybody bathrooms and/or single-user restrooms.

- Establish a zero-tolerance policy for gender-based discrimination, harassment, and bullying.

- Create a workplace culture of respect and inclusion so that all employees (regardless of their beliefs and opinions) can work together in a cohesive and healthy manner.

- Encourage and empower all employees to use their pronouns in their email signatures and other forms of written communication.

- Establish employee resource groups (ERGs) to promote the goals and/or concerns of LGBTQIA2+ employees.

On a larger scale, organizations can demonstrate their support by sponsoring and/or participating in LGBTQIA2+ community events, using LGBTQIA2+-friendly job sites for recruitment, and providing employee benefits for same-sex partners.

Scope Two: Racial or Ethnic Diversity and Culture Clashes

Diversity includes so many factors, such as race, ethnicity, religion, nationality, class, gender, sexual orientation, age, and ability, that it can be quite overwhelming to initiate structural and social change in the workplace. Numerous modern-day organizations (and especially those that operate in several countries) have a multiracial and multicultural workforce, so it is expected that some individuals will have prejudices and biases toward those who they perceive as different. Whether employees believe that their immigrant coworkers are stealing *their* jobs or managers refuse to hire candidates from a racial group that they deem *lazy*, prejudice and discrimination can occur in any workplace and at varying degrees. As such, organizations must create, implement, and monitor DEI policies that are inclusive of all factors of diversity and that acknowledge how different elements of marginalization can intersect with each other.

For example, islamophobia—the prejudice against or dislike of Muslims and Islam—is very present in several workplaces and can be seen in instances where a Muslim employee wearing hijab while at work may be at the receiving end of discrimination based on her gender, race (as Muslims are racialized in the context of the US), and religion. Perhaps the Muslim employee is being called a "terrorist" by her coworkers who believe in negative stereotypes about Muslim people, or she is seen as meek and submissive simply because she expresses her beliefs by covering parts of her head and neck with a hijab. Whatever the reasons behind this discrimination, organizations must recognize that discrimination occurs on three distinct yet intertwined levels. While a critic of the term Islamophobia himself, legal scholar Khaled Beydoun gives context in a 2018 interview with Religion News around how social movements and culture clashes are not altogether separate and distinct. He contends:

> "The Muslim-American narrative is tied to the construction of whiteness, which in turn is heavily reliant on anti-Black racism in the sense that white identity was constructed to be the opposite. For a long time in this country, whiteness was a prerequisite for citizenship. When non-Black Muslims came from abroad, they had to demonstrate that they were in fact white to become naturalized citizens. So, the Muslim-American experience is rooted in the Black experience, because the first Muslim communities in this country were in fact, Black. There were enslaved populations in the antebellum South, largely, who practiced Islam and tried to persevere in their faith against persecution by slave masters and against the letter of the law."

In another instance, cultural differences in terms of communication may be negatively perceived in the workplace: Some cultures communicate with high levels of eye contact and hand movements, while other cultures deem direct eye contact as disrespectful. Relatedly, verbal communication can also get lost in translation, as employees who speak English as their second language may struggle to communicate with their coworkers who speak English as their first language (or vice versa). Even employees who speak proficient English (even as a second, third, or fourth language) may be subject to ridicule should they speak with an accent.

Culture clashes among any large group of diverse people are bound to occur, so organizations also need to have the relevant mechanisms in place to fully address and remedy these conflicts. If cultural conflicts or clashes in the workplace are not addressed in a timely manner, the organization may experience a noticeable decrease in productivity and employee morale and perhaps an increase in hostility among employees. On a larger, organization-wide scale, unresolved conflicts can also escalate from miscommunication and tension to full-blown discrimination, bullying, and abuse, and this can have a ripple effect across the organization. On a more individual level, such conflicts can harm the employees' self-esteem and self-confidence and can lead to symptoms associated with anxiety and depression.

Organizations (and their employees) can support racial, ethnic, and cultural diversity in the workplace by doing the following:

- Allow for workplace discussions or conversations on or related to race, ethnicity, and culture instead of avoiding the topic.

- Respect all employees' religious holidays, cultural festivals, and traditions.

- Boost cultural competence by attending cultural events, taking courses on cultural studies, and engaging with media (such as literature, music, and movies) created by those from diverse backgrounds.

- Celebrate employees' cultures and heritages by hosting cultural events, such as days where the staff canteen offers foods from various countries or days when employees wear their traditional attire to the office.

- Be inclusive of employees who speak English as a second (or third, or fourth) language and celebrate multilingualism in the workplace.

- Offer racial and cultural diversity training for all employees and leaders in the organization.

Scope Three: Generational Differences

One of the most prevalent yet overlooked forms of diversity in the workplace is generational differences. Organizations with employees from generations that are far apart may see miscommunication and misunderstandings among their workforce. The Baby Boomer generation, for example, is a generation that is rather traditional when it comes to their work and careers. In general, they value hard work, traditional workplace hierarchies, and rigid work schedules and are more likely to stay at the same company for decades. Indeed, many Baby Boomers believe in working their way to the top and investing their time and skills in helping a company or organization grow. The

Millennial generation, however, is considered far more flexible when it comes to their work, and because they are keenly aware that they are replaceable, Millennial workers usually keep an eye out for new opportunities or jobs. Millennials tend to value freedom and a healthy work-life balance, and they are more likely to change jobs or careers frequently than previous generations. Millennials tend to align their workplace goals with their personal goals and are far more open to organizational changes than their Baby Boomer counterparts. Millennials are also the generation that challenges traditional workplace norms: Open offices are favored over tightly packed cubicles and office walls, and their workplace attire, too, is relatively laidback.

Because of these differences in working styles and approaches, some Baby Boomers deem the Millennial generation as one that is lazy, less hardworking, and less loyal, but, in reality, this is not the case. Millennial employees' work ethic has to be strong as the current job environment is highly competitive and ever-changing. For instance, large corporations, as in the case of fast fashion giants, outsource their labor to countries with cheap labor and weak labor laws, and/or they replace their human employees with technology. In fact, many of the industries that were prospering during the Baby Boomers' generation have since disappeared. Then there is the "Gen Z" generation, which has recently started entering the workforce. As the digital native generation, Gen Zers are tech-savvy and oftentimes over-reliant on technology, but this also means that their preferred communication channels are via online workspaces (such as Slack) or via email. Gen Z workers are also known for prioritizing their mental health, not settling for poor or substandard working conditions, and demanding flexible and/or remote work options and more employee benefits.

Due to this, Gen Z is often labeled the "spoiled" generation that "demands things for free," but it is also important to remember that Gen Z is entering a workforce that is vastly different from that of their grandparents. Gen Z values diversity, equity, and inclusion policies in the workplace because they are a diverse generation, and the recent COVID-19 pandemic and rising concerns over climate change and social injustices have shown this generation that the old way of doing things is unsustainable and, in some cases, unhealthy. With calls for remote work options, greater awareness of mental and physical health, and stronger DEI policies, Gen Z wants to work for progressive organizations, and that also prioritize human well-being and health over profit. Nonetheless, organizations with generational gaps in their working environments must recognize how age differences can lead to "cliques" among employees or divisions within the organization. Here, the organizations must also recognize the value of older employees, as they have developed skills and experience over the span of decades. Instead of being seen as a burden on the organization and, to a greater extent, the economy, Baby Boomers occupy an important space in the workplace.

Despite being deemed the more traditional generation, Baby Boomers still lead the way in terms of innovation because of their years of experience and resilient nature. Prejudice and discrimination against older individuals based on their age is termed "ageism," and the United Nations' Global Report on Ageism (2021) highlights the need to shift our mindsets and challenge the narrative of older individuals as frail and vulnerable. Older people are often subjected to dismissive and patronizing language in the workplace and in their private lives, and this is further exacerbated when their age intersects with other marginalized identities and "-isms." In the context of the workplace, older employees must be guaranteed dignity, equity, participation, and independence, but this is not often the case. Organizations that focus their attention on innovation erroneously assume that mainly or only younger employees can provide fresh and unique perspectives, ideas, and experiences, while older employees are overlooked.

In the US, the average age of retirement has increased from 62 to 66, yet some of these employees opt to stay at their companies because they enjoy their jobs and/or they cannot afford to retire. Those who remain in the workforce—whether voluntarily or because of financial issues—often experience ageism in the workplace through biased practices and other inequities. In fact, 62% of employees over the age of 50 believe older workers experience age discrimination, and more than 93% state that ageism is a regular occurrence in the workplace (Choi-Alum, 2022). To tackle ageism in the workplace, organizations can establish a culture of care that seeks to listen to and understand employees across generations. The needs of different generations in the workplace may intersect, and it is therefore beneficial for organizations to facilitate the building of bridges between generations. While there are certain stereotypes associated with each generation, many employees transcend such stereotypes, and as a result, these employees should be viewed as individuals and not through the lens of their generation. Indeed, Gen Zers can be as hardworking as Baby Boomers, and Baby Boomers can be as tech-savvy as Gen Zers. By valuing employees as individuals rather than as products of their generation, organizations will be able to better address their needs in the workplace and leverage generational diversity to advance DEI efforts and business profits.

Generational gaps are present in many modern workplaces, so here are a few ways to bridge this gap:

- Establish a strong company culture that is devoid of ageism and preconceived notions about different age groups.

- Allow for a blend of various communication styles (including in-person and online meetings and discussions) to cater to employees of all ages, communication preferences, and technological abilities.

- Increase collaborations between employees of different age groups, such as two-way mentorships.

- Encourage flexible work options, as some age groups have childcare and schooling responsibilities, while younger hires may prefer remote work options.

- Avoid stereotyping of different age groups by seeing employees and coworkers for their unique skills, experiences, and ideas rather than judging them by their age.

- Protect the workplace against age segregation as some employees may clump together with coworkers or peers who are a similar age to them.

- Reject ageist perspectives and sentiments at all costs and constantly monitor internal practices and processes to ensure that the organization has not inadvertently built ageism into the system.

Scope Four: Disabilities and Accessibility

The term "disability" refers to how physical or mental injuries and/or illnesses influence an individual's senses, movements, or activities. While disabilities do not totally prevent individuals from performing workplace duties and tasks, they can hinder the work capacity of disabled individuals. Disabilities can also exist in various forms and to varying degrees, so it is important for organizations not to see people with disabilities as a monolithic group. Indeed, an employee with autism spectrum disorder (ASD) may have different needs from a deaf employee or an employee who uses a wheelchair. Disabilities can be physical, intellectual, sensory, or mental and can be acquired at birth, during childhood, or during adulthood; consequently, they often affect individuals in different ways. Nonetheless, many people with disabilities globally face barriers entering and in the workplace, and this is due to stigmas and negative attitudes toward people with disabilities, workplaces that are inaccessible for those with physical disabilities, or working conditions that do not take into account the medical needs of people with disabilities.

The term "ableism" describes the "discrimination against and social prejudice against people with disabilities based on the belief that typical abilities are superior" (Eisenmenger, 2019). Ableism is rooted in the assumption that people with disabilities require "fixing," and much like sexism and ageism, it deems entire groups of people as "less than." This form of discrimination can be seen throughout recent history, with the popularity of the eugenics movement in the early 20th century, the segregation of disabled individuals in many medical institutions, the use of restraint to control disabled students in various schools, and the mass murder of people with disabilities in Nazi Germany. Yet, ableism is also rife in modern society: Movies and videos seldom have closed captioning; people talk down to and infantilize disabled people; they ask disabled people invasive questions about their disability and medical history; and they design spaces (be they apartment buildings or offices) that are inaccessible to people with physical disabilities. Even Hollywood's framing of disabilities as inspirations in their movies and television series is ableist.

Many people with disabilities are met with discrimination and harassment in the workplace, as their colleagues or leaders may be ignorant or may believe that those with disabilities are incapable of meeting workplace demands. Workplaces may not have adequate equipment or measures (such as ramps or elevators), disability benefits, or spatial planning (such as passages broad enough for wheelchairs) needed for employees with physical disabilities. According to a report from the U.S. Department of Labor's Bureau of Labor Statistics (2019), Americans with disabilities are dealing with recession-level unemployment rates (an 8% unemployment rate for people with disabilities in the job market). This is worrisome, as hiring people with disabilities is not only an important part of DEI programming, but it is also fantastic for the economy. That is, an organization that includes employees with disabilities has higher productivity levels and the ability to dispel stereotypes and change negative attitudes toward people with disabilities.

Including people with disabilities in the workplace also means that organizations must implement structural and policy changes at all levels, which include:

- Discouraging ableist language, labels, and disability jokes.

- Recognizing behaviors, communication styles, and body language that are related to disabilities.

- Ensuring that all work events (be they meetings or parties) are accessible.

- Allowing employees with disabilities to determine whether to disclose their disabilities to others in the workplace.

- Teaching able-bodied employees, the appropriate ways to offer help to disabled employees.

- Addressing ableist comments, bullying, and harassment immediately and effectively.

- Understanding the differences between visible and invisible disabilities.

- Acknowledging how disability can overlap with other forms of marginalization, such as race and gender.

Scope Five: Religious and Political Diversity

We are often advised to avoid discussing politics and religious beliefs in the workplace, but in the status quo, these topics are unavoidable. More and more organizations are employing individuals with varying political leanings, religious beliefs, and cultural identities, and while this diversity can lead to innovation and creativity, it can also result in polarization among employees. Yet, organizations can (and should) leverage political and religious diversity to create and maintain open, honest, and inclusive work environments for all employees. The organization's leader(s) should publicly acknowledge the divisive nature of political and religious beliefs to show employees that such topics can and should be discussed in a healthy and productive manner. Without these discussions and mutual respect among employees, the work environment may be plagued by hostilities, ignorance, and exclusion. Of course, there are risks associated with openly discussing controversial topics in the workplace, but with the help of guidelines and policies, these discussions can lead to a stronger and more resilient workforce.

For example, the organization's leader(s) may have to regularly make it clear to their employees that all discussions on or relating to political and religious beliefs must be underpinned by mutual respect and should never come at the expense of others. Improving political diversity is incredibly important, as political homogeneity can lead to employees with differing political views feeling isolated or excluded in the workplace. The lack of religious diversity, too, can create a workplace culture in which some employees may feel uncomfortable with or disconnected from their coworkers and leaders.

As such, organizations and employees can use the following measures to boost their political and religious diversity:

- Clearly distinguish between political or religious beliefs and discrimination or intolerance.

- Regularly reiterate the importance of mutual respect, acceptance, and inclusion.

- Host workshops in which employees are provided with the tools and skills needed to voice their opinions and beliefs while still being respectful to others.

- Avoid assumptions, biases, judgments, and stereotypes when discussing political or religious beliefs that differ from your own.

- Know when to depart an interaction before a conversation becomes disrespectful or uncomfortable.

- Enter any conversation on politics and religion with an open and curious mind.

- Leverage physical space in the workplace for prayer rooms so employees from Muslim identities and other religious groups can feel comfortable praying safely at work.

- Educate teammates and the organization about religious diversity as some religions like the Jehovah's Witness faith and Jewish communities do not celebrate most traditional Christian Holidays like Easter and Christmas.

Scope Six: Military Veterans

According to the Bureau of Labor Statistics, there were around 20.4 million veterans in the US in 2020, and despite accounting for about 7% of the civilian population, veteran job seekers are 15.6% more likely to remain unemployed in comparison to their non-veteran counterparts (Gonzalez & Simpson, 2020; Stern, 2017). There is a strong business case for boosting the recruitment or employment of military veterans in the workplace: Military service creates individuals who have great leadership and teamwork skills, better problem-solving and decision-making abilities (especially when under pressure), and who are attentive to details. It is, therefore, crucial that recruiters, hiring managers, and employers seek to understand how military skill sets can be translated into and beneficial for the workplace. Organizations should also acknowledge the various barriers faced by members of this talent pool, as many veterans may not know how to express their military skills and experiences as employable skills during job interviews.

Here are a few more ways in which workplaces can support the hiring and retention of military veterans:

- Educate leaders on the business case for recruiting or hiring more veterans.

- Boost the cultural competency of employees so that they understand how to interact with veterans in the workplace.

- Invest in the onboarding and career development of veterans and measure their performance and retention metrics for an increased return on investment.

- Use federal resources that help companies train veterans during the early stages of the transition process.

- Create mentorship opportunities between senior veteran employees and veteran newcomers.

- Learn about the military's culture and values to better help veterans transition into civilian employment.

- Offer remote work options for military spouses.

- Develop volunteer programs to help veteran employees engage in community outreach.

There are several scopes when it comes to representation and the contours of diversity, and unfortunately, marginalized individuals and communities continue to be misrepresented, stereotyped, and discriminated against in our media, workplaces, and societies. Whether this takes the form of a film that portrays Black students being "saved" by their white teacher or real-life situations in which disabled employees are treated as subhuman, we need to ensure that individuals from marginalized communities are fairly, equitably, and accurately represented. The lack of representation of marginalized peoples in all spheres of life not only makes them invisible to the dominant culture but also reduces them to monolithic groups that are devoid of complexities, diversities, and intrinsic value. In doing so, we give marginalized people only two options: to assimilate into the dominant culture or to remain at the periphery of power and prosperity.

Chapter 3:

Empathy Through Education

Education is the point at which we decide whether we love the world enough to assume responsibility for it and by the same token to save it from that ruin, which, except for renewal, except for the coming of the new and the young, would be inevitable. An education, too, is where we decide whether we love our children enough not to expel them from our world and leave them to their own devices, nor to strike from their hands their choice of undertaking something new, something unforeseen by us, but to prepare them in advance for the task of renewing a common world. –
Hannah Arendt

When it comes to understanding and working with others, empathy is a vital skill, as it allows us to create meaningful connections with others and respond appropriately to their thoughts and emotions. Sometimes, we listen to others mainly to form our own responses, or we pretend to listen to others when, in reality, we have other things on our minds. A lack of empathy can make an individual seem aloof, unfeeling, or apathetic toward people or situations, but more importantly, it can lead to minor or significant disagreements, hostility, and misunderstandings. Without empathy, we may struggle to interact with others, understand varying viewpoints, or recognize social cues in important conversations—making it all the more necessary to embed empathy in our DEI efforts. DEI education, for example, provides us with the time and space to learn about the experiences of others and helps us create a culture of community and belonging in our organizations.

Empathy vs. Sympathy

Empathy and sympathy are often used interchangeably, but understanding the differences between these terms is key to determining which one to use in any given situation. Empathy refers to the ability to understand and share another person's feelings, and this entails actively listening to the other person, attempting to see their perspective, and acknowledging their thoughts and feelings—all without judging them. An empathetic individual can connect to another person's emotions and thoughts without feeling forced to respond with (often unwanted) advice. In doing so, the empathetic individual can see themselves in another person's struggle and acknowledge the emotions of all those involved in a situation. This is one of several reasons why empathy is such an important skill for leaders: Understanding everyone's feelings and experiences regarding a specific situation helps leaders see the bigger picture and, subsequently, make better-informed decisions. The empathetic leader can, therefore, remain neutral in a workplace conflict while still acknowledging and giving value to each employee's emotions. Empathy can also help individuals develop and improve their communication skills, as the ability to actively listen to others and understand their perspectives is essential for having open, productive conversations.

Sympathy, on the other hand, refers to feeling sorry for another person's feelings. In contrast to empathy, the sympathetic individual judges the emotions of others and understands the situation mainly or only from their own perspective, provides unsolicited advice, and views the issue only at a surface level. Here, the sympathetic individual feels pity for the other person without attempting to understand how the other person may truly feel. While sympathy is appropriate in some situations, the sympathetic individual often emphasizes their own thoughts, emotions, and perspectives while listening to others. For example, perhaps one of your coworkers was reprimanded for missing a deadline, and as a result, they may feel sad, frustrated, or disappointed in themselves. If you want to express sympathy, you would tell them that you are sorry for what they are going through, but you would still judge them for missing the deadline. You may even reply with something along the lines of "At least you weren't fired!" If you want to express empathy, you would feel the sadness, frustration, or disappointment that your coworker feels. Instead of judging your coworker or providing them with unsolicited advice, you would be concerned about their well-being and may even respond with, "I'm sorry that you're going through this, and I'm here for you." Here, your main concern is to offer your coworker a moment of connection instead of trying to fix their situation for them.

In workplace environments, empathy trumps sympathy, as it can help you form a meaningful connection with your coworkers, employees, or leaders and better provide them with what they need. Of course, choosing whether to express empathy or sympathy largely depends on the context and your relationship with the other person. Empathy allows you to be more compassionate and understanding when communicating with others, whereas sympathy often comes from your ego and can move you into a problem-solving mode that potentially ignores the other person's feelings. Indeed, an empathetic individual provides others with the space to process their thoughts and emotions, while a sympathetic individual tells others what they should feel or do. Importantly, empathy is appropriate in any given situation, but sympathy should be reserved for times of difficulty.

Understanding History for Greater Empathy

Systemic change often takes time (and resources), whereas empathy is something that can be displayed almost immediately. Empathy can help us connect with others and understand thoughts, opinions, and perspectives that are different from our own, and when it comes to DEI strategies, empathy can help organizations and their leaders take action to spark long-term, systemic change. Trying to understand another person who has a different background, history, culture, and experience than you can be rather challenging, and it is all the more difficult when we try to understand the unique perspectives and needs of each employee in a large and diverse workforce. But this feat is not impossible! In current anti-racism and anti-sexism debates, the various parties involved must be able to employ an empathetic approach to find mutual understanding. This entails not only taking another person's perspective and experiences into account but also acknowledging your own positionality and privileges (or marginalization) in workplace contexts. Besides, if an organization seeks to successfully implement DEI strategies, it must take into account all of the possible privileges and/or marginalization of its workforce. One way to do this is to learn about the history of marginalized communities to better understand the political and socio-economic contexts that affect employees from underrepresented or historically oppressed groups.

The Clark Doll Test and the Brown-Eyed, Blue-Eyed Experiment

One key example is from the 1940s when husband-and-wife team in the US, Dr. Kenneth Clark and Dr. Mamie Clark, performed a psychological study on the self-image of African American children. Now referred to as the Clark doll experiment, the study found that African American children not only preferred dolls with white skin but also considered the Black doll the "bad" doll and believed that the white doll was the "good" doll. The study was relatively simple: The African American children (many of whom attended segregated schools) were asked to identify the dolls in a variety of ways, including choosing which doll they wanted to play with, which doll looked "white" or "colored," and which doll was "good" or "bad." Toward the end, the children were asked to identify the doll that looked like them, leading to some of them crying and running out of the room. Indeed, it may have dawned on the children that the doll they deemed "bad" actually looked more like them than the doll they considered to be "good."

The Clark doll experiment demonstrated the psychological impact of racial segregation on African American children and eventually formed part of the class-action case that later became Brown v. Board of Education. Here, Dr. Kenneth Clark testified in front of the Supreme Court and told the judges and juries that the children's preference for white dolls symbolized the psychological damage of racial segregation. The Clark doll experiment was pivotal to the Supreme Court's landmark decision that deemed racial segregation in public schools unconstitutional. Similarly, a white third-grade teacher from Iowa, Jane Elliot, performed an experiment of her own to make her students understand the brutal nature of racism. In 1968, the day after the assassination of Martin Luther King Jr., Elliot separated her all-white class into two groups—blue-eyed children and brown-eyed children—and told the blue-eyed children that they were genetically inferior to the brown-eyed children. The blue-eyed children were told by Elliot that they were not allowed to play on the swings or jungle gym, that they would not receive second helpings for lunch, and that they would have to use paper cups if they drank from the water fountain. Elliot also informed the blue-eyed children that they were not to do their homework because, even if they did it, they would probably forget to bring it to class the next day. On day two of the experiment, Elliot switched the children's roles.

After her experiment received attention in the local newspaper, Elliot appeared on The Tonight Show with Johnny Carson, where she explained that the experiment taught her white students what it was like discriminated against on the basis of uncontrollable identity. The experiment took the US by storm. Of course, this experiment did little to address the root causes of systemic racism in the US, but it helped demonstrate the impact empathy can have on people. Indeed, Elliot instructed her white students to put themselves in the shoes of African Americans, and while the students could not truly understand the brutal, violent extent of racism and racial segregation in the US, they were provided with a glimpse into the impact of racial segregation. The Clark doll experiment, too, yielded significant insights into internalized racism and the impact of racial segregation. Besides, some of the African American children were distraught after realizing that they looked more like the doll that they had rejected. These two experiments occurred during a time of racial segregation and Jim Crow laws, and while we exist in a different context today, the legacy of systemic racism (and slavery, for that matter) continues to subjugate many BIPOC peoples in modern-day America.

The Sociological Imagination

While organizations do not have to separate their employees according to eye color, nor do they have to place dolls of various skin tones in front of their employees, modern-day organizations have the responsibility to ensure that their leaders and employees are willing to learn how historical systems of oppression contribute to privileges and/or marginalization among employees today. Because what happened in the past has consequences for the modern-day US, organizations that wish to successfully implement DEI strategies must understand the connections between the past and the present in order to address the complexities faced by marginalized peoples today. Here, the concept of "multi-perspective" comes into play. Referring to the idea that history is subjective and comprised of multiple, co-existing narratives, multiperspectivity allows people and organizations to understand why some groups are underrepresented in various industries, why some groups have higher rates of unemployment, health issues, and housing problems, and why some groups may experience workplace discrimination owing to their identities.

In 1959, sociologist C. Wright Mills introduced the notion of the sociological imagination as a way to encourage us to place individual hardships or challenges in the context of broader and more public issues. For example, if an employee often shows up late for work, we may view this tardiness as an individual choice. But the sociological imagination asks us to consider how such a choice is connected to structural realities and issues; perhaps the employee is late because they have to drop off their kids at school or they have to use public transportation to travel to work. As stated by Stacey (2020), the sociological imagination "not only coaxes us to listen to others and imagine the circumstances of individual behavior; it also asks us to consider broader realities that condition and shape a person's life and decision-making." In terms of DEI strategies, the sociological imagination serves as a tool to foster empathy across differences and divides.

Within workplace contexts, the sociological imagination encourages leaders to ask questions about why their coworkers, employees, or peers act the way they do without judging them for their actions. Whether the leaders do independent research or gather information from the employees in question, their willingness to put themselves in the shoes of others not only demonstrates their empathy but also their commitment to DEI strategies. This process, however, is not simply altruistic, and it does not mean that leaders must accept or excuse any form of disrespect or discrimination. Instead, the leaders must partake in this process to gain a deeper understanding of the employees' beliefs or actions while also holding employees (or others) accountable. For instance, an empathetic manager has noticed that employee 1's work performance has significantly decreased in the past week. After having a productive, meaningful conversation with the said employee, the manager realizes that another employee, employee 2, has made a few microaggressive remarks about or to employee 1. As a result, employee

1 no longer feels comfortable in the workplace and is fearful that they may face further discrimination by employee 2.

In this example, the manager may have also held a one-on-one meeting with employee 2 to understand why they have acted in a microaggressive manner toward employee 1. Whatever the reason for such behavior and as challenging as it may be, the manager must remain empathetic throughout the meeting. Here, the manager has lent both employee 1 and employee 2 an empathetic ear, but because of their positions of power and responsibility for the organization's DEI strategies, the manager must still hold employee 2 accountable for their words and actions. This is just one hypothetical scenario that demonstrates how empathy and sociological imagination can help organizations and their employees boost their DEI strategies. What is most important here is the willingness of organizations and leaders to acknowledge how and why privileges and marginalization remain present in the workplace (and in broader society) and to find culturally relevant and empathetic ways to empower all employees.

Practicing Empathy in the Workplace

Expressing empathy for others can be rather challenging and, in some cases, emotionally exhausting. A 2021 report by Businessolver revealed that 70% of CEOs struggle to demonstrate empathy consistently in the workplace, while 68% believe that they will be less respected if they show empathy at work. Empathy is an essential skill in the workplace, as 90% of Gen Z employees are more likely to remain at their jobs if their employer is empathetic. So, how can a leader or employee develop and improve their empathy skills?

Strategy One: Improve Your Active Listening Skills

When you listen to others, do you focus on what they are saying, or do you instead focus on your own thoughts? Oftentimes, we get carried away thinking about what we want to say next or how we want to respond, but a major aspect of good communication is to be an active listener. This entails fully focusing on what the other person is saying and paying attention to their non-verbal communication. Here, recognizing the other person's body language and tone of voice can help you better understand their emotions. You may even need a moment or two to process the conversation and all of its nuances. Moreover, active listening often entails listening to others without judging their emotions or actions. This may be rather challenging, as many of us cannot help but judge high-conflict situations or petty squabbles, but refraining from making judgments is all the more important in workplace contexts. If you are a leader, then you absolutely need to withhold judgment and remain neutral—especially when it comes to mediating conflicts.

In some cases, active, empathetic listening requires you to affirm the other person's emotions even if you do not fully understand or agree with their contents. This can help you become more accepting of others (especially those who come from a background that is vastly different from yours) and help you develop a deeper understanding of others' perspectives and experiences. For instance, if your coworker talks to you about a time that they were discriminated against, as an empathetic, active listener, you should focus on their thoughts and emotions, acknowledge their experiences, and remind them that they are not alone in their situation. If relevant, you can share your own experiences with discrimination in the workplace but be sure to wait until they are done speaking (lest you want to interrupt and, therefore, undermine the other person's experiences and emotions).

Strategy Two: Develop Your Emotional Intelligence

Emotional intelligence (EQ) refers to the ability to understand and manage your own emotions, communicate effectively, relieve stress in healthy ways, and empathize with others. Many believe that emotional intelligence is more important than intelligence quotient (IQ) when it comes to workplace communication and professional success. This is because our ability to interpret, evaluate, and control our emotions in a healthy and constructive manner plays a major role in various workplace interactions, such as team meetings, coaching or mentoring sessions, or presentations. Individuals who have high levels of emotional intelligence are usually more self-aware, can recognize non-verbal communication cues, are able to manage their emotions and stress levels, and are fully capable of managing and developing their relationships with others. Moreover, a high level of emotional intelligence is ideal if you need or want to improve your empathy skills.

Empathy entails seeing and understanding the feelings of others, and here, emotional intelligence can help you manage your own feelings while being empathetic toward others. That is, empathy requires active listening, but this should not stop you from managing your own moods and emotions while listening to others. In the workplace, leaders have the responsibility to rise above their own feelings to take action, and this must come from a place of understanding. In order to lead effectively, the leader must let go of their own needs and ego, step outside of their own perspectives and experiences, and focus on the emotions of others to be able to see the bigger picture. Yet, a good leader does not become lost in the emotions of others but rather is able to remain neutral and listen to all sides of the story. This process is called "cognitive compassion," and it refers to the ability to recognize another person's emotions without allowing these emotions to affect your own.

Cognitive compassion works hand-in-hand with empathy, and a high level of emotional intelligence is needed to ensure that you are not consumed by the emotions of others. This is why self-awareness and self-management are important tools for improving your emotional intelligence and practicing empathy. In diverse workplaces, leaders, and employees must be able to understand and accept each other's opinions, experiences, and ideas—even the ones with which they disagree. Acknowledging diverse viewpoints and seeking to understand the perspectives of others is incredibly important for the successful implementation of DEI in the workplace. Plus, combining DEI with empathy (and, therefore, emotional intelligence) allows employees to see their coworkers, leaders, and peers in a new, more accepting way.

Strategy Three: Seek to Understand the Needs of Others

We are all different, and therefore, we all have different needs. A person who is grieving the loss of a loved one has different needs than someone who is celebrating a professional achievement. Or your emotional needs during times of stress may be very different from another person's needs during such times. In order to practice empathy, we must recognize that our needs may differ from the needs of others, and therefore, we must resist the urge to jump to conclusions about another person's needs. For instance, a coworker may reveal to you that another coworker has been making advancements at them both at and outside of work. You may immediately think about what you would do if you were in that situation and subsequently respond with your own thoughts and opinions on the matter. Perhaps you recommend that your coworker "take it as a compliment," or you tell them to just ignore the interaction, but in such a situation, it is best to withhold your judgment and instead practice active listening to identify your coworker's emotional needs. If you are not sure about their needs, you can simply ask them instead of moving into problem-solving mode or providing the wrong kind of support. Sometimes, your coworker may simply want to vent, or they may want to be reassured that they are not alone in this situation.

Strategy Four: Leverage Empathy to Foster Belonging

It is part of human nature to want to create meaningful connections with others and to feel a sense of belonging. Here, empathy is the key that unlocks the door to these connections by forming a complex psychological network in which knowledge, memories, and observation allow us to develop a deeper understanding of the thoughts and emotions of others. In turn, empathy is the basis of our understanding of each other and helps to build meaningful professional (and personal) relationships so that we may create a deeper sense of belonging in the workplace.

As stated by Ciaramicoli & Ketchum (2016),

> Empathy creates the invisible connections that hold us together, one human to another, neighborhood to village, community to country, nation to planet. With the connectedness that empathy engenders, the world itself becomes a less frightening place. A sense of belonging replaces loneliness, strangers appear less strange, defenses seem less necessary, and hope replaces

hopelessness... This is power—and the promise—of empathy. (p. 244)

For any organization that serves the public, embracing empathy in the client or consumer experience is an essential part of success. Indeed, empathy helps organizations offer culturally relevant and quality products and services that meet the specific needs of their consumers or client base. Here, organizations that weave empathy into the fiber of their being are able to recognize the obstacles faced by their clients or consumers and, in response, develop holistic services or products to remedy these obstacles. Simply put, organizations that employ empathetic approaches to their products and services can boost their client or consumer experiences and create life-long loyalty among their audience.

Empathy is also a key part of DEI, as leaders must be able to put themselves in the shoes of their colleagues and employees to create DEI strategies that are culturally relevant, sensitive to the needs of marginalized populations, and that can truly help employees from underrepresented groups prosper. Empathy can also spark open and meaningful conversations on DEI, as it allows leaders to decenter themselves and instead actively focus on the experiences and perspectives of others. When organizations and their leaders open themselves to input from employees from marginalized or underrepresented groups, they include their employees in DEI strategies and in moving the organization forward. Besides, when employees feel like their organizations care about them, they are more likely to feel a sense of belonging in the workplace. But empathy in DEI strategies must also come from an informed or knowledgeable place, as ignorance can undermine both empathy and a sense of belonging in workplaces.

Paying the Emotional Tax

When there is a lack of empathy in the workplace, employees from marginalized or underrepresented backgrounds are more likely to pay an emotional tax. The term refers to the "heightened experience of being treated differently from peers due to race, ethnicity, or gender, triggering adverse effects on health and feelings of isolation and making it difficult to thrive at work" (Travis et al., 2016). According to research by Catalyst (Percil-Mercieca, 2018), almost 60% of men and women of color have experienced the burden of emotional tax when they feel they must be on guard to protect themselves against racial bias. This constant state of alert also leads to employees struggling with their overall employee well-being and wanting to leave their jobs, yet in some cases, employees who are always on guard have a stronger drive to succeed at their jobs. While this may seem like a good thing, the added pressure to succeed can also have adverse effects on the employees' mental, physical, and emotional health. Catalyst's research also reveals that women of color (24%) are more likely to be on guard than their male counterparts (11%) because they expect to face both racial and gender bias in the workplace and in their personal lives.

The emotional tax is often referred to as the "Black Tax" because of its significant impact on Black individuals in the US and beyond. In fact, data from the Pew Research Center (Anderson, 2018) shows that 62% of Black employees, 44% of Asian employees, 42% of Hispanic employees, and 13% of white employees in STEM fields have experienced various forms of race- or ethnicity-based discrimination at work, such as receiving less support from managers and earning less than their coworkers with the same jobs or positions. When subjected to racial discrimination and/or microaggressions, Black employees may feel pressured to code-switch, downplay their racial differences to connect with their coworkers or suppress their racial identity and heritage. The suppression of their identity, however, comes at the cost of the employee's self-confidence, sense of belonging in the workplace, and authenticity.

The emotional tax also renders Black employees' racial identity hypervisible while systematically erasing their unique talents, skills, and personalities. That is, Black employees are seen through the lens of their racial identity rather than for their value as working professionals. More specifically, Black female employees shoulder the burden of both racial and gender bias as they are on constant alert should they be interrupted while speaking or asked to do office housework (such as washing the dishes). There is also the lingering threat of having their hair touched (without their permission or consent), being told that they are "one of the good ones," or having their coworkers tell them that they are articulate. While white women are often told to be more assertive to succeed at work, such advice seldom works for Black women, who—owing to racial stereotypes—are labeled as "angry" or "aggressive" when they speak up for themselves. Having to remain alert to the threat of discrimination, bias, and/or microaggressions in the workplace leads to many Black employees (and other employees of color) focusing their energy on self-regulation and self-control. This becomes an exhausting job-within-a-job, and the financial and professional repercussions can be devastating for employees and their families.

The racial and gender wage gaps can have a long-term impact on their earning potential and coupled with the limited opportunities to advance their careers, Black employees may struggle to gain socio-economic mobility to uplift themselves, their families, and their community. Indeed, the Black tax hinders many Black families from building generational wealth and casts a far-reaching shadow over the economic health and well-being of multiple generations of Black families. When employees are held back by the emotional tax, there is an unspoken pressure on marginalized employees to be more qualified, harder working, professional, and polite in the workplace to be seen or valued on par with their non-marginalized coworkers or peers. In a sense, these employees may be forced to overcompensate as their marginalization(s) render them invisible and hypervisible: Marginalized employees feel pressured to overperform to increase their chances of being recognized for their often-ignored work ethic and skills in the workplace, but they are also exposed because their marginalization(s) sets them apart or makes them the "Other" in the workplace.

This is a tricky paradox to navigate, and with all of the energy that goes into being on constant alert and overperforming, marginalized employees burdened with the emotional tax may find themselves struggling to be productive, suffering from health issues, and being disenchanted with their employer(s) and workplaces. When marginalized employees are burdened with the emotional tax, it often means that there is a gap or disconnect between the organization's diversity efforts and inclusion initiatives. Here, organizations can have a diverse workforce, but without inclusion (and empathy) in the workplace, the marginalized employees may be subjected to various forms of emotional tax, microaggressions, and hostilities. This is why diversity efforts must go hand-in-hand with inclusion, as organizations may struggle to retain their diverse workforce if their employees feel unwelcomed and excluded from their jobs. Ideally, an organization needs to establish an inclusive work environment from the very beginning, but with DEI gaining significant popularity only recently, it can be assumed that most organizations are attempting to develop and implement DEI policies, strategies, and initiatives in a pre-existing workforce and corporate culture. The more leaders invest in educating themselves on the impact and implication of issues like the emotional tax, the better suited they are to lead more inclusively, equitably, and across lines of difference.

Bridging the Diversity and Inclusion Gap Through Empathy

If organizations truly wish to make an impact with their DEI strategies, they must be willing to learn about the experiences of others and integrate these experiences into their structures and daily operations. Empathy does not require us to have the same experiences as others to fully understand their perspectives, opinions, and emotions, but rather, it provides us with the opportunity to try to understand them.

Here, empathy allows leaders of an organization to ask themselves the following:

- If I were in a similar situation, how would I feel?

- Have I experienced a similar situation or emotion that can help me better understand my employees and, therefore, provide them with support?

- How would I want to be treated if I were in their shoes?

- How well do I understand the needs and concerns of my team members?

- Am I listening actively and with an open mind to what my team members are saying?

- Do I take the time to acknowledge my team members' emotions and validate their experiences?

- How can I adjust my communication style to be more empathetic and supportive?

- Am I making assumptions about my team members' perspectives without seeking to understand their point of view?

- Do I prioritize the well-being and mental health of my team members?

- How can I demonstrate more compassion and understanding toward my team members?

- Am I creating a safe and inclusive environment where my team members feel comfortable sharing their thoughts and feelings?

With ongoing social issues and the ever-increasing pressure of economic volatility, these questions are all the more important should an organization wish to uplift all of its employees. A Deloitte Global report (2021) found that 80% of the women surveyed left the workforce as their previous places of employment did not provide them with a healthy work-life balance during the COVID-19 pandemic. Indeed, women (and especially women of color) are often pressured into working formal, paid jobs *and* performing informal, unpaid, and laborious tasks. This example demonstrates how organizations and their leaders are often unaware of the unique experiences of others and/or are unwilling to understand the perspectives and feelings of others. The lack of understanding and, therefore, empathy in these organizations is driving employees away.

Employees from marginalized groups often struggle when they are forced to conform to the dominant culture in the workplace, but for those of the dominant group, their way of doing things is the default, so they may not even be aware of the immense impact workplace discrimination and microaggressive behavior can have on marginalized employees. For those who are aware, they may not see workplace discrimination as a serious enough issue to address (because they may not be affected by such discrimination), or they may downplay or ignore the experiences of others. In turn, employees from marginalized groups may feel ashamed of their identity, which can have a detrimental effect on their physical, mental, and emotional well-being and negatively impact their work performance. To counteract this lack of understanding and empathy, organizations need to develop or improve their DEI strategies by adding a more empathetic approach. This entails embracing transformational and inclusive leadership, initiating healthy and open dialogues on DEI where all employee input is taken into consideration, creating, empowering, and properly resourcing employee and/or business resource groups to empower employees from marginalized backgrounds, and providing employees with professional support networks.

Research has shown that comprehensive DEI learning education is essential to creating a more psychologically safe, welcoming, and inviting workplace. A study by the Society for Human Resource Management found that employees who receive comprehensive DEI training are more likely to recognize and respond to unconscious bias and are more likely to report non-inclusive behaviors that may arise in workplace cultures. Furthermore, research by the University of Toronto found that comprehensive DEI training leads to increased awareness, improved attitudes, and more inclusive experiences for all. Empathy through education ensures that all employees, regardless of their role or function, understand the importance of core DEI practices and principles. Furthermore, DEI education also helps organizations build trust and credibility with external stakeholders, such as customers, investors, and community partners, who expect companies to take a stand on social and environmental issues. A study by Edelman found that 64% of consumers now buy or boycott brands based on their social or political stances, and that companies with a strong reputation for social responsibility tend to have higher customer loyalty and advocacy.

Empathy through education is underpinned by the willingness to be a life-long learner, as we cannot practice empathy without educating ourselves on the triumphs and hardships experienced by those who are different from us. We may not come from the same backgrounds, we may not share the same opinions, and we may not have the same values, but we must try to understand each other so that we may form a culture of community and belong in the workplace and in broader society. In doing so, we will be able to work together to translate DEI policies and strategies fully and effectively into reality. It is through this empathetic lens that we acknowledge that while DEI aims to dismantle the systemic barriers that preclude marginalized individuals from succeeding in the workplace, it is a framework that is beneficial for all employees.

Chapter 4:

Decolonization of the Mind and

Organization

Our minds must be as ready to move as capital is, to trace its paths and to imagine alternative destinations. –Chandra Talpade Mohanty

A culture of community and a sense of belonging in the workplace are essential for an organization's successful development and implementation of diversity, equity, and inclusion strategies and initiatives. As such, the employees of an organization all have a responsibility to each other, and this interdependence not only strengthens our professional relationships but also makes us acknowledge our inherent belonging to a network, organization, or community. This also means that leaders and employees must also operate ethically at their jobs to maintain a healthy, cohesive workplace culture. The values of community, interdependence, and cohesion have been prioritized by many cultures and societies throughout history, but the advent of colonialism sought to undermine these values. The consequences of European colonialism are far-reaching and continue to affect countless populations around the world even today. The colonization of the Americas between 1492 and 1800 is often called the "Age of Discovery," yet the Americas were not simply "discovered" by the Europeans.

Indeed, Native Americans, or Indigenous Americans, have inhabited the American landscapes for centuries. Nevertheless, European empires, including Britain, Spain, Portugal, and France, arrived on the American coast and claimed the land, natural resources, and humans as their own. This resulted in the forced removal and displacement, enslavement, and slaughter of many Indigenous Americans. The Indigenous Americans who did not fall victim to genocide were eradicated as a result of the many diseases the Europeans brought with them. In addition to spreading diseases and famine, the European colonizers established settler colonies in the Americas and, thus, the "New World." Even centuries later, Indigenous Americans are still reeling from the trauma of being removed from their ancestral lands, subjected to unjust government policies, and forced to assimilate into dominant American culture.

The Americas were not the only regions conquered by European colonial powers; Africa and much of South and East Asia, too, were colonized. During the Scramble for Africa, European colonial powers carved up and established arbitrary borders in Africa, separating various ethnic groups and seizing control of the natural resources and human labor that would later give rise to the powerful economies of European colonial powers. While European leaders and citizens were enjoying the fruits of colonial forced labor, the colonized countries were suffering. There were outbreaks of war, famine, and massacres throughout the colonized regions, and the African terrains were being plundered for gold, timber, rubber, cocoa, coffee, and other popular raw materials. Even before the Scramble for Africa, the transatlantic slave trade transported millions of enslaved Africans to the Americas and forced them to work under cruel, inhumane conditions on the plantations. Yet, even after the abolishment of slavery, enslaved Africans and their descendants, now African Americans, continued to face discrimination and persecution. The Jim Crow and racial segregation laws of the 20th century, too, led to racial trauma among African Americans and other communities of color and deeply embedded racism, sexism, classism, and other social "isms" into the fabric of American society.

Decolonization in Theory

Colonization is not just a form of political, economic, and cultural domination of one group over another; it also encompasses the forced assimilation of BIPOC communities into the dominant culture, systemic inequalities, and lack of access to adequate healthcare, education, and employment, and the explicit or subtle discriminations against those deemed "inferior." While the legacy of European colonialism is embedded in American society, it is also present in our organizations, businesses, and companies. Clearly, the legacy of colonialism (and racial segregation) continues to harm employees from underrepresented or marginalized groups and undermines any attempts at diversity, equity, and inclusion in the workplace.

This makes it all the more important for us to actively decolonize our organizations, our workplace cultures, and our minds. As stated by Belfi and Sandiford (2021):

> Decolonization is work that belongs to all of us, everywhere. It asks us to think about our relationship with Indigenous lands that colonizers have unjustly claimed, re-defined and repurposed all over the world. It asks us to embrace responsibility as opposed to accepting fault. Lastly, decolonization is a path forward to creating systems which are just and equitable, addressing inequality through education, dialogue, communication, and action. (para. 3)

The term "decolonization" describes economic, cultural, and psychological freedom for all those negatively impacted by (the legacy of) colonialism. For Indigenous Americans, for example, the goal of decolonization is to gain sovereignty and self-determination over their cultures, histories, lands, and political and economic structures. In general, decolonization for BIPOC communities also includes confronting racial injustice, the overlapping oppressions of race, gender, and class, and internalized racism and colorism, to name a few examples. We often focus on colonization in terms of politics and socio-economic conditions, but colonization also established a sense of cultural inferiority and shame among BIPOC communities while also forcing many BIPOC to forget their own histories and cultures and, instead, to assimilate to white, Eurocentric norms and traditions.

While BIPOC communities should actively challenge erasure, oppression, colonial beliefs and narratives, and historical amnesia, we must also look at decolonization as a DEI tool that can work against systemic inequalities. We must also recognize that decolonization is not necessarily an end goal but rather an ongoing process that requires active engagement from all parties and can adapt to changing social norms. That is, decolonization, much like diversity, equity, and inclusion, is not something organizations and their leaders can simply tick off on a checklist. As the environments around us become more diverse and our identities become more fluid, our decolonization strategies and processes must be evaluated and changed when needed. Relatedly, we must also recognize how and why the term "decolonization" has been and can be commercialized, commodified, weaponized, or relegated to being a diversity buzzword.

Decolonization is often discussed and debated in academic circles, on social media, and in social justice spaces, and when these discussions lack nuance, the meaning of decolonization can become warped and even decenter the narratives of marginalized communities. In fact, a warped, weaponized, or problematic conception of decolonization may even further dismiss and/or oppress marginalized communities. Instead of overly relying on decolonization discourse, we must also translate decolonization into practice. For instance, it is not enough to read books written by BIPOC authors or to watch movies with a diverse cast; we must actively work toward deconstructing the many ways in which colonization manifests and is expressed in our healthcare system, in our school curricula, in our social circles, and in our workplace cultures. This also requires confronting racialized and gendered hierarchies, placing values on indigenous knowledge systems, and framing decolonization as a tool, process, and strategy that cannot be weaponized or commercialized by the mainstream, dominant culture.

Decolonization of the Mind

Because it involves the restructuring of political and socio-economic systems, decolonization is not an easy process. So let us first look at decolonization on a more individual scale. Kenyan American academic, author, and poet, Mũkoma wa Ngũgĩ, writes that decolonizing the mind also applies to the areas of our lives that are "away from immediately recognizable power relationships between the colonizer and the colonized, or oppression and avenues of resistance." Here, decolonization is a life-long process that focuses on how power imbalances and inequalities are culturally, socially, economically, and politically encoded so that they appear normal or the default. Despite being pervasive, these power imbalances are often hidden, and to identify them, we may need to identify how we hold onto colonial knowledge systems, beliefs, traditions, and norms.

Ask yourself the following questions:

- Do I consider my English-speaking, writing, and reading abilities as markers of my intelligence and skills?

- Do I feel ashamed of my family, community, culture, or traditions?

- Do I code-switch when I am in professional spaces or in social situations?

- Do I acknowledge my and my community's history?

- Does my workplace have a gendered and/or racialized hierarchy?

- Do I struggle with internalized racism and unconscious bias?

- Do I see myself as culturally inferior to others?

These questions are only the first step toward implementing decolonization strategies in your personal life, but they can also be used to confront colonial traditions and beliefs in the workplace. Of course, decolonization on an organization-wide scale is far more challenging than decolonizing your own mind, but it is not impossible. Besides, decolonization strategies need to be translated into practice and implemented on a larger scale to ascertain whether these strategies truly uplift leaders and employees from marginalized communities.

Decolonization in Practice

Decolonization in organizations, businesses, or companies entails reversing the inequalities and discrimination that form part of the legacy of colonialism and other systems of power imbalance. From discriminatory hiring and promotion practices to covert and overt racism in the office, organizations must address these power imbalances in all of their iterations and expressions and develop new ways of thinking (and doing) that are empowering for all employees. While there are no legal requirements for decolonization in the workplace, organizations with colonial histories must recognize their role in upholding or perpetuating colonial beliefs and traditions and prioritize the ethical and moral process of reparations. This does not mean that organizations must completely forget their colonial histories, but rather, they should identify how their histories linger in their daily operations, in their systems and policies, and in their relationships among employees, leaders, business partners, and collaborators, and clients or consumers.

For instance, businesses that use raw materials from previously-colonized countries in their manufacturing processes have the moral, ethical, and sometimes legal responsibility to address how they may contribute to the inequalities and hardships faced by the farmers, laborers, and civilians of those countries. In a more specific example, it is no secret that several fast fashion retailers have used forced, slave, child, and/or underpaid labor in countries like India, Bangladesh, Nepal, and Cambodia to produce garments at ridiculously low prices. These retailers exploit the cheap labor and lax labor laws of countries in the Global South to meet the unreasonable demands of fast fashion consumers, and as a result, the garment workers (who are mostly women of color) are subjected to terrible (and sometimes deadly) working conditions, sexual harassment, abuse, toxins, and inhumanely low wages, all so that fast fashion retailers can bring in massive profits and fast fashion consumers can stay on-trend. Moreover, once the garments are no longer in fashion, they are dumped in landfills or exported to countries in the Global South, which now have the burden of dealing with the Western world's trash. Obviously, the fast fashion business model is not sustainable in terms of the environment or in terms of human labor.

While being one of the main culprits of environmental degradation and human rights abuses in exploited countries, fast fashion is not the only global industry that needs to address its unsustainable business model and acknowledge its role in the ongoing oppression and exploitation of colonial power imbalances. Indeed, companies that engage in mining gold and diamonds or the manufacturing of coffee, cocoa, tea, and leather, to name a few examples, are most probably complicit in or active participants in labor rights violations, slave labor, and other practices that form part of the legacy of colonialism. Of course, we, as individuals, may not have the political and economic power to challenge these exploitative industries, but as consumers, we can make a difference with our wallets. Yet, the onus should not fall on consumers and employees to change the system; rather, those in power can (and should) make decolonization a major part of their diversity, equity, and inclusion strategies and policies. So, how can organizations take the first steps toward decolonization?

Strategy One: Research the Organization's History

Organizations that wish to decolonize may be required to not only delve into their histories but also perform an equity audit to identify whether their founders, business partners, and leaders have benefited from colonial exploitation and/or the slave trade. Here, organizations can work with historians and research companies to perform in-depth research into the organizations' histories, political and economic ties, and funding. Even organizations that were established relatively recently may need to research their histories to identify any ties to colonialism and the slave trade. For example, the British brewer and pub chain Greene King recently apologized for its historical links to the slave trade because one of its founders, Benjamin Greene, owned a couple of highly profitable plantations in the Caribbean. Following the abolition of slavery in 1833, the UK government compensated slave owners for their loss of "human property" rather than compensating those who had been enslaved. Benjamin Greene was one of the many recipients of this compensation. As part of their reparations, Greene King promised to invest in the Black, Asian, and minority ethnic (BAME) communities. Nevertheless, formal apologies and financial promises are not enough to atone for businesses or companies' profits from slave labor, but the acknowledgment of their role in colonialism and slavery is a good start.

Strategy Two: Be Actively Anti-Racist

Once an organization has identified any links to colonialism, slavery, or historical power imbalances, the organization should release an official statement acknowledging its role in such histories and pledging to take action toward remedying any current power imbalances or inequalities within the organization. Whether this involves organizational changes, forming alternative business partnerships, re-branding, or making financial commitments to make reparations, the organization must translate its acknowledgment into clear actions. Moreover, these actions should have a noticeable and apparent impact on marginalized employees and/or communities. It is also worth noting that many organizations or companies may not have to do their own research into their histories as many activists have continuously performed the (unpaid) labor for them. In the Amazon region, for instance, indigenous leaders and activists have called out Western banks and businesses for their support of the ongoing degradation of Amazonian rainforests.

Owing to the oil, logging, and mining industries—that mainly or only benefit Western companies and economies—the ecosystems of the Amazon are on the brink of collapse. A recent report by the Association of Brazil's Indigenous Peoples (APIB) reveals that the manufacturing of many of the hardware products by several major technology brands is tied to the illegal mining of gold in the Amazonian region. The executive leader of APIB, Dinamam Tuxá (quoted in Milman 2022), states that the activities of these companies directly threaten the indigenous people's way of life and that the "destruction and violence stems from the interest of these giant corporations in the advancement of industries, such as agribusiness and mining, within Indigenous lands." In cases such as this, indigenous activists, leaders, and organizations have done and continue to do the work that many organizations or companies ignore to protect their economic interests and profits. As such, it is not enough for organizations to acknowledge their role in continuing the legacy of colonialism and slavery; they must also actively work to eradicate these legacies.

Strategy Three: View Decolonization as a Process

As our workplace norms change, so too must our decolonization efforts adapt. Many colonial practices that are embedded in our socio-political, economic, and workplace structures are no longer socially appropriate or acceptable. As we focus our attention on decolonization and DEI, we must also revisit our existing policies and business practices that explicitly or subtly perpetuate colonial beliefs. This process is ongoing, and all decolonization approaches must be evaluated and, if necessary, adapted regularly to ensure that the needs of marginalized employees and leaders are being met. As a whole, organizations need to encourage the hiring, mentoring, and promotion of employees from diverse backgrounds while also ensuring that these employees are not tokenized and are not expected to perform extra, unpaid labor to achieve DEI and decolonization goals.

While the ongoing process of decolonization may incur short-term costs for the organization, decolonization must be prioritized by organizations. As explained by Horne et al. (2020), "Companies should think about ethical productivity and focus on new systems of value that are not purely financial" so that they may prioritize DEI and employee well-being over profits. But with all forms of organizational change, effective leadership is necessary to remedy any anxieties, hesitations, and confusion among employees. Business or organization leaders play a significant role in ensuring decolonization is an ongoing process rather than an end goal, and these leaders should also be willing to stand up against any form of exploitation, discrimination, or exclusion in the workplace. That is, business leaders must lead by example so that their employees, coworkers, and peers, too, can be empowered to address systemic inequalities. Indeed, implementing decolonization and DEI strategies in the workplace can make employees uncomfortable, as such strategies challenge what they may consider "normal" in the workplace.

Strategy Four: Read, Research, and Reflect

In order to decolonize DEI strategies in the workplace and decolonize workplace cultures, organizations (and their leaders) must gather as much information from books and other resources as possible to identify and understand how and why colonial ideologies may still plague their workplace environments. This entails reading not only books on the topic but also staying up to date with current research and studies on the topic of decolonization in the workplace. Here, leaders can diversify their sources of information by listening to podcasts, watching documentaries, attending local cultural events, or speaking to experts in such fields. Remember, using a diverse array of sources also prevents us from understanding only mainstream or dominant perspectives. While undertaking in-depth research is a significant part of the decolonization process, organizations must also reflect on what they have learned. This ultimately involves the employees and leaders of an organization confronting their own privileges and disadvantages and possibly shifting their mindsets.

Strategy Five: Acknowledge, Act, and Collaborate

Once an organization has researched, read, and reflected on ways in which colonial ideologies and structures continue to exist in workplaces, the organization must also take the necessary steps to implement change. This can entail anti-racist and anti-sexist or inclusive culture workshops for all employees, short classes, or courses on how history and systems of oppression inform workplace cultures and environments, or group sessions that provide employees with the opportunity to have healthy discussions and conversations on decolonization in the workplace. Whatever actions it may undertake, it is important for the organization to be public about its decolonization strategies. In doing so, it will be easier for the organization to reach out to the public for help (as an organization, be it a corporation or small business, exists and should be contextualized within broader society). By publicizing its decolonization strategies, an organization may even influence other companies or businesses to also decolonize their organizational structures and workplace environments.

Organizations can join forces with each other or collaborate with activist movements and research organizations to expand their decolonization networks. Decolonization does not have to be an individualistic experience for an organization; rather, it can (and should) be a process where the organization works with activists, researchers, and community leaders to identify the key areas in the workplace that are in urgent need of immediate decolonization. By collaborating or partnering up with others, your employees will see your commitment to decolonizing the workplace, and they, too, may be inspired to challenge their own colonial beliefs or ideologies. Moreover, collaborating with community leaders and organizers from marginalized or underrepresented groups can help organizations identify their cultural missteps and general lack of cultural competency and awareness and find ways to remedy them for greater employee well-being and a healthier, more inclusive workplace culture.

Let us take the politics of hair as an example: The natural hair movement began in the 1960s in the US as a way to encourage all individuals of African descent to celebrate their natural, afro-textured hair. With further encouragement from other Black power movements, many African Americans began embracing their natural hair and other racialized physical features. This was empowering on both an individual and community level, so unsurprisingly, there was a renewed interest in the natural hair movement in the 2000s. Despite these individual and community-level forms of empowerment and, arguably, decolonization, not everyone was as welcoming to natural, Black hair. Several workplaces, in particular, viewed natural Black hair as "unruly" and "unprofessional," and through policies and/or discriminatory remarks, they made it known that natural Black hair was unacceptable in professional settings. Indeed, decolonization on an individual level can be empowering, but we also need society- or country-wide decolonization efforts so that African Americans can be empowered even when they step outside of their homes.

A Case Study of Hair Politics in the Workplace

In 2010, an Alabama woman, Chastity Jones, accepted a job offer as a customer service representative from Catastrophe Management Solutions. Wearing a business suit and with her hair in short, natural locs, Jones attended the interview only to be told by an HR manager that her locs were in violation of the company's grooming policy. When Jones refused to cut her hair, the job offer was rescinded, and thus began a years-long legal battle. Whereas Catastrophe Management Solutions argues the decision to rescind the job offer was based on a grooming policy unrelated to race, Jones claims that the decision was a clear example of racial discrimination. In 2013, the Equal Employment Opportunity Commission (EEOC) filed a suit on Jones' behalf and argued that Jones was denied the job based on the racial stereotype that African American hair is unprofessional. The EEOC subsequently lost when the federal district court stated that claims of racial discrimination must show evidence of bias based on traits a person cannot change (such as skin color). In 2016, the 11th Circuit Court of Appeals dismissed the case. With the support of the NAACP Legal Defense and Educational Fund, Jones' case went to the Supreme Court, but the Court ultimately declined to hear her case.

Jones' situation, however, is just one of the many instances of Black employees alleging discrimination against their natural hair in the workplace. There is a long history of anti-Black hair sentiment in the US. Back in the 1700s, enslaved women who worked in the fields often covered their hair in head rags, while those who worked in their enslavers' households would often attempt to mimic Western hairstyles. In the latter's case, this meant donning trendy wigs or styling their natural hair to be straighter. In some parts of the US, such as in New Orleans, free Black and Creole women wore their hair in elaborate hairstyles that emphasized their coils and kinks to fight against the laws that required them to wear a tignon over their hair. Hair for Black people, and Black women in particular, was also politicized. In the 1960s, the "Black Is Beautiful" movement took center stage, with activists assuring Black men and women that their skin, natural hair, and facial features were beautiful and should, therefore, be celebrated. Black women, for example, were encouraged to embrace their natural hair instead of trying to emulate Eurocentric standards of beauty. Afros also became a symbol of Black power in the fight for racial equality and justice, with several activists, including Angela Davis, sporting an afro to rebel against white beauty standards and to declare solidarity with the Black community in the US.

The banning of discrimination in the workplace (as part of the Civil Rights Act), however, did not foresee how prevalent hair discrimination in the workplace would later become. Despite the landmark 1976 Jenkins v. Blue Cross Mutual Hospital Insurance case that ensured the protection of afros under the Civil Rights Act and the rising popularity of the natural hair movement, federal courts continue to dismiss cases of hair discrimination. There is, however, an exception to this: In 2019, the New York City Commission on Human Rights argued that natural hair is inextricably linked to race and is, therefore, protected under Title VII of the Civil Rights Act. The Commission also declared its commitment to protecting New York residents' legal right to wear their hair in braids, afros, locs, and other culturally specific hairstyles. The Commission (cited in Griffin 2019) stated that the "[b]ans or restrictions on natural hair or hairstyles associated with Black people are often rooted in white standards of appearance and perpetuate racist stereotypes that Black hairstyles are unprofessional" and that these policies "exacerbate anti-Black bias in employment, at school, while playing sports, and in other areas of daily living."

While the New York City Commission on Human Rights' efforts shows a step in the right direction, natural Black hair and hairstyles continue to be seen as "unprofessional" in numerous workplaces—forcing many African Americans to choose between embracing their natural hair (and, by extension, their Black identity) or being or remaining employed. It is a difficult choice that employees should not have to make, and yet, the issue of natural hair remains rife in American workplaces. As recent as December 2022, the C.R.O.W.N. (Create a Respectful and Open Workplace for Natural Hair) Act, which would have banned hair discrimination nationwide was blocked by the Senate and did not pass. As such, it remains legal to discriminate on the basis of hair texture in 27 states in the Union. The above examples of racial discrimination demonstrate the need for organizations to decolonize not only their DEI policies but also their workplace culture. Besides, an organization may have fantastic DEI policies, but these policies may not prevent or deter employees from discriminating against each other. As such, decolonized DEI strategies must translate into practice and be fully and clearly communicated to all the employees of an organization. This is where empathy through education comes into play: Discrimination among employees may be a result of unconscious biases or cultural ignorance, and should an organization want to ensure a healthy, productive, and decolonized working environment for all employees, the organization must encourage employees to learn about different people, cultures, countries, traditions, beliefs, and customs.

By encouraging its employees to learn about each other and diversify their knowledge, the organization also helps employees confront their prejudices, unconscious biases, or ignorance. In turn, this can help foster even greater employee-client or consumer relations—especially if the organization has a larger or more global client or consumer base. Having a truly inclusive workplace culture is important for the professional growth and well-being of an organization's employees, but an organization's decolonization processes or efforts must also be reflected in its advertising, marketing, and other communication channels. Here, organizations must ensure that the images and words conveyed to their clients or consumers via various communication channels do not reflect any intentional or unintentional prejudice, bias, or negative stereotypes.

Decolonizing Branding, Advertising, and Marketing

Advertisements are created to appeal to mass audiences, but many brands and companies assume that these masses are white. With changing demographics in the US, brands are not only losing out on potential consumers, but the absence of ethnic minorities or racial stereotyping in their advertisements can directly or indirectly harm ethnic minorities. The same can be said for when women, LGBTQIA2+ people, people with disabilities, and other underrepresented groups are excluded from or stereotyped in advertisements. Decolonization seeks to disrupt the status quo, and, therefore, organizations must also decolonize their communication strategies, including branding, marketing, and advertising. In many cases, branding, marketing, and advertising bridge the gap between organizations and their clients and consumers and show their audiences the values, ethics, and objectives of the organization. From billboards alongside highways to sponsored posts on social media platforms, advertising is almost inescapable in modern society, so it makes sense for organizations to ensure that their communication strategies do not perpetuate colonial beliefs, discrimination, or prejudice. Owing in part to the Black Lives Matter movement and various other forms of mostly-online social justice activism, many brands and companies have started paying greater attention to what they are communicating to their clients and consumers.

Addressing colonial beliefs in its advertising is a must for any brand or company that wants to market its products or services online. Nowadays, many social media users are quick to point out any hypocrisies or double standards in a brand's advertising and marketing. A 2018 social media campaign by luxury brands, Dolce and Gabbana, for example, featured a Chinese model clad in D&G clothing clumsily attempting to eat Italian food with chopsticks. The dialogue in the video advertisements was also sexually suggestive. Many Chinese luxury consumers were offended by the campaign, and D&G soon buckled under public pressure: D&G issued a formal apology, the advertisements were taken down, and D&G's runway show in Shanghai was canceled. But the racial stereotyping in the ads was further exacerbated when screenshots of racist comments allegedly made by D&G's co-founder, Stefano Gabbana, were posted. In these screenshots, Gabbana allegedly called China the "Ignorant Dirty Smelling Mafia" and a "country of shit," and, in response, D&G claimed that the brand and Gabbana's social media accounts had been hacked. Yet this is not D&G's first-time receiving backlash for their advertising. In 2007, for instance, the brand had to pull an ad in Spain that depicted a man holding down a woman on the ground while a group of men watched. Spain's Labor and Social Affairs Ministry stated that the campaign was humiliating to women, and some journalists claimed that the advert glorified gang rape.

Cultural Appropriation vs. Appreciation

There is also the issue of cultural appropriation versus cultural appreciation in the marketing and advertising of products and services. From cuisines, music, and clothing to ways of life and beliefs, cultural exchanges are bound to occur in our increasingly globalized world. While sharing cultures and learning from each other are usually positive experiences, there are cases where cultural appreciation veers into the territory of cultural appropriation. Appropriation occurs when the individual(s) of a privileged group or culture adopts or takes certain aspects of a different, marginalized group or culture without their consent. Cultural appropriation is underpinned by the economic, social, or political exploitation of a marginalized culture, whereas cultural appreciation involves a desire to learn about and a deeper understanding of another culture. In the latter case, there is a deep respect and appreciation for the other culture and its members, and there are no intentions to exploit the culture for profits, power, or aesthetics.

The problem with cultural appropriation is that it often reinforces negative stereotypes about and misrepresents the appropriated culture, misuses the culture for one's own gain, and takes credit for and/or compensation for objects, philosophies, and lifestyles that were originally created and used by the appropriated culture. For example, purchasing mass-produced "Native American-inspired" headdresses for a Halloween costume, wearing sacred items or religious symbols without understanding the meaning(s) or origin(s) of them, whitewashing the practice of yoga, or taking credit for "inventing" matcha or turmeric beverages. In addition, when members of a privileged group appropriate another culture, they are often praised for it, whereas the members of the appropriated culture are punished for doing or wearing the same thing. For instance, when a white celebrity wears cornrows or locs, the media deems their hair "edgy" and "trendy," but when a Black celebrity wears cornrows or locs, they are met with racially-underpinned criticism and stereotypes.

Moksha (2018) describes cultural appropriation as "the silent racism of marketing and advertising" and something that marketers moving into a diverse field must be aware of if they want to avoid potentially catastrophic blunders for their companies. In marketing and advertising, cultural appropriation steals and capitalizes on the cultural experiences, creativity, property, and hardships of an oppressed group without making any efforts toward easing the oppression and marginalization of the said group. Cultural appropriation relies on a power imbalance between the appropriating and appropriated cultures, and advertisers and marketers should acknowledge that, nowadays, marginalized cultures and communities have far more platforms to voice their concerns than ever before. Indeed, the proliferation of the internet and social media allows marginalized communities (and their allies) to unite against injustice, misrepresentations, and the appropriation of their cultures.

In 2019, for example, luxury brand Dior faced controversy over a Native American-inspired advertising campaign for its Sauvage fragrance, forcing the brand to swiftly delete the campaign from their digital channels. Despite consulting with the Americans for Indian Opportunity (AIO), Dior juxtaposed Native American imagery with the fragrance name Sauvage, and this drew criticism as Native Americans have often been stereotyped, misrepresented, and falsely labeled as "savages." While the brand was quick to release a statement and a behind-the-scenes video to evince their appreciation of Native Americans, the campaign's imagery, and dialogue ("an authentic journey deep into the Native American soul in a sacred, founding, and secular territory") capitalized on colonial beliefs, stereotypes, and cultural symbols to sell a perfume while doing little to empower Native American communities.

Dismantling Colonial Beliefs in Advertising

These are only a few of the countless examples of advertisements that perpetuate colonial beliefs, but there are several ways that organizations can decolonize their advertising and marketing. Firstly, organizations should ensure their advertising and marketing team(s) (or their outsourced advertising agencies) are conscious of the colonial legacies and systemic inequalities that are prevalent in the organization's client/consumer base or target market. For instance, an advertisement for a Dove body product featured a Black woman removing her top to reveal a white woman. The white woman, in turn, removes her top and turns into a Middle Eastern woman; it is implied that these "transformations" come as a result of using the Dove body product.

At best, the advert can be seen as Dove missing the mark, but when we contextualize the images and implications of the advert, Dove's message to consumers becomes murkier. Indeed, this was not the first-time Dove posted a racially insensitive advert, and in general, there is a long history of beauty advertising that portrays Black people as dirty and unhygienic and as becoming clean once they have used a body product. Such portrayals play into colonial notions that associate cleanliness and purity with white skin and uncleanliness and impurity with black or dark skin. As such, having a diverse, historically-aware advertising and marketing team can prevent organizations from posting advertisements that are culturally or racially insensitive and/or explicitly racist.

Secondly, organizations can establish their own internal regulatory body to ensure that their advertising and marketing strategies are free from colonial ideologies and biases. This can form part of the organization's overall DEI strategy or part of the organization's efforts to adhere to national and international advertising regulatory boards. Here, the internal regulatory body can determine whether the organization's advertising campaigns are truly free from prejudice or discrimination *before* the campaign is posted or viewed by the public. Besides, if organizations want to avoid facing a public backlash for insensitive or discriminatory advertising campaigns, they need to have mechanisms in place to monitor all processes relating to the advertising and marketing of their products or services.

An alternative to establishing an internal regulatory body is for the organization to create sensitivity viewer groups. In the publishing industry, for example, sensitive readers are hired to review a book or script before its publication to help identify any unconscious biases, stereotypes, or insensitive content that may appear in the book or script. Sensitivity readers are particularly important in cases where authors are not from the often-marginalized group(s) that is being portrayed in their work. As such, if a novel features a main character who is Native American, the novel may be reviewed by a sensitive reader who is also Native American. Similarly, organizations and/or advertising agencies can make use of this process by hiring sensitive viewers for their advertising and marketing campaigns.

The proliferation of European colonialism had devastating impacts on various countries and cultures around the world, and we should remember that the anti-colonial struggle for independence in several countries was fairly recent. Indeed, the early to mid-20th century was marked by anti-colonial protests and a push for decolonization. We must see decolonization as a significant part of not only DEI in the workplace but also social change in the broader global social, political, economic, and environmental context. Decolonization is no easy feat as it requires ongoing reflection and action, but it is incredibly rewarding for communities that have been marginalized throughout recent history. Whether it is a small but growing business or a larger, multi-national company, all organizations have the responsibility to uplift their marginalized employees so that they may thrive without the fear of colonial barriers in their way.

Chapter 5:

Equity as a Means to Achieve

Equality

The difference between equity and equality is that equality is when everyone gets the same thing, and equity is when everyone gets the things they deserve. –DeRay Mckesson

Defining Equity and Equality

Despite being two different concepts, "equity" and "equality" are often used synonymously in the workplace. Both equality and equity play a major role in developing and strengthening DEI policies in the workplace, but we must be able to distinguish between these concepts to fully grasp how we can make our organizations truly inclusive and welcoming toward those from marginalized groups. "Equality" as a concept and practice seeks to provide all employees of an organization with access to the same resources, but it does not take into consideration any pre-existing, systemic barriers the employees may face. As such, an organization that prioritizes equality ensures that there is an equal distribution of opportunity, resources, and money among employees who work at similar levels. Equality is a fantastic idealistic practice to implement in any organization, as it helps push the organization and its employees in the right direction. However, equality (as a concept and in practice) does little to remedy the problem of underrepresentation and marginalization among employees, nor does it truly challenge the status quo at the workplace.

Equity, however, is the concept and practice of providing all employees with fair opportunities, but it differs from "equality" in the sense that these opportunities are doled out based on the employees' individual needs. An equitable organization does not provide every employee with the same resources or opportunities but instead acknowledges that its employees already have varying access to opportunities, resources, and privileges. As a result, the organization provides its employees with less access to resources or opportunities so that they may have a fairer advantage in the workplace.

Simply put, equity in the workplace levels the playing field by ensuring that all employees have the skills, resources, and opportunities they need to succeed. Because employees have different needs and may require specific resources or support, organizations must be adaptable and willing to work with their employees to identify these needs. Like many other DEI strategies, promoting equity in the workplace takes a lot of work and can be even more challenging in larger or more global workforces. Luckily, there are numerous methods organizations can employ to make their work environment more equitable, such as having greater diversity in interview panels, creating and investing in resource groups for employees to share their experiences with each other, taking into consideration the different or unique contexts or situations of each employee, and examining all existing policies and strategies to ensure that they are fully inclusive. For example, to create a more equitable working environment for employees with children, an organization may need to offer more flexible working hours or, when it comes to benefit packages, an organization should provide employees of all backgrounds and gender and sexual identities with the opportunity to share health insurance benefits with their partners.

Why Equity Trumps Equality in the Workplace

While "equality" suggests sameness, "equity" connotes fairness and uses a needs-based approach. Equity focuses on giving employees what they need rather than assuming that all employees have the same needs, and as such, equity can be described as a form of corrective action against systemic and structural barriers. For example, an equitable workplace recognizes that those from low-income backgrounds may not have had the resources to further their formal education. The hiring practices of such a workplace will look at more than just the candidates' formal qualifications; the interviewers will also focus on skills, work experience, and cultural add. Relatedly, equity highlights the importance of social and racial justice, inclusion, and social change as it seeks to empower those who specifically have less access to resources and opportunities. Coupled with the fact that equity is a means to achieve equality, equity is preferred over equality in workplaces that wish to diversify their workforce, initiate systemic change, and create an equal workplace culture. An equitable workplace is, therefore, one that acknowledges differences and works toward bridging the gap between those who are privileged and those who are marginalized.

When organizations treat all of their employees equally, they fail to consider that employees do not start at the same point. For instance, those who are born into families with generational wealth will have different resources and opportunities than those born into lower-income families. Here, the wealthier employees may have attended private schools and an ivy league university (that may even be their parent's alma mater), have traveled across the world and been exposed to various people and cultures, and may have all the tools needed to succeed handed to them on a silver platter. This greatly contrasts the circumstances of more indigent employees who had to work from a young age to support their families, who were unable to travel beyond their city (let alone their country), or who may have had limited access to formal education and training. The wealthier, more privileged employees and the less socio-economically disadvantaged, more marginalized employees come from vastly different circumstances and, therefore, have different needs. It is the responsibility of an equitable workplace to ensure that marginalized employees have greater access to resources and opportunities so that they do not remain in the lower echelons of the organization throughout their careers while their more privileged coworkers climb the corporate ladder.

Equity is often seen as the government's responsibility. Indeed, most country's government has the power and resources to challenge systemic injustices and empower their marginalized citizens. Yet, owing to a myriad of reasons, many governments struggle to level the playing field among their citizens. This is especially true of countries that have experienced colonialism, slavery, racial segregation, genocide, and civil wars in their recent history. If we take the US as an example, class inequalities and inequities exist along racial lines because of the country's history of slavery and racial segregation. These class and racial inequities and inequalities are often further exacerbated by other factors, such as gender, religion, nationality, age, and physical ability. If a government's public policies and equity initiatives fail or are inadequate, private organizations—from corporations to small businesses—have the moral and ethical responsibility to promote fairness and social justice among their employees.

Strategies for Promoting Equity in the Workplace

Strategy One: Equity in the Hiring Process

An organization can claim to have fantastic DEI commitments and goals, but if diversity is not reflected in its workforce, it may be challenging for the public (including clients and consumers) to believe the organization's claims. From the cleaners and administrative staff to the managers and supervisors, the workforce is what keeps an organization running. Sure, transformative and inclusive leadership is essential to any organization, but its employees, too, are an integral part of ensuring the organization's financial success and sustainability in an ever-competitive global market. As such, diversifying a workforce begins during the recruitment and hiring process. To create a more equitable workplace, the organization must ensure DEI strategies are implemented within the hiring team. Here, those selected to be part of the hiring team should represent a diverse set of perspectives, ideas, and opinions, and, more importantly, they must be heard. Every person on the hiring team should feel like their opinion matters and that their contributions have value.

If an organization has pre-existing DEI infrastructure, the hiring team should be diverse, but if the organization is in a transitional phase, then having a diverse hiring team may not be an option. In either case, the people on the hiring team should be trained on structural and unconscious biases that may affect the hiring process. For instance, resumes with "Afrocentric-sounding" names on them should be given just as much consideration as those with "Eurocentric-sounding" names on them. Indeed, there have been cases where resumes that subtly indicated the candidates' race were discarded toward the initial stages of the hiring process (Asare, 2020). As such, hiring teams must recognize that such situations exist and actively address their own biases so that the hiring process can lay the groundwork for a more diverse, equitable, and inclusive workplace.

Once a hiring team has been selected or formed, the recruitment process, too, should prioritize diversity, equity, and inclusion. Here, organizations can make their job descriptions more transparent and accessible by including the following factors: Wage ranges for different positions, available resources for career growth, opportunities for skill development and training, and employee benefit schemes. The hiring process can also be skills-based rather than mainly or only qualification-based. Many people have limited access or resources to attend and graduate from a college or university, but this should not prevent them from being employed if they have the necessary skills and/or work experience to do the job. There are many professionals who attended community college or vocational school who are perfectly capable of doing many jobs in corporate spaces. Besides, formal qualifications do not necessarily guarantee that the candidate is the best for the job.

Strategy Two: Equitable Pay

There is a key difference between equal pay and equitable pay: The former looks at whether there are pay discrepancies within the same (or similar) jobs, while the latter focuses on the systemic issues that lead to pay gaps. Equal pay, therefore, suggests that every employee who does the same job should get the same pay—regardless of the employees' race, ethnicity, gender, sexuality, age, physical ability, and nationality. Pay equity, however, is more nuanced: An organization may have equal pay for the same jobs, but if male employees disproportionately dominate the higher-paying positions while female employees are more likely to be found in lower-paying positions, then the workplace is not equitable. Similarly, if white employees hold most of the high-paying, high-status positions while employees of color occupy the low-paying, low-status positions, then the organization needs to implement equity strategies to level the playing field.

As such, organizations need to identify whether skills and qualifications or systemic issues (such as gender and racial discrimination) keep certain employees in lower-paying jobs at the organizations.

The organization may need to ask itself the following questions:

- Are women's jobs valued as highly as men's jobs? Similarly, is the work of employees of color seen as equally valuable as the work of white employees?

- What factors (systemic or otherwise) prevent certain employees from progressing in the workplace or in their careers?

- Do employees from marginalized groups have the same access to resources and opportunities as employees from privileged groups?

- Does diversity only exist in the low-paying, low-status positions of the organization, or is there greater representation in the high-paying, high-status positions?

- Are there any systemic issues outside of the workplace that hold certain people back in their careers? For example, lack of access to childcare may prevent female employees from advancing their careers at the same rate as their male counterparts. It is important to note that male employees with children are also affected by a lack of childcare options, but because female employees (and women in general) are disproportionately expected to take on or pressured into taking on the bulk of childcare and household labor, a lack of adequate childcare options is a gender issue.

Pay equity is not just a social justice and DEI issue; it is also required by labor laws in numerous countries. So, unless there is a justified reason for pay inequities (such as significant differences in qualifications and work experience), organizations must ensure that they are bridging any pay equity gaps. Whether the organization conducts a pay equity analysis or evaluates each employee's unique circumstance, pay equity not only strengthens the likelihood of ethical outcomes in the workplace but also improves employee retention. In fact, a 2018 Deloitte report revealed that companies with equitable and inclusive workplace cultures have 22% lower turnover rates.

Strategy Three: Reasonable Accommodations in the Office

According to the Americans with Disabilities Act National Network (2018), a reasonable accommodation is "any change to the application or hiring process, to the job, to the way the job is done, or the work environment" that allows employees with mental and/or physical disabilities "to perform the essential functions of that job and enjoy equal employment opportunities." This accommodation is considered "reasonable" if it does not create any undue hardships in the workplace and instead seeks to level the playing field. Any organization that wants to establish an equitable working environment should provide these accommodations, even if they are not a legal requirement. For example, an employee with a chronic illness may ask to work from home one or two days per week, or an employee who uses a wheelchair may require a ramp to enter the office building. Because mental and physical disabilities can vary from person to person, not every disabled person will require the same accommodations, and some will most likely need more accommodations than others.

It is best for an organization to determine which reasonable accommodations to implement in the workplace by looking at the request(s) made by the disabled employee(s), and thereafter, the organization can ascertain whether the accommodation is reasonable. Accommodations that are usually considered reasonable include reserved parking spaces, flexible work schedules, improved accessibility in the work environment, changing equipment and software, and providing alternative formats or presentations of training materials and communication channels. For instance, if an employee is unable to walk long distances, they may require a reserved parking spot that is close to the office building, or if an employee requires a service animal, the organization may have to change its "no animals in the office" policy. Importantly, organizations or employers are only required (by law) to accommodate disabilities of which they are aware, so organizations must first ensure that their employees feel comfortable and psychologically safe enough to disclose this information. Because there is a long history of discrimination against disabled people in the workplace, some employees may be hesitant to disclose their disability (especially if they have an invisible or hidden disability). As such, the request for reasonable accommodation(s) must be an interactive process between the organization or employer and the employee.

Strategy Four: Equitable Employee Benefits and Incentives

Employee benefits and incentives are a fantastic way to boost employee engagement and well-being, but they should be inclusive of all the possible circumstances in which employees find themselves. For instance, having event-based incentives that require a formal dress code or that center around alcohol can potentially exclude some employees. In another example, spousal health insurance that is not available to non-traditional or same-sex couples can also be alienating.

Here are a few ways to ensure that employee benefits and incentives are inclusive and equitable:

Flexible Holidays and Greater PTO

Flexible holiday days allow employees of different religions and cultures to celebrate the days that are important to them or to their specific religion and culture. This is especially important for employees who follow religions other than Christianity, as many organizations allow for days off during Easter and Christmas but may not allow time off for Eid or Diwali. Moreover, when an organization increases paid time off (PTO) for all employees, the organization demonstrates its trust in its employees and shows its commitment to boosting employee morale. Here, employees can use their PTO to rest and re-energize to not only avoid burnout but also to take care of their physical, mental, and emotional health. Besides, employees may struggle to work at optimal levels if they are exhausted, stressed, or physically ill. Organizations can also host a company-wide wellness week every few months, offer incentives for employees who use all their vacation days or offer half-day working days once a week.

Paid Parental Leave for All New Parents

Paid maternity leave is mandated in most countries, but organizations should also offer paid parental leave for all new parents, not just those who have given birth. This includes parents who have adopted a child or children, parents who have used surrogates, or parents who foster children. Paid, gender-neutral parental leave can help new parents create a positive and healthy work-life balance and help them form deeper and lasting bonds with their child or children. This also reduces the stigma many women face about taking maternity leave or informing their workplaces that they are pregnant until they absolutely must do so. Plus, with months-long paid parental leave, employees will be able to find adequate childcare options and will be more comfortable returning to the workforce once their paid parental leave has ended. Relatedly, organizations can also offer family-building employee benefits, such as fertility tests, egg freezing, surrogacy, and adoption, to name a few examples.

Financial services company JPMorgan Chase & Co. offers its eligible employees financial assistance to help offset the high costs of fertility treatments, adoption, and surrogacy. In late 2019, the company started offering its American employees up to $30,000 for in vitro treatments and between $10,000 and $30,000 in reimbursement for surrogacy costs. Assistance with all types of family-building demonstrates the company's commitment to helping LGBTQIA2+ employees (and their partners), who have historically been excluded from such employee benefits. Family-building assistance, however, should not end after the paid parental leave period, as employees who are nursing may need access to on-site lactation rooms, lactation consultants, and milk shipping services (should the nursing employee need to travel for work). These benefits, along with many others, ease some of the stress that new parents may face and show them that having a family and a successful career does not have to be mutually exclusive. Plus, such benefits help companies or organizations attract new talent and give them an edge against their competitors.

Domestic Partner Benefits

To help create and maintain an inclusive workplace, organizations can offer employee benefits that also support their spouses and domestic partners. This can include allowing the domestic partners of employees to join the organization's healthcare plans and increasing family responsibility leave for all employees. As relationship and marriage norms are changing in our society, organizations need to keep up and adapt. For example, some employees may be in long-term, committed relationships but may not feel the need to get married legally and/or may get married via a religious ceremony.

Flexible Work Schedules

As we have seen during the COVID-19 pandemic, flexible work schedules and hours can help employees create and maintain a healthy work-life balance and have the time to meet demands outside of the workplace. Indeed, employees who struggle with the usual nine-to-five work hours but are still able to complete their work will benefit from working according to their own schedule. With flexible work hours and schedules, employees will be able to schedule drop-off and pick-up times for their school-going children, run errands (such as grocery shopping or attending doctor's appointments), and have the time to participate in their hobbies. Flexible work schedules are especially beneficial for employees with children, employees who take care of their parents or elders, and disabled employees. Yet even able-bodied and/or childless employees can benefit from flexible work schedules, as they, too, have responsibilities outside of the workplace.

Caregiving Benefits

Whether an employee is raising children or taking care of their aging parents, caregiving benefits are an important part of creating an inclusive workplace and can ease some of the emotional and financial stress that often comes with being a caregiver. These benefits are especially important as a recent survey by Genworth Beyond Dollars reveals that 53% of caregivers face additional stress as a result of their caregiving responsibilities and spend an average of nine hours a week on caregiving responsibilities (Nisenson, 2021). Here, organizations can offer professional guidance for caregivers or leverage and invest in benefits that provide employees with backup care for their children or elders. Without caregiving benefits, organizations may experience increased employee absenteeism, decreased productivity levels, a loss of employee and team morale, and increased turnover rates.

Strategy Five: Measure Equity Progress

There is no standard method to accurately measure equity in the workplace, but it can be tracked, analyzed, and improved through employee satisfaction surveys and other forms of employee feedback channels.

For example, to determine whether an organization's equity policies need improvement, employee satisfaction surveys can ask the following questions:

- Do you think that your company treats you fairly?

- Do you think that your company's promotion practices are fair?

- Do you believe your benefits package is fair (according to your work responsibilities, skills, and work experience level)?

- Are you able to maintain a healthy work-life balance?

- Do you believe your company is accommodating to your needs?

Of course, employee satisfaction surveys are not the only way to track equity in the workplace. The organization's leaders or management team, such as managers or supervisors, should also be trained on how to initiate and hold productive and open discussions or conversations on equity with their employees. Here, the leaders should build rapport and trust with their employees so that they can solicit honest feedback on equity.

In addition, organizations should track equity according to the stages of the employee life cycle by determining the following:

- What is the percentage of candidates who believe that the recruitment and hiring process is fair and equitable?

- What is the percentage of employees who believe that they are treated fairly and equitably in terms of skill development and learning in the organization?

- What is the percentage of employees who believe that their benefits package and incentives are fair for their job position, experience, and skills?

- What is the percentage of employees who feel that the organization meets their reasonable accommodations and/or unique needs?

The answers to these questions can help organizations track their progress in terms of equity in the workplace and determine which areas need immediate improvement. Here, organizations need to ensure that their surveys and other feedback channels are accessible to all employees. For instance, can the text of the survey be enlarged? Is the survey anonymous? It is important for equity in the workplace to be tracked, analyzed, and improved regularly, as equity is an ongoing process rather than an end goal. Indeed, the end goal of equity is equality.

Strategy Six: Implement Workforce Education Programs

There are systemic barriers that can prevent people from marginalized or underrepresented groups from accessing quality education, and as such, organizations that use a skills-based hiring approach can improve equity in the workplace by offering education programs to their employees. Whether this includes funding employees' university or college education, sending employees to skills development workshops and training sessions, or offering employees short online courses and coaching sessions, organizations that invest in their employees are also investing in their own growth. Significantly, organizations should offer incentives and/or time off for employees to participate in these education programs, as employees may be deterred from these programs if it means spending extra hours outside of work to complete them. Moreover, these education programs must be accessible and provide employees with flexibility and an array of learning options, such as online learning through a series of videos, podcasts, e-books, pre-recorded or live lectures, and interactive lessons.

Education programs also take the pressure from mentors and coaches, who may be spread thin as a result of their DEI duties, and they establish a culture of learning and innovation in the workplace. Besides, education no longer has to take place in a traditional classroom setting or include tests or exams at the end of the course. Nowadays, education initiatives can include apprenticeships where employees learn hard and soft skills under the guidance and training of highly specialized leaders, one-on-one mentorships that are mutually beneficial for junior and senior employees, and informal independent learning options in which employees can access volunteer opportunities or attend industry-relevant conferences, workshops, and events. Industry-relevant events and conferences also provide employees with the opportunity to grow their professional support networks and foster collaborations or partnerships with other organizations.

Strategy Seven: Build Diverse Pathways to Leadership

Equity in the workplace entails fostering diversity in the leadership and management positions of the organization. In far too many cases, the leaders of an organization can be biased when it comes to choosing their successors or the organization's new leaders and may choose successors who are most like them. Choosing someone who reminds them of themselves is not necessarily a bad thing, but it can hinder the organization's DEI progress and ensure that the new leaders adhere to the status quo instead of inciting positive change in the workplace. A survey by Gartner (Zeuch, 2020) found that 88% of DEI leaders have perceived bias in their company's succession and/or promotion processes. To promote equity in the workplace, organizations may need to redefine or adapt their standards for what it takes for employees to become the organization's next leaders. This means that organizations should select future leaders based on skills, experience, and feedback from employees rather than selecting someone who is most like the organization's previous leader(s).

One way to redefine the pathway to leadership and to tackle bias in the succession processes is "to presume everyone is eligible for promotion and to discuss why a nominated employee is not ready, rather than presuming they are not and pushing for advancement" (Zeuch, 2020). This method levels the playing field when it comes to the selection of the organization's future leaders and has the potential to advance the careers of marginalized talent. However, creating a more diverse, non-traditional leadership path sometimes entails reducing the input from those who are leaving the organization and/or developing personalized leadership development strategies. This involves far more work for the organization, but creating a non-traditional leadership path can spur innovation and social change. Nevertheless, organizations must be wary of tokenizing future or potential leaders if they are from marginalized or underrepresented groups. When the future leader is the only leader from a marginalized group, it can be quite an isolating experience for them, and they may feel the need to represent their entire group (be it their racial group, gender, etc.). While it may seem progressive to select someone from a marginalized group to be the organization's next leader, tokenism can and does, in fact, negatively impact purposeful progress in the workplace.

Strategy Eight: Create and Invest in Employee and/or Business Resource Groups

Employee resource groups (ERGs) (also called employee networks or Business Resource Groups) are "internal communities of workers with shared identities and interests" in which their leaders and members seek "ways to offer the support employees are actually looking for" (Catalino et al., 2022). The ERGs are voluntary and employee-led and provide employees with the opportunity to build a community, receive support, and reach the objectives of DEI in the workplace. Of course, the goals of ERGs must align with employees' expectations and needs in order to boost well-being and feelings of inclusion for marginalized or underrepresented employees. In 2017, 90% of Fortune 500 companies had ERGs, and the number is steadily growing (Huang, 2017). ERGs can serve several purposes, as they are a safe space and networking hub for marginalized employees to bring together their unique skills and collaborate to create meaningful change within an organization. For instance, ERGs can lead campaigns to raise awareness of the key issues affecting marginalized communities, partner with non-profit organizations to raise funds for social issues, and promote the causes that are closest to them.

ERGs can also foster inclusion and belonging in the workplace by:

- Offering spaces for open discussion, conversations, and debates.

- Promoting the empowerment of marginalized employees through mentorships and professional development programs.

- Allowing employees to directly contribute to or influence DEI policies and initiatives in the workplace.

- Providing employees with the opportunity to connect with others who have the same culture, heritage, or identity as they do.

- Educating others on the issues faced by their communities and demonstrating how others can be allies.

In addition, ERG leadership can help yield personal and professional growth as these groups can help bridge the skills and experience gaps between employees. In doing so, the employees in an ERG can work together to create new approaches or solutions to issues in the workplace, drive innovation, and become a key resource for organizations that are struggling with employee dissatisfaction and systemic issues in the workplace.

ERGs are based on a common identity or shared interest among members, such as race, gender, sexuality, or age, but these groups also need to be intersectional in their approaches and work. Indeed, people are made up of complex, often-overlapping identities and interests, so ERGs based on a single shared interest can be quite exclusionary. For instance, if an employee is Black and lesbian, it would be unfair to make her choose which part of her identity is more important or should be placed at the forefront. Even women-centric ERGs can be problematic, as not all women have the same experiences and struggles. A religious woman may not have the same needs as a non-religious woman; a white woman may not experience discrimination in the workplace in the same way as an Asian American woman, or a cisgender woman may not advocate for the same things as a transgender woman would. Thus, ERGs have the potential to empower some while still excluding others, which is why they need to be actively intersectional.

In addition, participation in ERGs must not feel compulsory so that its members are enthusiastic about their participation instead of feeling pressured to represent their identity or marginalized group. This is especially problematic if we consider how often employees from marginalized groups are tokenized in the workplace and have to take on extra, unpaid, and underappreciated work. Volunteer roles are usually uncompensated, but this lack of compensation can potentially exacerbate wealth inequities among employees. As such, organizations may need to budget to financially compensate the leaders of their ERGs and ensure that the main tasks and responsibilities of their roles are not compromised. Here, organizations can tie the employees' active leadership in the ERG to their contributions to the organization's culture and operations so that they are paid for their labor and are not burdened by additional labor. If done correctly, ERGs can boost the DEI strategies and goals of an organization while also providing employees from marginalized groups with the necessary support and resources. Indeed, ERGs do not have to be confined by pre-existing DEI policies and approaches but can rather improve or adapt them. In turn, organizations have the responsibility to take the feedback and contributions of ERGs seriously. This entails listening to the needs, obstacles, and proposed solutions of the ERG and finding ways to translate the ERG's work into reality.

While organizations should strive for equality, they must also ensure equity among their employees to provide marginalized employees with the resources and tools from which they have historically been barred. Organizations should acknowledge that not all employees enter the workplace on equal footing, and as such, they must ensure that their equity commitments level the playing field. Besides, greater equity in the workplace usually leads to higher employee engagement, productivity, and well-being. As in the case of other DEI strategies, equity is an ongoing process that needs to adapt to changing social and workplace norms and cultures. Therefore, equity should be measured and monitored to ensure that those who need them are truly benefiting from them. Whether this involves providing reasonable accommodations and/or adopting flexible work schedules and hybrid work options, organizations that focus their attention on equity are a few steps closer to reaching equality in the workplace.

Chapter 6:

Neurodiversity and the Practical

Benefits

The enormous diversity among individual human minds is a product of multiple factors, including environment, culture, family, and personal history. But human minds also possess an innate diversity, which interacts with these other factors to produce the unique individuality of each human being. –Nick Walker

Neurodiversity: Definitions, Types, and Misconceptions

What Is Neurodiversity?

According to Armstrong (2011), neurodiversity "describes differences in brain function from person to person that affect daily mental functions" and encompasses all differences in learning, mood, and attention. The term is believed to have been coined in 1999 by a social scientist, Judy Singer, when she used "neurodiversity" in her sociology thesis. While the term may have been used before Singer, she popularized the concept and contextualized it in terms of biodiversity and the politics of disability. "Neurodiversity" is commonly used in reference to people on the autism spectrum, but nowadays, it also includes all people whose brain functioning falls outside of what is considered "normal" or "typical." On the other hand, people who are neurotypical (those with standard brain processing and function) are considered "normal" because their brains function similarly as many other people. As a social justice movement, the neurodiversity movement challenges prevailing stereotypes and misconceptions about neurodevelopmental disorders and seeks to destigmatize neurological differences in humans. The movement embraces neurological differences and advocates for the acceptance and inclusion of "neurological minorities," who have long been considered "abnormal."

Neuro-differences are recognized as a social category, much like race, gender, ethnicity, sexual orientation, and ability. Because neurodivergent people's brain functioning deviates from the standard, they are often made aware of and discriminated against because of their atypical brain functioning. There is a long history of neurodivergent people being treated as problems, with many medical professionals have attempted to "fix" them and make them neurotypical (that is, "normal"), but as we improve our understanding of neurodiversity, we find that there are alternative methods of engaging with neurodivergence. As many advocates have pointed out, neurodivergence is not a problem to be fixed but rather a different way of brain functioning that can actually be beneficial. As stated by Resnick (2022), neurodivergent people have "brains that work differently than most of the population… [and the] qualities and traits that neurodivergence creates are widely varied and include everything from high perception to strong abilities with computer systems to enhanced creativity." Indeed, there should not be a right or wrong way for the brain to function but, rather, a spectrum of ways in which the brain can function.

In schools, for example, neurodivergent students may have atypical needs, such as completing tasks in their own way, learning under alternative teaching methods, or needing noise-canceling headphones in the classroom to prevent the overstimulation of their senses. Neurodivergent people may also need extra time to adjust to the work environment—especially if they struggle to block out distractions or pick up on social cues when interacting with their coworkers. Over time, this can take a toll on a neurodivergent employee's work performance and physical, mental, and emotional well-being. In the same way, heterosexuality is seen as the so-called default or norm in society; neurotypical brain functioning and behavior have been deemed the norm in the workplace, classroom, and in broader society. Thus, if organizations wish to develop or improve their DEI strategies and policies, they need to accommodate neurodiversity in their work environments. Plus, with the stigma surrounding neurodiversity, neurodivergent employees may fear judgment from their leaders and coworkers.

The Spectrum of Neurodiversity

There is a spectrum of neurodivergent experiences and identities that includes learning disabilities and/or medical conditions. In some cases, people can be neurodivergent or display neurodivergent traits without having been formally diagnosed, making it particularly difficult to identify neurodivergence in those who lack access to adequate healthcare. Nevertheless, "neurodivergent" is not necessarily a medical term but rather a way to describe people whose brain functioning differs from what is deemed "normal." This raises the question: Are neurodivergent people disabled? While neurodivergent experiences and identities differ from mental and physical disabilities, neurodivergent people are still marginalized because many processes or systems are not designed to accommodate brain functioning that is atypical. For example, school curricula that do not take into account the needs of students with dyslexia or neurodivergent candidates who struggle in social situations may find it challenging to express themselves during job interviews. This does not mean that neurodivergent students will fail their tests and exams, nor does it mean that neurodivergent employees will not be able to perform at their jobs. Instead, the usual ways in which we teach the curriculum or conduct job interviews are barriers for neurodivergent people. Indeed, neurodivergent people may struggle during a job interview, but their heightened attention to detail may make them excellent for a variety of technical roles in finance or engineering, for example.

To ensure diversity, equity, and inclusion in the workplace, organizations must accommodate the needs of neurodivergent employees to help them succeed. In the same way, ramps at the entrance of office buildings accommodate employees who use wheelchairs; organizations can adopt various means of helping their neurodivergent employees.

People who are neurodivergent usually have one or more of the following disorders or conditions:

Attention Deficit/Hyperactivity Disorder (ADHD)

ADHD is a mental health condition that causes unusual levels of impulsive behavior and hyperactivity. People with ADHD may experience fluctuating energy levels and may struggle to concentrate on or complete tasks, sit still or remain seated, organize their daily tasks, maintain focus when conversing with others, or complete tasks quietly.

Autism Spectrum Disorder (ASD)

ASD refers to a developmental disability that affects how people perceive and socialize with others and may cause people to have repetitive or restrictive interests or behaviors. People with ASD may struggle to maintain eye contact with others, understand what others are feeling or thinking, express their emotions, understand social cues, and deviate from their daily routines. Other possible symptoms of ASD include noticing patterns, small details, or smells that others do not notice, having an avid interest in specific activities or topics, or not wanting others to get close to them or touch them. People with ASD have varying challenges, abilities, needs, and strengths; some can communicate verbally and live independently, while others may not be able to communicate their emotions and needs and may be dependent on support to live their lives. For some autistic people, their challenges may not necessarily arise from their disorder but rather from the social norms and prejudices that lead to their being unfairly treated or socially excluded.

Tourette Syndrome (TS)

As a neurological disorder that affects the central nervous system, Tourette syndrome causes a person to make sudden, involuntary sounds or movements, often referred to as "tics." These tics cannot be prevented or controlled and can include arm or head jerking, distorted facial expressions, eye blinking, shouting, grunting throat clearing, or barking.

Dyslexia

Dyslexia is a learning disorder in which people have difficulty identifying and using speech sounds. Here, people who are dyslexic struggle to process language and, therefore, have difficulty reading, writing, and spelling words.

Dyspraxia, or DCD

Dyspraxia, or developmental coordination disorder (DCD), affects physical coordination, which affects a person's posture, balance, movement, and hand-eye coordination. Moreover, those with dyspraxia may struggle to learn new skills, plan, or organize tasks, or type on a keyboard.

Obsessive-Compulsive Disorder (OCD)

This is a disorder characterized by frequent, unwanted sensations (obsessions) and thoughts that lead to a person performing repetitive behaviors (compulsions). OCD is often a life-long, chronic disorder that can adversely affect a person's social interactions and carrying out daily tasks and activities. Common examples of OCD include feelings of doubt, an excessive need for order, symmetry, or neatness, a fear of coming into contact with perceived contaminated items, a need for constant reassurance, or a fear of acting on an impulse. Moreover, compulsions can include excessive washing of one's hands, arranging items in a specific way, repeatedly checking things (such as doors, locks, or light switches), hoarding things of no personal value, repeating certain words while performing unrelated tasks, or doing something a specific number of times.

Common Misconceptions: Why We Need to Educate Ourselves

While neurodivergent conditions and disorders are not necessarily new, our understanding of neurodivergence is changing as we learn more about the diversity of human behavior and ways of thinking. Nevertheless, the stigma surrounding neurodivergence prevails, and many workplaces are still not inclusive of neurodivergent employees. Without understanding, recognizing, and accommodating the needs of neurodivergent employees, these employees may experience various systemic challenges and discrimination in the workplace, leading to many neurodivergent employees underperforming. To support neurodivergent employees, we must break down some of the most common misconceptions about neurodiversity in the workplace and in broader society.

The first misconception is that neurodiversity includes only autism (ASD), but in reality, neurodivergent people may have dyslexia, ADHD, or Tourette syndrome, amongst other areas. It is important for organizations and employers to recognize the various neurodivergent identities or conditions so that they may better support the unique needs of their neurodivergent employees. Secondly, neurodivergent people are not a monolithic group, as each individual occupies a different place on the cognitive spectrum. That is, neurodivergent individuals' thought processes and behaviors are unique, and they may also face challenges or obstacles in the workplace that are unique to them. The third misconception is that neurodivergent employees cannot succeed in the workplace. Here, neurodivergent employees may face unique challenges and obstacles in the workplace, despite clear contributions to the creative nature and innovative commitment of organizations. This allows neurodivergent employees to have higher productivity levels than their neurotypical counterparts, and if the barriers and challenges they experience in the workplace are removed, neurodivergent employees can prosper. Fourthly, neurodiversity is often considered a mental health condition, but this is a myth. Indeed, neurodivergent individuals are at a higher risk of experiencing mental health issues (often as a result of the systemic barriers and social exclusions they face) but being neurodivergent means that the individual thinks and processes information in a different way than neurotypical individuals.

The fifth misconception is that neurodivergent individuals are best suited for jobs with repetitive tasks. While some neurodivergent individuals work well with and enjoy repetitive tasks, others prefer more innovative and less repetitive tasks. Much like neurotypical individuals, those who are neurodivergent have an array of strengths, talents, and skills that can be beneficial for all types of jobs. The sixth misconception or stereotype is that neurodivergent individuals lack communication skills and cannot form interpersonal relationships. In many cases, neurodivergent individuals may struggle with social interaction, understanding social cues, or recognizing the thoughts and feelings of others. Organizations must take into account the needs and preferences of neurodivergent employees, as these employees can be a great asset to organizations if reasonable or minor accommodations are made in the workplace. Moreover, neurodivergent individuals can form long-lasting, meaningful relationships with others if others are aware of and accepting of their differences. As such, it is of the utmost importance that all employees of an organization are educated on neurodiversity so that workplaces can be productive, prejudice-free, and welcoming spaces for neurodivergent employees.

As explained by Barnes (2020), advocates for neurodiversity believe in giving neurodivergent people "the tools to succeed in the workplace" without "shaming or pitying those who will never be financially (or physically) independent... [since a] person who needs lifelong care can also be happy and reach personal goals." Organizations should view neurodiversity as just another way of being human and, consequently, challenge assumptions about what is "good work" and who is deemed "intelligent" in the workplace. Much like other diversity, equity, and inclusion efforts, accommodating the needs of neurodivergent employees requires changes in the organization's structure and work cultures. While such changes are no easy feat, they are an essential part of DEI and social justice.

Neurodiversity in the Workplace

Some researchers argue that neurodiversity in the workplace has become the new normal, not because people have changed, but because our understanding of people has changed. What we deem a "normal" brain has changed, and nowadays, more and more organizations are expanding how they design their work environments, cultures, and processes. Nonetheless, some managers and leaders are still hesitant to hire neurodivergent employees as they worry that these employees will require too many accommodations, will not be a good cultural addition to their organizations, or will not have the necessary skills, talents, or work ethics to perform well at their job. Around 15%–20% of the population worldwide is neurodiverse, and while the capabilities of neurodivergent individuals range from challenged to gifted, even those who are highly capable, talented, and skilled may struggle to find and maintain employment (Doyle, 2020). In the US, only around 29% of individuals with cognitive disabilities (including neurodivergent individuals) were employed in 2018—making them one of the biggest underrepresented groups in the workplace (Haynes, 2022).

While we cannot (and should not) generalize neurodiversity, many neurodivergent individuals have heightened attention to detail, can easily recognize patterns, are visual thinkers, and can come up with creative ideas. Recent research from Deloitte shows that work teams that include neurodivergent employees can be 30% more productive than teams without neurodivergent employees (Mahto et al., 2022). It has also been reported that employees of JPMorgan Chase's Autism at Work are 48% faster and 92% more productive than their neurotypical counterparts (Haynes, 2022). By not hiring neurodivergent candidates, organizations are missing out on the opportunity to include unique perspectives and fuel innovation in the workplace. According to a report by the Korn Ferry Institute (Haynes, 2022), organizations that include neurodiversity in their DEI strategies have experienced increases in engagement, profits, and performance—to the extent that greater neurodiversity in the workplace gives organizations a competitive edge.

A Competitive Advantage? The Benefits of Neurodiversity in the Workplace

Many individuals with ADHD, autism, dyslexia, and other neurodivergent conditions have higher-than-average abilities, and with the right workplace accommodations, organizations can leverage the unique skills and capabilities of neurodivergent employees to spur innovation. Indeed, neurodivergent employees have unique challenges and, therefore, need various accommodations, but the potential returns on these accommodations have long-term benefits. Several companies, including JPMorgan Chase, Microsoft, Ford, Deloitte, and Dell Technologies, have extensive neurodiversity programs that, despite being relatively new, have already yielded success. Whether it boosts innovation and productivity or higher employee engagement, companies that provide their neurodivergent employees with the necessary tools and accommodations to succeed have a significant edge over their competitors. At Hewlett Packard Enterprise (HPE), a multinational information technology company, the neurodiverse software testers found that certain clients' projects would always go into crisis mode before the launch. The software testers questioned the client's apparent acceptance of the chaotic launch process, and together they were able to successfully redesign the launch process. Preliminary results from HPE's neurodiversity program show that neurodiverse testing teams operate at 30% higher productivity than other teams (Austin & Pisano, 2017).

Organizations with a neurodiverse workforce are provided with unique perspectives, skills, and ways of thinking, as well as greater capabilities when it comes to problem-solving, pattern recognition, and mathematics, as neurodivergent employees often outperform their neurotypical counterparts. This is why organizations that want to lead in terms of innovation should be hiring more neurodiverse employees. Besides, the so-called bad traits of neurodivergent individuals are seen in a negative light mainly because these traits do not conform to what society has historically deemed "normal." Depending on where they fall on the spectrum, neurodivergent employees may lack socially appropriate communication skills, salesperson-like personalities, the ability to network and work in a team, or the ability to connect effectively in social settings. As echoed by Haynes (2022), the behaviors of neurodiverse individuals can "run counter to what is typically considered the makings of a "good employee"—emotional intelligence, gregariousness, persuasiveness, strong communication, and networking skills, to name a few." For instance, employees with ADHD are 18 times more likely to face discipline at their jobs—owing to their perceived behavioral problems, including short attention spans, challenges in time management, and long periods of extreme focus—and are 60% more likely to lose their jobs (Haynes, 2022).

Neurodiverse candidates also face several challenges during the recruitment and hiring processes. For instance, candidates with ASD may struggle to mimic neurotypical ways of thinking and behaviors during job interviews; perhaps these candidates cannot maintain eye contact, or they are unable to disguise any distracting behaviors. If neurodiverse candidates are unable to mask their neurodivergent conditions during job interviews, they are less likely to be hired (even if they have the qualifications and skills to back them up). Even in cases where neurodivergent candidates or employees are able to cover their atypical behaviors, this covering requires constant self-awareness and self-regulation, which can take an intense physical, emotional, and mental toll on the individual. For instance, neurodivergent employees may force themselves to maintain eye contact during social interactions, ignore any sensory discomforts, or force themselves to constantly rehearse responses while they are at work. All of these identity covering behaviors may help neurodivergent employees avoid stigma or exclusion in the workplace, but the incredible amount of energy it takes to self-regulate may prevent them from performing at optimal levels.

That is, instead of focusing their energy and efforts on innovation, neurodivergent employees spend this energy on trying to appear "normal." This not only undermines a sense of belonging in the workplace, but being unable to be their authentic selves in the workplace can lead to neurodivergent employees having higher rates of anxiety, stress, and depression. This constant covering and mimicry of what is considered a "good employee" is not always necessary, and while some organizations continue to discriminate against neurodivergent individuals, others prioritize innovation and creativity over neurotypical behaviors that are often associated with being a "good employee." Neurodiversity adds greatly to an organization's overall cultural diversity and business outcomes, as neurodivergent employees have built-in advantages. A Harvard Business Review study (Lagace, 2008) found that owing to their steady focus, employees with Asperger's are better suited to perform attentive and thorough work. The University of Michigan (2022) also revealed that individuals with dyslexia often exhibit out-of-the-box thinking and are adept at finding hidden connections, patterns, and trends in data. Moreover, individuals with ADHD tend to be more creative than their peers, work well under pressure, and are better at adjusting to change (White & Shah, 2011).

The varying traits of neurodivergent employees mean that a one-size-fits-all approach to including them in the workplace does not exist. Instead, organizations can (and should) acknowledge that each employee—whether they are neurodivergent or neurotypical—thinks and works in different ways. While not every employee will need the same accommodations, it is vital for organizations to take into consideration the various reasonable accommodations that their employees may need to succeed in the workplace. In this case, neurodivergent and disabled individuals are protected under the Americans with Disabilities Act (ADA), but many of them are hesitant to disclose their neurodivergent conditions for fear of stigma and discrimination in the workplace. This makes it especially important for organizations to create inclusive and welcoming workplace environments and to encourage trusting and honest relationships between their leaders and employees so that neurodivergent employees feel safe enough to disclose their neurodivergence to their managers, supervisors, or leaders. In general, organizations should prioritize accessibility and provide reasonable accommodations for their employees, whether or not the employees have disclosed their neurodiversity. However, this is not always the case, as many organizations are only now learning about neurodiversity and are still in the beginning stages of developing and implementing DEI strategies in the workplace.

Many organizations that are more advanced in their experience with hiring, promoting and developing neurodiverse talent continue to see the benefits and competitive advantage from an operational efficiency, cultural and product innovation, and revenue generation perspective. Their examples are great case studies to continue to assess and highlight as organizations make even more investments in DEI.

Strategies for Ensuring the Success of Neurodivergent Employees

Similar to people with disabilities, neurodivergent employees may need reasonable accommodations in the workplace. If organizations want to strengthen their DEI strategies and truly be inclusive and welcoming to a diverse workforce, then it is essential for these organizations to take these accommodation requests into serious consideration. Besides, many of these accommodations benefit *all* employees, not just those who are neurodivergent. As Haynes (2022) writes, "When you design for neurodiversity—and the structures and practices established to support neurodiverse talent—you build something that works for everyone...[and] the accommodations made can make the work environment more sustainable for all." For instance, when a workplace makes accommodations for neurodivergent employees who have sensory sensitivities, these accommodations are also beneficial for neurotypical employees who may get migraines due to a sensory overload in the workplace.

The Job Accommodation Network outlines the following potential accommodations for more inclusive workplaces: noise-canceling headphones, flexible work hours and remote work options, neurodiversity coaching, workspaces that are distraction-free, mental health days and greater PTO, and offering reference materials and job interview questions in advance. Moreover, workplaces can offer decompression rooms or spaces, allow their employees to wear sunglasses inside, and allow employees to keep their cameras turned off during online, remote meetings. The leaders of an organization also have the responsibility to be clear and consistent in ensuring these accommodations in the workplace, as well as following up on or gathering feedback on whether these accommodations are truly beneficial for neurodivergent employees. Here, managers should be clear and consistent in their communication of these accommodations, as some neurodivergent employees may struggle to read body language or social cues. In addition, managers should be aware of signs of timing or fidgeting, restlessness, confusion, zoning out, and other ways in which employees experience sensory overload. But some accommodations require structural changes in all stages of the employee life cycle.

Strategy One: Adapting the Hiring Process

While almost 20% of the global population is neurodivergent, unemployment rates among neurodivergent individuals remain disproportionately high. As such, organizations need to adapt to the initial stages of the employee life cycle by adapting their recruitment and hiring processes so that they are not overlooking or dismissing neurodivergent candidates. Organizations can cast a wider net during their recruitment process instead of mainly or only recruiting recent graduates from a set of universities or colleges. Here, the organization can partner with employment support agencies that source neurodivergent candidates and/or expand their recruitment efforts by including universities, colleges, and education programs that cater to neurodivergent individuals. Once the organization has widened its talent pool, it should also ensure that the hiring process (including job interviews) is free from recruiter or interviewer and algorithmic bias. Indeed, Artificial Intelligence (AI) hiring systems are often biased against candidates with atypical speech or facial expressions, and similarly, interviewers and recruiters, too, may have an unconscious bias when interviewing neurodivergent candidates who may struggle to maintain eye contact, read body language, or understand figurative phrases.

It is, therefore, important for recruiters and interviewers to be sensitized to different personality types and aware of signs of neurodivergence so that they can adjust their expectations of what is considered a "good employee." Besides, the inability to make and maintain eye contact does not make a candidate any less qualified for the job. Moreover, organizations can assess the non-traditional traits of a "good employee," such as risk-taking tendencies, emotional intelligence, and perseverance, along with the more traditional traits, such as quantitative and logical reasoning, communication skills, and networking skills. Job interviews, too, can be adapted to be more inclusive of neurodivergent candidates, and this may entail asking specific questions (instead of abstract ones), focusing on the skills needed for the job during the interview process, and scheduling interviews across several days to help ease the stress the candidates may experience. The candidates should also be allowed to bring their own devices, such as laptops or tablets, for tests instead of having to use company-provided devices.

Some organizations have found success by allowing candidates to determine how they would like to interact with the interviewer or employer. By placing some of the control in the hands of the candidates, they may feel more at ease during the interview process. Organizations can also make use of collaborative interviews (where the candidates meet with both interviewers and the organization's employees) and trial work periods where candidates can demonstrate their skills and talents. Relatedly, organizations should be wary of assigning neurodivergent candidates and employees certain jobs or roles based on stereotypes about neurodivergence. Neurodivergent candidates can be hired for roles other than the ones with which they are usually associated. For example, neurodivergent individuals can excel in more creative roles and not just in analytical positions. Indeed, assigning neurodivergent individuals roles based on stereotypes about neurodivergence can undermine an organization's DEI strategies and efforts.

Strategy Two: Create an Inclusive Work Environment

Understanding the nuances of neurodiversity is key for an accommodating, healthy, and welcoming workplace, and organizations can offer opportunities to all of their leaders and employees to learn more about neurodiversity and how to accommodate neurodivergent coworkers and employees. Here, it should not be the responsibility of neurodivergent employees to educate their coworkers and leaders, so when organizations offer education programs, workshops, and meetings that educate others on neurodiversity, it prevents neurodivergent employees from being tokenized and performing additional, often unpaid labor. By educating everyone in the workplace, organizations may even help existing employees who are neurodivergent feel a greater sense of belonging, seek support, and request accommodations if needed. All employees of an organization should also be encouraged to respect individual differences and working styles so that they can interact with their coworkers and leaders in an open, clear, and conducive manner. Here, some neurodivergent employees may need clear, multi-step instructions to perform certain tasks, and they should feel comfortable enough to ask their leaders questions or ask their leaders to repeat themselves and their instructions.

In turn, managers and leaders should find out how each of their employees perform optimally and how they best understand instructions and tasks so that these leaders can adapt their leadership style accordingly. This is especially important when it comes to remote, hybrid, or virtual work, as some neurodivergent employees may need follow-up virtual meetings or emails that reinforce the messages of the work meetings. To create a workplace that is inclusive of neurodiversity, organizations should provide their employees with notes, transcripts, and recordings of virtual meetings. Such an accommodation is also incredibly beneficial for neurotypical employees. Depending on how large a neurodivergent workforce is, organizations can provide their neurodivergent employees with mentors who can provide these employees with much-needed support. Providing mentors to employees with a disability and/or who are neurodivergent leads to a 16% increase in productivity, a 12% increase in customer loyalty, and an 18% increase in productivity (Mahto et al., 2022). Mentors not only provide neurodivergent employees with career advice, but they can also help advocate for them and their accommodations and empower neurodivergent employees by helping them network with other professionals. This is all the more important for organizations that hire neurodivergent employees from non-traditional colleges, as these employees may not have had access to alumni networks, affinity groups, or other professionals in comparison to employees from traditional universities and colleges.

Employee resource groups (ERGs) are beneficial for any organization wanting to foster a diverse, equitable, and inclusive workplace environment, and organizations must ensure that there are resources available for neurodivergent employees. This may include creating an ERG specifically for neurodivergent employees, and depending on how large a neurodivergent workforce an organization has, the organization may even need to create separate ERGs for employees with ADHD, employees with ASD, and employees with dyslexia, for instance.

Indeed, lumping together all neurodivergent employees into one ERG can undermine the diversity of neurodivergent conditions.

Strategy Three: Provide Flexible Work Options

Flexible work schedules and options help support the productivity, mental and physical well-being, and career growth of the entire workforce. Neurodivergent employees, too, benefit from flexible work options, as they will be able to choose the hours and environment that work best for them. For instance, a neurodivergent employee who has sensory sensitivities may prefer working from their quiet household rather than in a busy, noisy office space. Moreover, a flexible work schedule allows neurodivergent employees to better schedule self-care activities and/or therapy appointments. In these cases, organizations should make flexible work options a part of their policies instead of placing the responsibility on the employees, who may be hesitant to request time off. In the post-COVID-19 era, more and more organizations are switching to work-from-home or hybrid work options, and this works well for some neurodivergent employees who perform better on their own and in a comfortable environment. Other neurodivergent employees, however, thrive with routine and the predictability of their jobs, so working in an office allows them to be more productive.

Understanding the unique needs of neurodivergent employees helps organizations create and implement strategies that help all neurodivergent and neurotypical employees succeed. As such, organizations need to be flexible and adaptable when it comes to DEI strategies and ensure a work culture and environment that are knowledgeable (about neurodiversity), accepting of neurodivergent individuals, and inclusive of all reasonable accommodations. Should organizations offer a hybrid approach to work, then reasonable accommodations in the workplace are vital for neurodivergent employees who opt to work from their organization's office. One example of reasonable accommodation is providing employees with noise-canceling headphones, dimming overhead lighting, offering a room or space for decompression, or ensuring that employees' cubicles have enough space between them.

Strategy Four: Collaborate With Experts

DEI strategies are quite vast and nuanced and often require in-depth research and reading. Many companies can benefit from collaborating with social partners, such as non-profit or government organizations, community leaders, and activist groups, from gaining expertise that they may lack. These organizations and groups can help companies navigate local employment laws and regulations, assist with the hiring and recruitment process, provide training, mentorship, and general support, and raise public funding for training to help neurodivergent employees succeed in the workplace. As seen in Germany, companies can work with government organizations, as including more neurodivergent individuals in the workforce allows these individuals to move from public assistance to jobs that can generate tax revenue. In turn, this revenue can fund the retention of mentorships for neurodivergent employees.

For example, a Danish social innovator company, Specialisterne (The Specialists), promotes the idea that the traits of neurodivergent individuals can be used as competitive advantages in the market. Specialisterne provides data conversion, quality control, and software testing for businesses in Denmark and Canada, as well as trains individuals with ASD to improve their professional, social, and personal skills. With over 50 employees, 75% of whom are on the autism spectrum, Specialisterne works with international clients such as Microsoft, Oracle, and KMD to turn disabilities into abilities: This includes "hangouts," in which "neurodiverse job candidates can demonstrate their abilities in casual interactions with company managers," and by the end of these half-day hangouts, "some candidates are selected for two to six weeks of further assessment and training (the duration varies by company)" (Austin & Pisano, 2017). In another example, HPE creates "pods" in which around 15 neurodivergent employees work alongside neurotypical coworkers in a 4:1 ratio. Here, a consultant and two managers are also included in this "pod," and they are tasked with addressing any neurodiversity issues or concerns that may arise.

Importantly, these commitments to neurodiversity inclusion and advocacy should be mainstreamed in organizations so that all parts of the employee life cycle are neurodiversity-friendly and that all neurodivergent employees can work in a supportive corporate ecosystem. Neurodiversity programs have yielded significant results. Reports from HPE and SAP (a multinational software company based in Germany) reveal that the greater participation of neurodivergent employees has led to higher rates of productivity, lower defect rates in products, and significant increases in innovation. Moreover, by making communication more direct (as autistic employees may struggle to understand sarcasm, irony, and figurative language), organization-wide communication has improved, which, in turn, boosts employee engagement and morale. Organizations that have pioneered neurodiversity programs are also able to boost their reparations and improve public opinion, as these organizations are often recognized by the United Nations and have won numerous corporate citizenship awards across the globe.

Strategy Five: Amplify Accommodations, Training, and Support

Similar to other DEI strategies and initiatives, it takes time for organizations to build a neurodiverse workforce—especially when it comes to organizations that have unintentionally excluded neurodivergent employees for years. The recruitment and hiring processes, training and mentorship sessions, ERGs, and other neurodiversity programs often occur over several weeks or months. Plus, DEI is an ongoing process, so neurodiversity programs, too, may need to be evaluated and adapted over the years. Nevertheless, these programs must be expert-driven and must also provide neurodivergent employees with hard and soft skills so that they may succeed in both their professional and personal lives. Neurodiversity training sessions should include all of the organization's employees, as neurotypical employees, too, need to be educated about neurodivergent conditions and accommodations in the workplace. Besides, in many organizations, neurodivergent and neurotypical employees have to work together to complete projects and tasks and to reach the organization's targets or goals. By providing neurodiversity training for all employees, organizations can prevent and/or remedy interpersonal difficulties and conflicts so that all employees can perform at optimal levels.

Organizations should also amplify the importance of neurodiversity in the workplace, both internally and externally. Internally, organizations must ensure that their employees are not only aware of their neurodiversity programs but also encouraged to participate in them. Organizations should also promote their focus on neurodiversity outside of their workplaces so that they may be able to collaborate with or partner with other organizations, including community or activist groups and nonprofit or governmental organizations. Besides, organizations exist and operate within the context of broader society, and by publicizing their acceptance and celebration of neurodiversity, these organizations can incite social change and empower neurodivergent employees both in and outside of the workplace. These efforts also help mainstream neurodiversity programs and initiatives in the corporate sector so that neurodiversity becomes the new normal in the workplace.

As we try to advance our societies, we must acknowledge our past attitudes toward neurodiversity. We should no longer see neurodiversity as a problem in need of a cure but rather as a unique way in which our brains function. Indeed, many neurodivergent conditions need long-term treatment to improve the daily lives of neurodivergent individuals, but we also need to place some responsibility on our social norms and systems that continue to deem neurodiversity a problem. Since workplace norms and systems serve to benefit neurotypical individuals, organizations must identify how they can provide reasonable accommodations to neurodivergent employees. This can involve increasing support (through mentorship and training programs), adapting the hiring process so that it is more inclusive, and/or educating employees to dispel common misconceptions and stereotypes surrounding neurodivergence. These accommodations must fall under the organization's larger DEI efforts to ensure a workplace that is fully accepting of neurodiversity.

Chapter 7:

Team and Talent Strategies

If you haven't hired a team of people who are of color, female, and/or LGBT to actively turn over every stone, to scope out every nook and cranny, to pop out of every bush, to find every qualified underrepresented founder in this country, you're going to miss out on a lot of money when the rest of the investment world gets it. –Arlan Hamilton

Team and talent management is a vital part of DEI, as hiring managers along with Talent Acquisition professionals are responsible for recruiting underrepresented talent, while people managers and supervisors, along with organizational leadership and human resources teams are responsible for retaining, developing, and advancing this talent. Many organizations spend more than one-third of their revenue on employee benefits and salaries, and as such, their return on (people) investment needs to reflect this. That is, organizations must be able to attract and retain talent that will help drive the organization forward and give the organization an edge in a competitive market. According to research from LSA Global (Mobilio, 2016), companies that align their strategy with their culture and talent outperform their peers when it comes to profits, revenue growth, employee engagement, and customer satisfaction. Talent is a significant asset in an organization: skilled, qualified, and motivated employees drive innovation, and with the right guidance, learning, and management, they can become the organization's future leaders. This makes it all the more important for organizations to nurture talent at all stages of the employee life cycle and to link talent to their DEI efforts.

Effective team and talent management requires the integration of DEI practices and principles into every stage of the employee candidate and employee experience from attraction and engagement to hiring and onboarding, to promotion and development, and even in retirement.

Accessing a Diverse Talent Pool

The One-In-The-Pool Effect

Many organizations have invested hundreds of millions of dollars in their diversity, equity, and inclusion policies and programs, yet relatively homogenous populations continue to dominate the higher echelons of companies and businesses. Indeed, having cisgender, heterosexual white men in CEO and other leadership positions is so normalized in modern American society that status quo bias often leads to board members promoting more cisgender, heterosexual white men to leadership positions. This seemingly never-ending cycle not only keeps this demographic at the top, but also excludes their equally qualified yet marginalized counterparts from gaining even a fraction of their professional success. Should organizations (and society in general) wish to change this status quo, they must have access to a wider or more diverse talent pool so that those who are privileged are not the default choice for leadership positions.

In research from Johnson et al. (2016), two studies were conducted to examine the effects of changing the status quo among the finalists for a job position. The first study had 144 undergraduate students reviewing the qualifications of three candidates from a finalist pool of applicants. The three candidates had the same credentials, yet they differed in terms of race, and, here, the names of the candidates either sounded stereotypically Black or stereotypically white. The participants of the study were split into two groups: One group reviewed the finalist pool with two white candidates and one Black candidate, while the other group reviewed the finalist pool with one white candidate and two Black candidates. The study found that when white candidates were in the majority, the participants were more likely to recommend hiring a white candidate, and when the Black candidates were in the majority, the participants tended to recommend hiring a Black candidate.

The second study involved 200 undergraduate students, but instead of reviewing candidates based on race, the study instead focused on gender. As seen in the first study, the candidates' gender was assumed through their stereotypically male and stereotypically female names. This study found that the participants are more likely to recommend hiring a woman when two of the three candidates are women and are more likely to recommend hiring a male candidate when two of the three candidates are men. Johnson et al. (2016) explain the results from the two studies: "When there were two minorities or women in the pool of finalists, the status quo changed, resulting in a woman or minority becoming the favored candidate." That is, having only one woman or racial minority in a candidate pool leads to people (interviewers or board members) opting to adhere to the status quo and undermining DEI efforts in the recruitment, hiring, and succession planning processes. When there is only one woman or racial minority in the pool of finalists, the woman's or racial minority's deviation from the norm is highlighted, making them more likely to be ostracized by interviewers, recruiters, or board members—regardless of their qualifications, experience, and skills. Johnson et al. (2016) state that for "women and minorities, having your differences made salient can also lead to inferences of incompetence."

This is also referred to as the "one-in-the-pool" effect, as having only one candidate from a marginalized or underrepresented group means that their odds of being hired or selected for a leadership position are quite slim. Once this becomes a "two-in-the-pool" situation, the odds of a woman or racial minority being hired increase, *which* changes the status quo.

In essence, the study found that when there was only one woman or minority candidate in a pool of applicants, their likelihood of being hired or promoted was statistically zero. However, when there were multiple women or minority candidates in the pool, their likelihood of being hired or promoted increased dramatically. Specifically, the study found that a woman's odds of being hired increased by 79 times when there were at least two women in the finalist pool, while a person of color's odds of being hired increased by 193 times when there were at least two minority candidates in the finalist pool. These findings provide strong evidence for the one-in-the-pool effect and suggest that diversity recruitment and talent promotion approaches must go beyond simply hiring one or two minority candidates or considering one or two underrepresented teammates for promotion to truly have an impact on organizational diversity and inclusion.

Changing the status quo can incite social change and pave the way for more candidates and employees who are marginalized or underrepresented to be hired and promoted in the future. While some may see the "two in the pool" approach as a form of affirmative action, it is important to note that women and racial minorities are just as qualified and skilled as (if not more than) white men in workplaces. As in these two studies, unconscious sexism and racism are still prevalent in cases where women and racial minorities have the same qualifications or credentials as white men. It is, therefore, essential for organizations to dismantle unconscious sexism and racism when it comes to recruitment and hiring, promotions, and leadership pathways. The studies conducted by Johnson et al. (2016) focus on measuring unconscious racism and sexism, but the one-in-the-pool effect is also present when it comes to other marginalized groups, including queer, disabled, and immigrant candidates. With this concept in mind, how can organizations build recruitment, promotion, development, and retention strategies that prioritize DEI every step of the way?

DEI Recruitment Strategies

Strategy One: The Diverse Slate Approach to Hiring

Patel (2021) describes diverse slate hiring as the "talent acquisition strategy that requires recruiters to start with an already diverse pool of qualified candidates" so that the candidate pool features individuals from an array of identities, backgrounds, and experiences. While this strategy began during the National Football League's efforts to increase minority representation among coaches, many global organizations have since employed it to develop and improve DEI. Recruiting a diverse candidate pool helps organizations expand their talent and skill sets, create an inclusive and adaptable work culture, increase employee engagement, and approach innovation from fresh and unique perspectives. Besides, diversifying the early stages of the employee life cycle is an effective way of building a diverse workforce within the organization. As with almost all DEI commitments, this is easier said than done, as diverse slate hiring can only work if it is supported by recruitment teams who have had DEI training and who, therefore, understand the nuances of DEI in both theory and practice.

The diverse slate hiring strategy is not about reaching quotas or diversity for the sake of diversity; instead, this strategy must make a genuine impact on the organization and its culture. This strategy is also a vital part of the "two in the pool" effect, as recruiting a more diverse candidate pool increases the chances of underrepresented candidates being hired and helps to change the status quo in an organization. Katica Roy (2020) elaborates on this: A diverse slate of candidates "helps mitigate similarity bias, or our natural inclination to surround ourselves with people who think, act, and look like us," and, in turn, the weakening of similarity bias allows organizations to increase their gender and racial representation among their ranks. Again, it is equally important that organizations invest in ensuring belonging and inclusion in the organization's culture that supports underrepresented candidates-turned-employees to retain these employees. Indeed, the integration and embedment of DEI must be prioritized at all parts of the employee's life cycle.

Strategy Two: Inclusive Employment Brand Interactions and Talent Attraction

In today's digital age, the significance of inclusive employment branding and talent attraction cannot be overstated. With the proliferation of social media, interactions with brands occur well before the recruitment and hiring processes even begin. Brands have harnessed the power of social media platforms to engage with their clients and customers, shaping their reputation through consistent content creation, direct interactions, and promotion of user-generated content. However, the implications of this go beyond customer engagement, reaching deeply into the realm of attracting underrepresented talent.

Job seekers are increasingly turning to social media, company websites, and platforms like Glassdoor to evaluate potential employers. They scour an organization's social media accounts, read reviews, and examine the brand's online presence to gauge its commitment to diversity, equity, and inclusion (DEI). When candidates fail to find visible evidence of a DEI focus on these platforms, it can significantly impact their perception of the brand's workplace culture and their eagerness to apply.

Brands must recognize that their online presence serves as a window into their organizational values and practices. By showcasing their DEI strategies and successes across accessible platforms, brands send a powerful message to both their customers and potential employees. A company's website plays a pivotal role in this effort. The website should not only feature inclusive language that is devoid of bias but also provide a clear outline of the brand's DEI initiatives and overarching commitments. When crafting an inclusive digital presence, authenticity matters. Incorporating authentic images of employees, accompanied by their consent, delivers a potent message of real inclusivity. Eschewing generic stock photos in favor of real faces underscores the brand's commitment to fostering an equitable work environment. Employing larger, easy-to-read fonts further enhances the accessibility of the website, catering to a diverse audience with varying needs.

Recognizing the diversity of preferences and abilities, brands should aim to make their websites as inclusive as possible. This can be achieved by offering a range of content formats, such as text, images, videos (with captions), audio files, and downloadable information sheets. This multifaceted approach ensures that the brand's message is accessible and resonates with a wide spectrum of individuals. In essence, inclusive employment branding and talent attraction are not just about appealing to customers but also about fostering a culture that attracts, engages, and retains underrepresented talent. An organization's commitment to DEI must be evident across all touchpoints, leaving a lasting impression on job seekers and potential future employees alike.

Strategy Three: Adapt Job Requirements and Descriptions

Traditional job requirements can be rather exclusionary and undermine the organization's DEI efforts. Organizations can broaden their talent pool by focusing on the candidates' skills (such as problem-solving and decision-making abilities), experiences, and willingness to continue learning over the more traditional traits associated with "good employees." Organizations can demonstrate their openness to a diverse talent pool by writing neutral job descriptions that include the following: competencies needed to succeed in the position (instead of listing specific skills), skills that can be gained through on-the-job training, and gender-neutral language. In fact, jobs that use gender-neutral language in their posts are filled 14 days faster than posts that contain feminine or masculine bias (Taylor, 2021). Moreover, should the job position require a qualified candidate, the specific qualifications needed must be listed in the job description, as opposed to simply listing the preferred qualifications. This makes it easier for job seekers to filter through job descriptions and makes the recruitment and hiring processes far more efficient.

Many organizations also recruit and hire individuals based on "cultural fit"—that is, the cultural impact the individual can potentially have on the organization—but this, too, can be rather weighted and subjective. Besides, organizations that want to diversify their workforce and change the status quo of their work environments may not want to hire individuals who "fit" into a culture that is undergoing significant change. In this case, the organization may need to develop an objective method to determine which candidates share the values and goals of the organization *and* whether the candidate(s) can add or enhance the future culture of the organization. This method should be developed before the recruitment and hiring processes to avoid any ambiguity, and a more objective and broad approach to cultural add and alignment helps organizations consider the new traits, experiences, and perspectives the candidate(s) will bring into the organization.

Strategy Four: Reduce Recruiting Bias

Whether the organization uses human recruiters and interviewers or AI systems, the recruiting process must actively mitigate bias if the organization seeks to access a wider talent pool.

Reducing bias in the recruiting process involves:

- Identifying and remedying the existing biases in the recruitment process.

- Identifying any barriers and inequities that underrepresented candidates may face before and during the recruitment process.

- Ensuring that all candidates are asked the same interview questions and assessed on the same competencies.

- Requesting work portfolios or samples or conducting proficiency tests to verify the skills of the candidate rather than asking them self-evaluation questions; and

- Having a committee of interviewers of different races, ethnicities, genders, abilities, or levels rather than just one interviewer during the process.

Ideally, recruiters or interviewers should undergo DEI training so that they may dismantle their own unconscious biases, be able to effectively communicate with candidates from a variety of backgrounds, and envision how non-traditional candidates can add value to the organization.

Strategy Five: Understand the Labor Market

Companies can use labor market data (and if in the US, Equal Employment Opportunity Commission (EEOC) data) to better understand diversity in the market by level, industry, and type of role as a means to guide the setting of representation goals. Labor market data provides information about the demographics of the workforce, including information about the size and distribution of various groups, such as gender, race, ethnicity, and age, among others. This data can help companies identify gaps in representation and develop strategies to increase diversity and inclusion.

EEOC data provides additional insights into workforce demographics by requiring employers to report data on the gender, race, and ethnicity of their employees. This data is collected annually and is used to monitor compliance with equal employment opportunity laws. Companies can use this data to identify trends and patterns in their own workforce and benchmark their representation against industry standards.

While labor market data and EEOC data are not perfect or the most optimal data sources, they are incredibly useful and legally defensible. They provide a starting point for companies to assess their own diversity and inclusion efforts and to set goals for representation. By leveraging this data, companies can better understand the talent pool available to them and develop targeted recruitment and retention strategies to increase diversity and inclusion.

Strategy Six: Actively Diversify Where Talent is Sourced

While the location of the jobseekers or candidates can have an impact on the recruitment and hiring process, far too many organizations blame the lack of a diverse, qualified talent pool on the location(s) from which they recruit. Of course, if an organization mainly or only recruits candidates from a majority-white population, their DEI efforts can be significantly hindered. With the change in working norms that arose from the COVID-19 pandemic, it is clear that organizations can (and should) broaden the locations from which they recruit—especially if the organization offers remote and/or hybrid work options. Job advertisements should be posted on a variety of platforms, including print media, social media platforms (such as LinkedIn), the organization's website, and virtual or in-person job fairs. Relatedly, organizations that recruit candidates from prestigious universities and colleges may, too, have to adapt their recruitment processes, as many individuals from marginalized groups are still excluded from applying to and entering (let alone graduating from) prestigious education institutions. Not only are these traditional recruitment processes limited in their access to a diverse talent pool, but they also erroneously assume that individuals from marginalized groups cannot perform certain roles or occupy certain positions in the organization.

Indeed, this assumption is often based on negative stereotypes and disregards the systemic barriers faced by marginalized individuals and communities. Rather than mainly or only using traditional recruitment processes, organizations should look to expand the geographical locations of their candidates and target candidates from educational institutions and professional programs that are dedicated to the development of individuals from marginalized communities. For example, organizations can increase their recruitment of candidates from Hispanic-Serving Institutions (HSIs) and Historically Black Colleges and Universities (HBCUs). Understanding the labor market also involves identifying what candidates are looking for when searching and applying for jobs. As the most diverse generation and the age group that is starting to enter the workforce, Gen Zers value DEI in practice, flexible work options, and a healthy work-life balance when it comes to employment, and should organizations wish to hire young and underrepresented talent, then they must be clear in their prioritization of these values. Gen Z job seekers apply to companies that reflect their values, beliefs, and goals and may focus their attention on the organizations that are more culturally aligned and relevant for them.

Strategy Seven: Set Hiring Goals

It is beneficial for an organization to set clear hiring goals when they start recruiting from a more diverse talent pool. This does not necessarily mean that organizations should aim for x number of women employees, y number of racial minority employees, or z number of neurodivergent employees, but organizations should rather assess their current gaps in representation and work toward addressing these gaps. As we know, "representation" encompasses diversity in gender, race, ethnicity, sexuality, ability, age, nationality, religion, neurodiversity, and socio-economic status, and these factors often overlap. As such, an organization may have great female representation in its workforce, but if an overwhelming number of these female employees are white, the organization may need to improve its racial diversity efforts. Using the same example, if the organization's female staff disproportionately occupy its lower job positions or ranks while male staff disproportionately dominate the higher ranks, the organization also needs to focus on retaining its underrepresented employees and providing them with clearer or better pathways to leadership. Alternatively, the organization can set a clear goal of hiring women who have the qualifications, experience, and leadership skills to add to the higher ranks of the organization. An example of a DEI hiring goal is for an organization to build a diverse workforce that reflects its diverse clientele or customer base. Clients and customers are attracted to organizations that reflect their values and goals, so having a workforce that reflects the client or customer base provides organizations with a competitive edge (while also boosting their profits).

This is also where targeted universalism comes into play. As a means of "setting universal goals pursued by targeted processes to achieve these goals," targeted universalism ensures that universal goals are achieved based on "how different groups are situated within structures, cultures, and across geographies" (Powell et al., 2019). Targeted universalism is an inclusive approach that recognizes the needs of specific groups, promotes belonging, and aims to undermine structural exclusion and marginalization. For example, an organization that seeks to achieve gender equality in the workplace might use the targeted universalism approach to develop and implement strategies to increase the representation of not just women but also women of color, disabled women, neurodivergent women, and queer women in the workplace. This is because gender equality policies and strategies can increase the representation of women in the workplace, but these policies and strategies tend to serve mainly white, middle- to upper-class women.

Targeted universalism can be implemented in four intensive steps. Firstly, an organization must form a coalition with stakeholders who agree on a universal goal as a response to a social issue, such as gender or racial equality or greater access to education. The second step entails the coalition examining how the population is categorized by gender, race, class, and geography in relation to the universal goal. This specifically means identifying the groups that are most impacted by inequity and exclusion. Thirdly, the coalition must identify any barriers that these groups may face. For example, the lack of access to quality education in communities of color means that employees of color may not have the same on-paper qualifications as their white counterparts. This interventionist approach is designed to address the specific and direct challenges faced by the specific group in question while also considering a lens on how to promote equitable outcomes for all through these provisions. The fourth and final step is to develop and implement targeted policies to achieve the universal goal. Here, the universal goal can be racial equality in the workplace, and the targeted policies include providing education programs for or funding the university education of employees of color. Successful programs have been implemented by many organizations with significant employee representation in retail, manufacturing, and distribution, etc.

To ensure the success of targeted universalism in the DEI space, it is essential to continuously monitor and evaluate the effectiveness of interventions. This can be done through regular data collection and analysis, employee feedback, and community engagement. This information can then be used to make informed decisions about which interventions are working and which may need to be modified or discontinued. It is important to now see the efforts that are not working as anticipated as a failure, but rather as an opportunity for continued growth, development, and revision of the organization's comprehensive DEI strategy and the goals aligned with it that foster progress.

Inclusive Talent Management and Development

Strategy One: Measuring Your Talent Program through a Current State Assessment

Once a diversity hiring strategy has been developed and adopted, organizations should also focus on guaranteeing that the strategy leads to a more diverse workforce. Indeed, many things can happen in the time between an employee getting the job and starting at the organization. For example, perhaps the candidate has to move to a high-cost-of-living (HCOL) area for their job, or the candidate finds the workplace environment to be unwelcoming and intolerant. Here, the hiring strategy may have been fantastic and inclusive, but retaining employees from marginalized or underrepresented groups is equally important. To remedy this potential problem, organizations can develop and implement measures to assess the progress of new employees. This can entail having regular check-ins with first-year hires to see how they are coping with the onboarding and training process and fitting into the company culture and/or reading performance reports to gather employee feedback.

Another significant way to measure the efficacy of the organization's talent strategy is to focus on employee retention rates according to a group, such as gender, race, or disability. In doing so, the organization can pinpoint whether its female employees, its disabled employees, or its racial minority employees are choosing to stay with the organization or to leave. For example, an organization may have great retention rates for its women employees but may find that their disabled employees are opting to leave the organization after a year or two. The organization will now know to place greater attention on and improve its disability inclusion practices and policies. Employee retention is vital for DEI efforts to have a long-term impact within the organization. In contrast to the Boomer generation, millennials, and Gen Z are more likely to leave or switch organizations if they struggle with job satisfaction, if their organizations are failing in their DEI efforts, or if their well-being and a healthy work-life balance are not being prioritized at their current organization. As such, it is all the more important for organizations to use various strategies to retain their employees.

Strategy Two: Acknowledge and Invest in the Importance of Retaining Employees

Research by Peakon (2019) reveals that worker loyalty and engagement begin to decrease nine months before they quit, and this is due to a myriad of factors: Being assigned unchallenging work, feelings of underappreciation, bad managers, no sense of psychological safety and belonging, or a lack of a clear path for personal development and professional growth. This raises the question: What makes employees want to stay at their companies? Firstly, multi-generational workforces bring an array of new perspectives, experiences, and soft and hard skills to the workplace. Older and younger generations often work well together as the former group shares their worldly experience and practical knowledge with the latter group. In turn, younger employees share their tech and digital skills and interest in purpose-driven responsibility with their older coworkers. Here, the mentor-mentee relationship can involve two coworkers rather than a manager and employee. This is not to say that all older employees struggle with new technology or that young employees do not have practical knowledge, but rather that the camaraderie between employees is an important factor in employee retention.

Secondly, healthy interpersonal and professional (or personal) relationships among managers and employees foster a greater sense of belonging in the workplace, which, in turn, increases an employee's desire to remain at their current organization. Here, employees are more likely to prosper in workplaces where they can freely and openly engage with their coworkers and form meaningful relationships with them. Meaningful workplace relationships and the ability to take risks go hand-in-hand with a sense of belonging, and to retain their employees, organizations must acknowledge the importance of and foster teamwork and collaboration in the workplace. Thirdly, successful effective and transparent DEI strategies are a way to retain employees, and more specifically, employees from marginalized or underrepresented communities. An organization may have fantastic, in-depth DEI policies, but unless they are fully and efficiently translated into reality and employees see real action and tangible results, employees may not wish to remain at an organization in which they are being tokenized and/or are experiencing discrimination and bias.

Organizations should also actively work toward retaining their underrepresented employees by developing employee engagement programs, wellness initiatives, and human resource strategies. Here, the organizations can address all aspects of their employees' lives and ensure that their employees are able to maintain a healthy work-life balance so that they may prosper in their professional and personal lives. Gardner (2021) states that the total rewards strategy is a means to "develop a workforce motivated toward excellence and growing with the organization through an effective and inclusive rewards package" that includes "all the benefits, perks, incentives, guidelines, processes, programs, and other types of rewards that an employer offers to its workers." Organizations can therefore improve their business performance by using the total rewards strategy to build an engaged, motivated, and satisfied workforce. In turn, the employees are eager to excel and reach the organization's goals or targets (with the hope of being rewarded).

Strategy Three: Implement Sponsorship and Mentorship Programs

While "sponsorship" and "mentorship" are often used interchangeably, these terms refer to two distinct forms of guidance in the workplace. Mentors provide employees with guidance, career advice, and constructive criticism, as they usually work in the same function as the employees. They can also act as a role model for their mentee(s) by helping the mentee(s) create a personal vision for their careers, answer any career questions the mentee(s) may have, and help their mentee(s) achieve professional goals. Moreover, people of all ages can be mentors, and a mentor-mentee relationship can even form between employees who have the same job or position in the organization. Reverse mentorships, for instance, form when a more junior or less tenured employee mentors a more seasoned employee by helping them stay up to date with industry trends, methods, and workplace norms. In some cases, mentors do not have to work in the same organization as their mentees (but it would certainly make things easier).

Sponsors, too, can provide employees with guidance, but their role is more focused on advocating for the employees in the workplace. Wooll (2021) explains that a sponsor "roots for you and your career development... [and they will] put your name in for promotions, recommend you for a raise, or provide you with other similar opportunities." Sponsors are especially important in larger organizations as they can ensure the employee(s) do not get overlooked. Because of their merit and an esteemed reputation, sponsors are usually those in leadership positions who can identify talent and potential in newer or early in career employees and help these employees succeed. For example, if an employee is in a sales position at an organization but wishes to be promoted to a sales team leader, the employee's sponsor can speak to their coworkers (who are already in management positions) about the employee's goals, work ethic, and credentials. The employee's mentor, however, may be more focused on helping the employee develop the skills needed to become a sales team leader. Of course, having both a mentor and a sponsor is incredibly beneficial for employees.

Employees from marginalized backgrounds may also find it beneficial to have a mentor and/or sponsor who shares one or more of their marginalized identities. For example, a Hispanic female employee can gain excellent insights and guidance from a mentor who is also Hispanic and female. In this case, the mentor can provide their mentee with the usual career guidance as well as advise them on navigating the workplace or organization as an employee who is both female and of color. The mentee may also feel more comfortable discussing experiences of workplace discrimination or other identity-related issues with their mentor.

Research continues to reveal though that underrepresented communities, specifically women of color are often 'over-mentored and under-sponsored', so it is imperative that organizations find the healthy balance between the two approaches to employee development to avoid cannibalizing well-intended efforts to grow and build talent within the company.

Strategy Four: Implement a Seven-Step Plan for Inclusive Talent Management and Succession Planning

Inclusive succession planning is a strategic and forward-looking organizational process that encompasses identifying, nurturing, and preparing a diverse spectrum of talented individuals within a company or institution to seamlessly transition into key leadership roles. This holistic approach not only focuses on skill and competency development but also actively cultivates an environment of equity and accessibility, ensuring that underrepresented groups are given equal opportunities to contribute and excel in shaping the future direction of the entity. Here is a seven-step approach that works:

Step 1: Establish Inclusive Leadership Development Programs

Creating robust and inclusive leadership development programs is a pivotal strategy for cultivating the potential of underrepresented talent. To achieve this, collaborate closely with HR to design programs that transcend traditional leadership training. Recognize that underrepresented individuals may face unique challenges and barriers on their leadership journey. By customizing content to address these challenges, organizations can ensure that these programs resonate with participants, making them more impactful.

A key aspect of these programs is tailoring the curriculum to tackle the specific skills and competencies that are essential for diverse leadership roles. Workshops and seminars should encompass a wide range of topics, including inclusive leadership practices, cross-cultural communication, conflict resolution, and emotional intelligence. Moreover, interactive sessions that encourage open dialogues about personal experiences can foster empathy and understanding among participants.

Mentorship and sponsorship opportunities are integral components of these programs. Pairing emerging underrepresented leaders with experienced mentors not only provides valuable guidance but also helps build crucial networks. These relationships can provide insights into navigating the organization's dynamics and career progression pathways.

Furthermore, experiential learning components should be integrated to bridge the gap between theoretical learning and real-world application. Encourage participants to engage in hands-on projects, simulations, and case studies that challenge their problem-solving skills and decision-making abilities. This multifaceted approach ensures that underrepresented talent is equipped with the holistic skill set needed to excel in leadership roles.

Step 2: Data-Driven Talent Analysis

Collaborate with HR to conduct a comprehensive analysis of workforce demographics, promotions, and retention rates. A deep dive into these metrics will reveal critical insights into the representation of underrepresented groups at different organizational levels. Beyond mere representation, this analysis will provide a nuanced understanding of how underrepresented talent progresses through the pipeline.

Consider disaggregating data by gender, race, ethnicity, and other identity markers to unveil potential disparities and barriers.

By leveraging these insights, organizations can make informed decisions about where to allocate resources and efforts for maximum impact. For example, if the analysis reveals a significant drop-off of underrepresented talent at mid-level management positions, this information can guide the creation of targeted development programs to address this specific challenge. Moreover, setting data-driven diversity and inclusion goals enables the organization to hold itself accountable for achieving meaningful progress.

Remember that data is not just a snapshot but a dynamic tool for continuous improvement. Regularly revisit and update these analyses to track trends and measure the effectiveness of interventions. Over time, this iterative approach will allow the organization to refine its strategies and adapt to the evolving needs of underrepresented talent.

Step 3: Holistic Onboarding Experience

Crafting an inclusive onboarding experience is instrumental in setting the tone for underrepresented talent's journey within the organization. Collaborate closely with HR to design an immersive and holistic onboarding program that acknowledges and addresses the unique needs of diverse employees. Recognize that a one-size-fits-all approach falls short in catering to the range of experiences and backgrounds that individuals bring.

One key element of this process is to integrate cultural competency training as a foundational component of the onboarding journey. This training should go beyond a simple overview of cultural differences. It should encourage participants to explore their own biases, assumptions, and blind spots. By fostering self-awareness, organizations can cultivate a more inclusive and respectful work environment where individuals from all backgrounds feel valued.

Additionally, consider incorporating affinity group gatherings during the onboarding period. These gatherings provide a safe space for new employees to connect with others who share similar identities, fostering a sense of belonging from the outset. Moreover, assign mentors or buddies to new underrepresented talent. These mentors can offer guidance, answer questions, and help navigate the intricacies of organizational culture.

By creating a holistic onboarding experience that acknowledges the diversity of backgrounds and experiences, organizations can make a powerful statement about their commitment to inclusion and set the stage for the success of underrepresented talent.

Step 4: Customized Development Pathways

Collaborate with HR teams to design individualized development pathways for underrepresented talent. Recognize that a one-size-fits-all approach to talent development falls short in leveraging the unique strengths and growth areas of each individual. These customized pathways aim to empower underrepresented talent with the resources and opportunities needed to achieve their full potential.

Working closely with people leaders, conduct thorough assessments that identify individual strengths, areas for improvement, and growth potential. These assessments should encompass not only technical skills but also leadership competencies, such as emotional intelligence, adaptability, and cross-functional collaboration. Drawing on this assessment data, partner with employees to co-create tailored development plans that align with their aspirations and the organization's strategic goals.

These customized plans may involve a combination of targeted training, stretch assignments, cross-functional projects, and mentoring relationships. For instance, an employee with exceptional analytical skills but limited experience in leading teams might be guided toward projects that enhance their leadership capabilities. Similarly, providing exposure to different parts of the organization can foster a holistic understanding of the business landscape.

By offering tailored opportunities for growth and development, organizations demonstrate their commitment to each individual's professional journey. This approach not only drives engagement but also fosters a sense of loyalty and belonging among underrepresented talent.

Step 5: Feedback-Driven Performance Management

Implementing a feedback-driven performance management process is a cornerstone of supporting the growth and advancement of underrepresented talent. Work closely with HR to train people leaders in delivering feedback that is specific, actionable, and growth-oriented. Encourage ongoing conversations that address both short-term goals and long-term career aspirations. By establishing a culture of open dialogue, organizations create an environment where underrepresented talent feels empowered to actively seek growth opportunities.

Structured performance conversations should encompass a holistic view of an employee's contributions, strengths, areas for development, and long-term career goals. These conversations serve as a platform for people leaders to provide guidance, offer coaching, and ensure that employees have the resources they need to succeed. By shifting the focus from evaluation to growth, organizations foster an atmosphere of continuous improvement.

To ensure that performance evaluations are unbiased and objective, introduce standardized criteria for assessing competencies and performance indicators. Regular calibration sessions involving multiple people leaders can further minimize the influence of individual biases. By taking these steps, organizations can ensure that performance discussions are fair, transparent, and contribute to the development of underrepresented talent.

Step 6: Cultivate an Inclusive Culture Through ERGs

Investing in Employee Resource Groups (ERGs) as a pivotal component of your inclusive succession planning strategy can significantly impact the advancement of underrepresented talent. Collaborate closely with HR to provide robust support to ERGs that focus on career development. These groups play a vital role in fostering connections, offering mentorship, and advocating for equitable opportunities.

Work together with ERGs to create a wide range of initiatives that align with the organization's goals. These initiatives may include mentorship programs, workshops, networking events, and speaker series. For instance, a mentorship program that pairs emerging underrepresented talent with seasoned leaders can provide valuable guidance and insight into navigating the complexities of the organization.

Moreover, ERGs can serve as a platform for underrepresented talent to voice their unique needs, challenges, and aspirations. By regularly engaging with ERG members, organizations can gain valuable insights that inform talent management and succession planning strategies. ERGs also create a sense of belonging and community, which is crucial for the retention and advancement of underrepresented talent.

Investing in ERGs demonstrates a commitment to creating an inclusive work environment where all employees can thrive. By providing resources, leadership guidance, and a platform for advocacy, organizations enable ERGs to play a pivotal role in shaping the trajectory of underrepresented talent's careers.

Step 7: Continual Measurement and Improvement

Collaborate with HR to establish a comprehensive feedback loop that ensures continuous improvement in your talent management and succession planning strategies. Regularly assess the effectiveness of these initiatives by utilizing a combination of quantitative and qualitative metrics. Employee engagement surveys, turnover rates, diversity metrics, and promotion rates can provide valuable insights into the impact of your efforts.

Analyze data to uncover patterns, trends, and areas for refinement. For example, if engagement surveys indicate that underrepresented talent feels disconnected from leadership opportunities, this could prompt a closer examination of leadership development programs and pathways. Similarly, if turnover rates among underrepresented talent remain high, it may be an indicator of underlying issues that require attention.

Based on the insights gained, make data-driven adjustments to strategies and interventions. This iterative process ensures that the organization remains agile and responsive to the evolving needs of underrepresented talent. By continuously refining these strategies, organizations can create an environment that maximizes the potential of all employees and fosters a culture of inclusion and equity.

The Role of HR

In addition to the work driven by talent leaders and hiring/people managers, Human resources (HR) leaders, specifically HRBPs and HR Managers play a key role in driving diversity, equity, and inclusion in the workplace, as they are tasked with integrating various strategies, values, and targets to create and maintain a cohesive and productive workplace culture. DEI strategies are multi-dimensional (and rather new for some organizations), but an organization's HR department can act as a catalyst for change by creating awareness on DEI topics, ensuring that leaders are committed to DEI efforts, and advancing inclusion in the structure and culture of the organization. For example, HR is responsible for developing and implementing equitable pay policies and employee benefits in organizations. Moreover, the role of HR is becoming more data-oriented as HR can assess and address data concerning employee demographics, existing diversity and inclusion policies, and the strengths and weaknesses of existing DEI policies.

Human Resources (HR) plays a crucial role in advancing team and talent strategies connected to this work. HR plays a key role in advancing DEI in an organization by ensuring that the organization's workforce is diverse, equitable, and inclusive. To achieve this, HR must implement strategies that attract and retain underrepresented talent, create a culture of inclusion, and promote equity within the organization.

Creating a culture of inclusion is essential for attracting and retaining underrepresented talent. Inclusive workplaces foster a sense of belonging and enable employees to bring their whole selves to work, leading to increased engagement and job satisfaction. HR can create a culture of inclusion by implementing policies and practices that promote respect, tolerance, and acceptance of all individuals, regardless of their race, gender, sexual orientation, or any other characteristic.

Recruiting underrepresented talent is an important first step for many organizations that wish to advance their DEI efforts, but these organizations should also pour as much energy and resources into retaining underrepresented talent. DEI is an ongoing process that seeks to implement long-term change to boost both "employee well-being" and business profits. As such, organizations need to align their DEI strategies and efforts with their corporate culture and staff retention goals. Whether this includes greater employee benefits and more training programs or the use of ERGs and mentorship sessions, organizations can stay ahead of the curve by nurturing and advancing at each stage of the employee life cycle.

Chapter 8:

Inclusion and Implicit &

Unconscious Bias

If we want to include everyone, we have to help everyone develop their talents and use their gifts for the good of the community. That's what inclusion means—everyone contributes. –Melinda Gates

Workplace inclusion refers to "treating all employees equitability [in terms of] availability of opportunities, resources, and the possibility of success" so that no employee has an "advantage based on race, gender, background, or other precursors to employment" (Todd, 2022). When implemented effectively, inclusion policies ensure that workplaces are free from discrimination, bias, and workplace cliques, and as such, these policies are all the more important in diverse workplaces. Yet, many organizations that have a diverse workforce and extensive diversity policies still struggle to develop and implement adequate inclusion strategies that work. As a result, these organizations may have a diverse workforce but may also have difficulty retaining their employees because of their lack of inclusion in the workplace. Employees, especially those from marginalized backgrounds, need their workplaces to be inclusive so that they can be their authentic selves at work, can listen and communicate effectively with others, and feel a sense of belonging at their organization.

Diversity cannot exist without inclusion, as workplaces that are both diverse and inclusive tend to have high rates of employee engagement, which in turn drives innovation and productivity in the organization. Inclusion must also begin at the top, as leaders have the power and authority to promote inclusion, cohesion, and engagement among their employees. Research from Korn Ferry (2022) reveals that inclusive work teams make better decisions 87% of the time, while 73% of employees are empowered to perform at optimal levels when they feel heard in the workplace. To ensure inclusion in the workplace, the leaders of an organization can promote diversity training among all employees to eradicate discrimination, prejudices, and biases and boost team morale and job satisfaction. Employee feedback is one of the most useful data sources for measuring inclusion in the workplace. Whether this involves check-ins with employees or anonymous surveys, organizations can identify where they are lacking in inclusion and/or succeeding in maintaining an inclusive workplace.

Creating an Inclusive Workplace

Inclusive workplace environments are ones that do not show favoritism toward certain employees. When employees are provided with the necessary tools and resources to succeed in the workplace, their merits and work ethic will help them receive a promotion and/or gain more career opportunities. However, in many cases, employees are promoted, or their careers are advanced due to having similar personalities or backgrounds to the organization's leaders. Sometimes, employees are promoted based on nepotism and other forms of preferential treatment. To combat this, organizations must ensure that promotions and pathways to leadership are free from bias and favoritism. In an inclusive organization, the employees know that their work ethic and performance are valued over favoritism, and as a result, they are more likely to improve their skills, abilities, and expertise so that they can get ahead.

Another major aspect of inclusivity in the workplace is transparency and visibility, and several companies, including Google and Facebook, publish annual reports detailing their diversity and inclusion data for the public's perusal. In fact, this practice is mandated by law in some countries. Organizations that want to establish and maintain an inclusive working environment must be transparent in their DEI efforts and make their DEI data accessible to their employees and the broader public. As such, organizations are held accountable for their DEI promises, and employees, too, can monitor the DEI strategies in their own workplaces. To boost inclusivity efforts, organizations can also create a channel for reporting non-inclusive behavior and actions misaligned with the company's values. Here, employees will be empowered to discuss issues and experiences with discrimination, bias, or harassment they experience or witness in the workplace without fear of repercussions. For instance, the organization can establish, elevate, and amplify the role of the employee relations team and other HR functional teams to manage these complaints and find speedy and effective solutions, while maintaining safe spaces for teammates.

Organizations can use pay audit software to analyze and identify any wage gaps or disparities in compensation or pay equity to provide corrective action. Ideally, inclusivity should be a priority from the onset, and organizations can (and should) provide culture training for all recent hires during the onboarding process. New hires will learn about the organization's inclusive workplace culture, its various DEI policies and strategies, and its behavioral ethics so that they know what to expect as an employee of the organization. Besides, if employees are provided with this knowledge from the very beginning, it will be easier to hold them accountable should they breach any policies or behavioral ethics in the future.

Measuring Inclusion in the Workplace

While there are numerous ways to measure inclusion in the workplace through a variety of different pulse and engagement surveys, the Gartner Inclusion Index (Romansky et al., 2021) is often viewed as a best-in-class measurement framework. The index asks seven questions or statements to gain a holistic view of inclusion in the workplace:

1. Fair treatment: The employees of an organization who help the organization achieve its goals or objectives are recognized and rewarded fairly.

2. Integrating differences: The employees of an organization value and respect their coworkers' opinions.

3. Decision-making: The employees fairly consider the suggestions and ideas provided by other members of their work team.

4. Psychological safety: The employees of an organization feel welcome to express their true feelings at work.

5. Trust: The communication employees receive from the organization is open and honest.

6. Belonging: Employees in the organization feel cared for.

7. Diversity: The managers at the organization are as diverse as the broader workforce.

The more the employees of an organization agree with the seven statements (that can also be posed as questions in an employee feedback survey), is an indication that the organization is trending positively in terms of inclusion and belonging. While the Gartner Inclusion Index uses a broad definition of inclusion, it shows how diversity is distinct from yet an integral part of inclusion. With inclusion being a priority for many modern organizations, we also need to examine the barriers to establishing and maintaining an inclusive workplace, namely implicit or unconscious bias.

Implicit Bias: A Barrier to Inclusion

In 2018, two African American men entered a Starbucks in Philadelphia to attend a business meeting. The manager, however, asked the two men to leave the premises, but the men refused and told the manager that they were waiting for their associate. The Starbucks staff reportedly called 911, and the two men were arrested and escorted out of the store. In an interview following their arrest, the men stated that they believed the manager of Starbucks had targeted them because of their race. In response to the situation, Starbucks announced that they would be holding company-wide training to address implicit bias and prevent discrimination.

Implicit bias, also known as unconscious bias, refers to the "attitudes or stereotypes that adversely impact or influence our understanding, actions, and decisions in an unconscious way, rendering them uncontrollable if unchecked and unmitigated" (Okonkwo, 2022). Some theorists believe that implicit bias occurs when the brain engages in fast, emotional, and unconscious thinking that requires little effort and that can be prone to error. Indeed, premature conclusions are often drawn from a lack of sufficient reasoning. For example, a manager in a company in the Global North may think poorly of an employee who was born and raised in a country in the Global South. Despite the employee now residing and working in the Global North and being qualified and skilled enough for their position, the manager may show implicit bias by being surprised by the employee's credentials. Implicit bias in the workplace is also evident in instances where recruiters or interviewers favor or are more receptive to "Eurocentric-sounding" names over "Afrocentric-sounding" names. When an individual is drawn to other individuals who are similar to them, this is also known as "affinity bias."

Implicit biases are often associated with various social "-isms" such as racism, sexism, ableism, and ageism, to name a few examples. Ability bias, for instance, is seen when hiring managers avoid selecting a disabled candidate because they unconsciously assume that the candidate will be more likely to take sick leave or will struggle to perform at their job. Name bias is linked to gender and race/ethnicity, as many candidates' and employees' names are indicative of their race and gender, whereas beauty bias occurs when people who are conventionally attractive are treated more favorably in the workplace (and in broader society).

Five Key Types of Implicit Bias (Note: This is not an entirely comprehensive list of all types of implicit and unconscious biases)

1. Confirmation Bias

This refers to our tendency to view, interpret, and analyze new information or evidence as a confirmation of pre-existing ideas or beliefs. For example, when a supervisor who believes that employees are most productive in the morning reviews employee feedback surveys, the supervisor may disregard survey responses that suggest otherwise. Instead of reviewing the surveys objectively, the supervisor only focuses on the responses that confirm their beliefs and ignores the responses that contradict what they believe to be true. Similarly, when individuals favor a certain politician, they tend to seek news articles and other forms of information that portray the politician in a positive light (while also ignoring any information that paints the politician in a negative light).

2. Anchoring Bias

This type of bias occurs when individuals are overly influenced by older information when they interpret a new situation. Simply put, the older information, or "anchor," is favored over newer information, and in the context of the workplace, anchoring bias can be seen in salary negotiations. The first offer made by the employer during the salary negotiation process serves as the "anchor" or reference point for the rest of the conversation. If the first offer is rather low, then any offer higher than the original seems like a win for the potential employee.

3. The Halo Effect

The Halo effect occurs when our perception or impression of an individual (or a thing) unconsciously affects our opinion of a different part of the individual. For instance, a candidate may dress elegantly for a job interview, and the hiring managers, therefore, assume that the candidate is more skilled than the candidates who are not dressed as elegantly. Here, the well-dressed candidate may be more likely to get the job even if the other candidates are more skilled, experienced, or qualified than they are. Similarly, an attractive employee is assumed to be smart and hardworking because of their physical appearance, and as a result, their attractiveness outshines the rest of their traits. In fact, this employee may not even be hardworking, but this is ignored in favor of their physical appearance.

4. Attribution Bias

This refers to when we project negative traits onto an individual when they make a mistake instead of understanding the mistake in the context of the individual's situation or circumstances. For example, an employee's coworkers may wrongfully deem the employee lazy, careless, and incompetent because they often arrive late for work. However, the coworkers do not consider circumstances: The employee may be late because they live in an area with unreliable public transportation, or they may have caregiver responsibilities that fill up much of their mornings. Whatever the reason for the employee's tardiness, their coworkers may use limited information to judge them.

5. Small Numbers Bias

This type of bias occurs when we overgeneralize a group of people based on very little evidence. For example, an individual may have had a negative experience with someone from a particular religion, and as a result, the individual may be biased against all people from that religion. In another instance, a manager has regular negative interactions with an employee of a certain race and based on this small sample, the manager may refuse to work with or hire employees from that race group.

The Consequences of Implicit Bias

Implicit bias can have several negative consequences for an organization and its employees. For example, research has found that in STEM fields, 48% of Black women and 47% of Latina women have reported being mistaken for custodial or administrative staff (Williams et al., 2014). Moreover, resumes with Black, Hispanic and Latino, and Asian names are less likely to receive callbacks for job interviews (Spencer, 2021). These are only two of the many cases in which implicit bias can adversely affect organizations, but implicit bias can hinder DEI efforts in the workplace and undermine the skills and work of employees from marginalized groups. Implicit bias in the recruitment and hiring process, for example, can lead to a less diverse or more homogenous workforce in the organization. This can lead to less diversity of thought, experiences, and perspectives in the workplace, which, in turn, can hinder creativity and innovation.

In addition, when employees experience implicit bias in the workplace, they may be less likely to remain at the organization, leading to higher employee turnover rates and a negative brand reputation. These employees may feel less engaged at work and may not perform at optimal levels, and this can negatively influence the overall corporate culture. Implicit bias often encourages (or forces) employees from marginalized groups to behave in a certain way in the workplace. For example, women employees may be hesitant to be assertive as they do not want to come across as "bossy" or "too difficult." Or women employees who have children may be unfairly excluded from receiving deserved promotions as their managers may assume that these women no longer care about their careers. In another instance, Asian Americans are often stereotyped as docile or meek, and in the context of the workplace, their coworkers or leaders may assume that they will not fight back when they are mistreated or will be ill-equipped to lead large teams or functions—a completely false, misguided and inappropriate perspective.

Examples of Implicit Bias: Microaggressions and the Model Minority Myth

Microaggressions in the Workplace

"But where are you really from?"

"You're one of the good ones."

"You speak English so well!"

These are just a few of the many offhand remarks many individuals from marginalized communities hear regularly. In most cases, the speaker does not mean to cause harm or offense, yet their words (or actions) can still hurt the recipient. Whether the speaker has good or bad intentions, what they have said is considered a "microaggression," which, similar to other implicit biases, perpetuates harmful beliefs and behaviors. As a professor of psychology and author of books on the effects of microaggressions, Kevin Nadal (cited in Luc, 2022) defines microaggressions as the "everyday, subtle, intentional—and oftentimes unintentional—interactions of behaviors that communicate some sort of bias toward historically marginalized groups." These biases are considered "micro" because they are the day-to-day words or actions that can accumulate and be measured on a "macro" scale. Microaggressions emerge from limited perspectives and deeply-embedded biases and prejudices toward those who have been and are still "Other," including women, racial or ethnic minorities, queer individuals, people with disabilities, neurodivergent individuals, those from low-income households, and immigrants, name a few examples.

Racial microaggressions, for instance, are the everyday insults, indignities, and slights aimed at BIPOC communities from people who may be well-intentioned but are also unaware of how their words and/or actions are imbued with racism. Microaggressions can be seen everywhere: In the workplace, in schools and colleges, in recreational activities, on social media, in advertising, and even in our own households. Examples of racial microaggressions include African Americans being asked if their hair is natural, being referred to in African American Vernacular English (AAVE) by their non-Black coworkers or friends, or others assuming they are in a role or fulfilling a particular duty simply because of their race. Many of these microaggressions extend to other communities of color: A store owner, for instance, following a Hispanic and Latino customer around the store, a white individual clutching their handbag when a Hispanic and Latino person passes, by or telling an Asian American that they are "pretty for an Asian girl." Being subjected to racial microaggressions on a regular basis can make BIPOC communities feel unwelcomed, excluded, or undignified in the workplace and in broader society.

In some cases, microaggressions are not even verbally communicated to those from marginalized backgrounds. Supermarkets that have shelves dedicated to "exotic" foods (usually Hispanic or Asian products) or Hollywood films that fetishize Black, Hispanic and Latino, and Asian characters, too, engage in microaggressive behaviors. Microaggressions are so pervasive that they even have subgroups, including microassaults, microinsults, and microinvalidations. Microassaults are the intentional or conscious forms of discrimination that include using racial slurs or having white supremacist symbols on display, whereas microinsults are verbal or non-verbal communications that subtly demean the recipient's racial identity or heritage. For example, subtly suggesting that a coworker of color got their job because of affirmative action constitutes a microinsult. In terms of microinvalidations, these are communications that subtly negate, dismiss, or undermine the experiences and feelings of marginalized people. This includes asking Asian American or Hispanic and Latino individuals where they were truly born, saying that racism, sexism, and other social "-isms" no longer exist in modern society, or white people claiming not to see color. Indeed, microinvalidations aim to make marginalized individuals and communities invisible. Here are a few more examples of the various types of microaggressions.

Verbal Microaggressions

- "You speak English well" or "You are so articulate" when conversing with an employee or coworker of color.

- "You are being bossy or aggressive" when being uncomfortable with a woman's (and especially a Black woman's) assertiveness.

- "Your people are so [insert stereotype]," as this implies that all people of a certain marginalized group are the same or monolithic. Here, diverse experiences and identities are reduced or minimized to a single, often incorrect, assumption.

- "You're one of the good ones." This masquerades as a compliment, but, in reality, it tokenizes the recipient and insults an entire group of people.

- Asking a gay or lesbian employee or coworker, "Who is the man/who wears the pants in your relationship?"

Behavioral Microaggressions

- Assuming a person of color in the workplace is a delivery person or part of the cleaning staff.

- Using a "Blaccent" or AAVE only or mainly when speaking to African Americans.

- Assuming that immigrant employees do not understand English.

- Speaking slower and/or more loudly when conversing with a deaf employee or coworker.

- Mispronouncing a non-Anglo name even after being corrected several times and/or giving your employee or coworker a nickname (without their permission) because you cannot pronounce their name.

- Assuming an older employee or coworker does not know how to use modern technology.

- Providing employee performance feedback that is mainly or only personality-based, such as "You should smile more" when evaluating a female employee's work.

Environmental Microaggressions

- Creating or having a work environment that does not accommodate disabled employees in meetings, work events, and so on.

- Not providing reasonable accommodations for neurodivergent employees (such as office spaces with dim lighting or noise-canceling headphones).

- Excluding employees from marginalized or underrepresented groups from promotions and/or pathways to leadership.

- Refusing to address and change pay inequities among employees doing the same job or occupying the same level or position.

Microaggressions can adversely affect the work environment and overall corporate culture of an organization by creating a toxic, unwelcoming, and uncomfortable atmosphere. In turn, this reduces employee engagement, team morale, and the employee experience while also subjecting marginalized employees to regular (albeit more subtle) forms of discrimination. Microaggressions can also undermine an organization's DEI efforts because they are too subtle or seem too insignificant to act against. This is also exacerbated by the fact that the perpetrators of microaggressions are often unaware of the harms of their words and actions and, in many cases, chalk up the problem to the recipient being too sensitive or creating problems where none exist. Interestingly, microaggressions are patterned, underpinned by negative stereotypes, assumptions, and generalizations, and can be difficult to identify in cases where microaggressions are framed as compliments.

Recent research demonstrates that microaggressions can take a serious psychological toll on the mental and emotional health of the recipients, which, subsequently, can lead to anger, internalized oppression, and depression among the recipients. Internalized oppression, for instance, occurs when a marginalized individual or community internalizes the negative stereotypes and assumptions about them and/or believes in their cultural inferiority or that they deserve to face discrimination. Besides, it is challenging for marginalized individuals to ignore the constant stream of insults, invalidations, and assaults on their identities and backgrounds. Microaggressions cause far more than fleeting moments of upset, as the cumulative effect of microaggressions actually leads to trauma and various health issues. In the context of the workplace, employees who are regularly subjected to microaggressions may feel less motivated to perform, lose their self-confidence, experience imposter syndrome, or isolate themselves from their coworkers and managers.

What makes microaggressions difficult to identify and address is the fact that microaggressions are distinct from yet form part of racism, sexism, homophobia, transphobia, ageism, ableism, xenophobia, and classism. At their core, microaggressions are underpinned by the belief that anyone who is "Other" is inherently inferior to those of the dominant culture. The perpetrators of microaggressions seldom have bad intentions or aim to cause harm; rather, they are ordinary people who view their microaggressive words and actions as non-problematic and non-discriminatory. The people who engage in microaggressions are not overt racists (like white supremacists) or sexists (such as incels), and this makes it all the more challenging to call them out on their words and actions. Because they believe that what they are saying or doing does not cause harm or is not underpinned by ill-intent, those who engage in microaggressions tend to become defensive when they are called out or criticized. As a complex and nefarious form of implicit bias, microaggressions often shift the blame from the perpetrators to the victims: The victims are deemed overly sensitive, unable to take a joke, or too politically correct.

So, how can individuals and organizations prevent and/or confront microaggressions in the workplace? Firstly, allyship must be seen as an ongoing action rather than a label for those who want to uplift marginalized people. Leaders and employees must look within to dismantle their implicit biases, educate themselves on the various types of microaggressions, and empathize with the everyday experiences of their marginalized employees or coworkers. Leaders, for example, can implement formal microaggression and implicit bias training programs and workshops as part of the organization's overall DEI efforts. Moreover, the leaders of an organization should also establish formal processes or channels to address instances of microaggressions in the workplace, and here, the focus should be placed on the perpetrators and not the victims. These processes or channels enable leaders to communicate directly with the perpetrators while also reinforcing a psychologically safe working environment for the victims.

Unfortunately, microaggressions are far too common in workplaces, and change must occur on a social and structural level. Leaders and employees have the responsibility to educate themselves on microaggressions, improve their cultural competencies, and engage with those who are different from themselves. On a more structural level, organizations have the responsibility to provide workshops or training programs to educate all employees on the various types and harms of microaggressions, as well as create clear communication channels for victims to report any instances of microaggressive words or behaviors. The alternative—placing the onus of microaggression education on marginalized employees—is far too time-consuming, unfair, and can take away from the employees' performance at work. Besides, all instances of microaggressions in the workplace need to be addressed and remedied without causing further harm or trauma to the affected employees.

Asian Americans and the Myth of Model Minorities

The "model minority" is a race-, ethnicity-, or religion-based minority demographic whose members are seen as achieving a greater degree of socio-economic success than the average population. In the US, the concept of the "model minority" is usually associated with Asian Americans, and it reinforces the stereotype that Asian Americans are a law-abiding, polite, and docile racial group whose socio-economic success is a result of innate talent and hard work. This concept is considered controversial as it not only generalizes an entire racial group in the US, but it also pits minority groups against each other. According to the concept of the model minority, Asian Americans are "good" American citizens who obey the law, work hard, and contribute to the economic well-being of American society, whereas African Americans, Native Americans, and Hispanic and Latino populations are prone to crime and laziness or are a burden on the country's welfare systems.

Deeming Asian Americans as high-achieving, law-abiding, and docile people erases the diversity of the Asian American population. The label "Asian American" refers to Americans of Asian ancestry, and given how large the Asian continent is, "Asian American" includes people of Chinese, Vietnamese, Korean, Indonesian, Filipino, Indian, Pakistani, Japanese, Malaysian, and other Asian descent. The model minority lumps this diverse population into a single, monolithic group, and while Asian Americans, as a whole, tend to earn higher incomes and hold higher degrees than the general population, things become murky when we actually look at the data. For every dollar earned by a white man in the US, an Indian American woman earns $1.21, a Burmese woman makes $0.50, and a Samoan woman makes $0.62 (Blackburn, 2019). The pay disparities among Indian, Samoan, and Burmese women in the US demonstrate that we cannot (and should not) view Asian Americans as a monolithic population. If we do, we implicitly ignore the socio-economic stratifications within this population.

The model minority myth also categorizes Asian Americans as perpetual foreigners: Asian American women are depicted as the exoticized "Other" and the submissive object of sexual desire, while Asian American men are stereotyped as effeminate cab drivers or IT guys. Moreover, the "model minority" myth undermines the past and current racism experienced by Asian Americans. The Chinese Exclusion Act of 1882 and the Japanese internment camps of the mid-20th century saw rampant racial discrimination and human rights violations against Asian Americans. The increase in anti-Asian hate crimes in recent years also demonstrates how unwelcoming the US still is to Asian Americans and Asian immigrants. Instead of confronting the past and present discriminations against Asian Americans, the model minority myth suggests that all Asian Americans are prospering and other racial minorities, too, can succeed if only they worked as hard as Asian Americans and "got over" the US history of systemic racism. Here, the "model minority" myth downplays the impact of systemic racism on people of color in the US and creates a racial hierarchy among people of color in which Asian Americans are at the apex while Black and Native Americans occupy the bottom.

There exists a significant disparity between Asian American representation broadly in the workforce versus in leadership roles. While approximately 13% of working professionals are Asian American, only an astonishing 6% of executive leadership positions are filled by this demographic. Asian Americans are often seen as hardworking and easy-to-manage (read docile) employees, yet they are seldom considered great leaders—usually because of cultural stigmas, implicit bias, and racist attitudes among those in top management. Of course, this is further exacerbated by other overlapping factors, such as gender, age, and ability. Without the representation of Asian Americans in management or leadership positions, it is even more challenging for Asian American employees to find sponsors or mentors to help nurture their talent and support their career progress. Thus, the cycle continues.

A Limitation to Inclusion: Gaslighting in the Workplace

Similar to microaggressions, gaslighting can be hard to identify, but its impact on individuals, workplaces, and communities is often destructive. The term "gaslighting" originates from Gaslight (1944), the film adaptation of a play in which a husband tries to convince his wife that she is crazy so he can get her committed to a mental hospital. The husband makes the gas lights in the house flicker, and when his wife confronts him, he claims not to see the flickering and subsequently leads her to believe that she is going crazy. In more modern contexts, gaslighting refers to when "a person or group of people deliberately work to distort your judgments, minimize your work, or distort your recollection of events" (Ajayi-Hackworth, 2020). In the context of the workplace, gaslighting occurs when an employee manipulates their coworker into doubting their own self-worth, value to the organization, and skills. In many instances, however, gaslighting can be seen in employer-employee relationships because of the inherent hierarchical structure of these relationships.

A few misunderstandings are expected in any professional relationship, but gaslighting is an intentional form of manipulation. For example, during an employee's first day in a new position, the employee meets their new boss, who gives them a certain project: The employee must compile a report comparing the mission statements of five software companies. The employee writes the report and gives it to their boss, and in response, the boss states that the employee was supposed to compile a report comparing the mission statements of five healthcare software companies. The employee is confused but presumes that they must have misheard the boss' instructions. However, the boss continues to change up their instructions, and as a result, the employee begins to question their own listening skills, work ethics, and abilities. In this example, we may ask ourselves why the employee doesn't speak up or question the boss' changing instructions, but it is important to note that those who are at the receiving end of gaslighting often are not aware that they are being manipulated. The employee may truly believe their boss is being truthful and that they, themselves, are a problem.

Because gaslighting makes the recipient believe that they are at fault, the recipient can go from being a high-performing employee to one who is struggling at work. Gaslighting can adversely affect an employee's motivation, self-esteem, self-confidence, and decision-making skills and cause the employee's career to stagnate. Over time, gaslighting can lead to the employee leaving their job, company, or even their industry. In some cases, gaslighting can lead to anxiety, depression, and even trauma. Gaslighting can exist in any situation or relationship, but in the workplace, it significantly undermines DEI efforts and harms marginalized or underrepresented employees. Gaslighting is often fueled by power imbalances, and the gaslighter may use the recipient's marginalized status to their advantage as they are aware of the recipient's lack of power or privilege. This makes gaslighting even more challenging to spot, as individuals are less likely to question those in power or those who have professional authority over them. Nevertheless, there are a few standard techniques that gaslighters use to manipulate their targets.

The Eight Most Common Types of Gaslighting

1. Isolation

Gaslighters seek to isolate their target(s) from other coworkers or employees to limit the number of people who question the gaslighter's intentions or contradict the gaslighter's version of events. Gaslighting can cause confusion and emotional distress in the target, and without anyone to help them, they are far easier to manipulate. Isolation techniques include circulating lies or rumors about the target, excluding the target from work or social events, inciting conflict between the target and the target's coworkers or peers, and portraying the target in a negative light when conversing with senior leaders or upper management.

2. Withholding

This occurs when the gaslighter withholds information, meeting and event invitations, attention, praise, assistance, access to resources, and bonuses from the target. Withholding not only leads to the target questioning themselves and their abilities, but it can also cause them to wonder why they are deserving of such treatment. Indeed, the target will most likely place the blame on themselves, and this may make it far more challenging for them to perform at work. In cases where the target is from a marginalized group, withholding access to resources is especially insidious as it adds to the many pre-existing systemic barriers that hinder the target's career advancement.

3. Deception

The gaslighter uses explicit lies, alternative explanations, or narratives, or omits key facts to deceive the target, and, subsequently, the target may become less and less sure of themselves and their work. An important part of this deception is the gaslighter's repetition of lies and alternative narratives so that these lies and narratives become solidified as fact or the truth. Similar to the previous gaslighting techniques, deception aims to destabilize the target while simultaneously masking the gaslighter's manipulative behaviors.

4. Discrediting

The gaslighter's goal is to discredit the target as often as possible so that the target's experiences, ideas, perspectives, and contributions carry little or no weight. There are two major effects of discrediting: The gaslighter wants to invalidate the target's contributions to portray them as incompetent, and the gaslighter wants to convince others that the target cannot (and should not) be trusted or that their contributions should not be taken seriously. In doing so, the gaslighter devalues the target's contributions while adding value to their own. For example, the gaslighter will often reject the target's suggestions and ideas, take credit for or dismiss the target's ideas, state that the target's work is subpar, and micromanage the target's work.

5. Intimidation

In most cases, the gaslighter has some form of power, authority, or dominance over the target, and they will use their superior position to ensure that their own account of events, contributions, and statements are more heavily weighted than those of the target. Even in cases where the gaslighter does not occupy a superior position, they will level themselves as the target's superior. Gaslighters who use intimidation often establish themselves as experts in their field or industry, overemphasize their own competence, and make it known to their superiors that they are on the same level as their superiors.

6. Codependency

Codependency occurs when the gaslighter tries to blur the lines between themselves and their target to remove the target's self-sufficiency, agency, and independence. The gaslighter may make decisions for or on behalf of their target, disregard personal and professional boundaries, or spread personal information about their target. Importantly, when the target struggles to distinguish themselves from the gaslighter, they will be more likely to accept the gaslighter's account of events, alternate narratives, or lies.

7. Degradation

While this is a more overt and recognizable form of gaslighting, degradation is still a core technique of gaslighting. Degradation includes the gaslighter yelling, name-calling, or insulting the target to make the target doubt their own experiences, decisions, and judgments and to think that they are at fault for their perceived incompetencies.

8. Periodic Suspension of Gaslighting

This occurs when the gaslighter ceases all gaslighting behavior, behaves normally, and then resumes gaslighting behavior to confuse their target. These fluctuations make the target think that they have imagined the gaslighter's bad behavior, and as a result, the target may lower their defenses—only for them to be subjected to the next round of gaslighting.

No matter which technique(s) the gaslighter uses, they tend to target people who are people-pleasers, tend to doubt themselves and see the best in others, enjoy helping others, and/or are from underrepresented or marginalized groups. Of course, anyone can become the target of gaslighting, but the above qualities can make it easier for gaslighters to target them. For example, employees from marginalized groups are more prone to imposter syndrome and isolation because they have been historically and systemically excluded from and in the workplace. This makes marginalized employees the likely target for gaslighters to exploit the pre-existing imposter syndrome and isolation and further manipulate them. Moreover, society tends to believe privileged people over marginalized people (as seen in several cases where female employees are subjected to sexual harassment in the workplace). Because employees from marginalized groups often lack power or representation in authoritative positions, they are more likely to unsuccessfully question or call out the gaslighter's behavior.

The difficulties in questioning the manipulation and intentions of gaslighters are further exacerbated by the fact that gaslighters excel at managing their reputation and going the extra mile to make sure that they are liked and respected in the workplace. This serves to further discredit the target and make it even more challenging for the target to confide in others about the gaslighter's manipulations. Gaslighters are hard to identify in the workplace, but they often lie, make excuses, or blame others for their mistakes or issues; have explosive reactions to feedback; lack personal and professional boundaries; mock their coworkers, employees, or peers; and are meticulous when it comes to protecting their reputation. It is important to remember that gaslighters act intentionally and offensively, and despite being keenly aware of their behavior, they will feign innocence and ignorance when called out.

In many instances, the gaslighter will even portray themselves as the victim, change the subject, deflect blame onto the target, or lie when they are called out. Gaslighters who have power and authority over their target(s) may use their position in the organization to retaliate against the target(s) if they are called out for their gaslighting. This includes silencing any accusations, creating a hostile working environment for the target(s), withholding pay or bonuses from the target(s), demoting or preventing the career progression of the target(s), or limiting the target's access to workplace resources.

Implicit bias and gaslighting in the workplace are inextricably linked, as they both perpetuate harmful attitudes and behaviors toward marginalized groups, ultimately hindering diversity, equity, and inclusion efforts. As described, gaslighting as a form of psychological manipulation ensures the maintenance of power and control over marginalized communities and implicit bias exacerbates the impact of these unconscious attitudes and beliefs. When these two phenomena intersect, it leads to a toxic work environment where employees feel disempowered and undervalued. By recognizing and addressing the links between these two issues, organizations can work toward creating more inclusive and equitable workplaces, where all employees feel valued and respected. It is essential that organizations take proactive steps to address implicit bias and gaslighting to foster a positive work culture and promote diversity, equity, and inclusion.

Confronting Implicit Bias in the Workplace

Strategy One: Identify Your Own Biases

The first step to confronting implicit bias is to acknowledge that we all have biases. Biases are part of human nature, so we need to be able to recognize when and why we hold certain biases and how these biases can affect both our professional and personal lives. It is also important to make considered decisions rather than fast, spur-of-the-moment ones, as the latter is more likely to contain implicit biases. This is particularly important in cases of attribution bias, as we need to take a step back and reflect on our coworkers' or peers' actions. Implicit bias often goes hand-in-hand with social "-isms" and while educating employees on racism, sexism, ableism, homophobia, and so on can help them dismantle their biases, organizations also need to take tangible steps to empower marginalized employees so that they feel accepted and included in the workplace.

Identifying (and overcoming) your own biases can be done in one or more of the following ways:

1. Learn to reduce stress and increase mindfulness, as individuals are more likely to display bias when they are under pressure.

2. Consider the perspectives and experiences of those who have been (and continue to be) marginalized to boost empathy and create meaningful connections with others.

3. Take the time to understand the impact that biases have on people from marginalized or underrepresented backgrounds.

4. Learn to reflect rather than react when you are interacting with those who are different from you.

5. Engage with others based on their personal characteristics instead of judging them based on the stereotypes associated with their culture, race, gender, ability, and religion.

6. Celebrate differences rather than awkwardly ignoring or downplaying them (for example, avoid saying "I don't see color").

7. Measure the extent of your biases by taking the Implicit Association Test (IAT) and/or participating in implicit bias workshops and training.

8. Understand that confronting your personal biases is an ongoing process that takes time and self-reflection.

Strategy Two: Implement the IDI Assessment in the Workplace

The Intercultural Development Inventory (IDI) is a 50-question online assessment that tests intercultural competence and the complexity with which an individual experiences cultural differences. The assessment includes five monocultural or intercultural worldviews: The monocultural worldviews of denial and polarization determine which individuals view the world mainly through their own cultural lens and which individuals do not experience much cultural difference. The polarization worldview, in particular, takes on two forms: The Defense has an uncritical view of their own culture but an overly critical view of other cultures, while the Reversal perceives cultural differences as an "us" and "them" situation. The Reversal is also overly critical of their own culture while being uncritical in their acceptance of other cultures. The third worldview is minimalism, which focuses on cultural similarities and universal principles and values while also assuming that, in essence, all individuals are the same.

The intercultural worldview of acceptance identifies individuals who understand cultural differences and similarities on a deeper level and who wish to learn about and experience other cultures. The fifth worldview, Adaptation, also takes on an intercultural approach, and here, individuals recognize and appreciate cultural differences. But, these individuals take their appreciation a step further by adapting their behavior to other cultural contexts so that they may behave in culturally-appropriate ways. The IDI assessment is an extensive and seemingly objective in which to test individuals' cultural competence and can be especially beneficial when implemented in workplaces.

Research has shown that individuals who score high on the IDI are more likely to exhibit behaviors that promote inclusion, such as valuing and seeking out diversity, engaging in perspective-taking, and adapting their communication style to fit diverse audiences. This makes the IDI a valuable tool for organizations looking to promote a culture of inclusivity and equity. Furthermore, the IDI is an effective tool for identifying areas where individuals may need additional support or training to develop their intercultural competence. For example, an individual who scores low on the IDI may benefit from additional training on how to communicate effectively with individuals from different cultures, while an individual who scores high on the IDI may be well-suited for leadership positions that require intercultural competence. By identifying areas for improvement, the IDI can help organizations to tailor their approach to cultural intelligence building and promote the development of intercultural competence.

Finally, the IDI is an effective tool for measuring the impact of DEI at work on individual and organizational outcomes. By administering the IDI before and after implementing DEI interventions, organizations can track changes in intercultural competence and assess the effectiveness and progress along the journey. This can be particularly useful for organizations that are looking to establish a baseline for their DEI efforts or evaluate the impact of specific interventions over time.

Strategy Three: Establish an Equitable Corporate Culture

Of course, the IDI assessment and implicit bias training can go a long way, but organizations must establish a corporate culture in which every employee has an equal chance to voice their opinion and has equitable access to resources. Confronting implicit bias can also occur on an individual level: An employee can make it a point to spend time and get proximate with coworkers from different backgrounds and experiences to not only build on their empathy but also to improve their cultural competence. On a larger scale, organizations can also perform internal analyses to identify the areas where employees may be more vulnerable to implicit biases from their coworkers. Besides, if an organization can identify where implicit bias is most likely to occur, it can take the appropriate steps to prevent or remedy it in an effective and timely manner to reduce the potential harm to marginalized employees. Implicit bias is not just a hindrance to an organization's DEI efforts; it can also cause psychological harm to the victims of this bias. As such, organizations must also prioritize accountability so that those who perpetuate bias and discrimination in the workplace can face the consequences.

With inclusion being one of the main objectives of DEI efforts, we must also explore all obstacles that stand in the path of creating and maintaining a truly inclusive and welcoming workplace. A sense of belonging, a culture of community, and an open, productive space for creativity and innovation are the makings of an inclusive workplace or organization, but these qualities can only be achieved once we have mitigated all forms of implicit bias and microaggressions. Of course, the workforce is composed of individuals with unique circumstances, backgrounds, and experiences, so we can (and should) assume that implicit and unconscious bias and microaggressions are an inevitable part of the work environment. In these cases, organizations must ensure that there are programs in place to educate all employees on the harms of implicit bias and microaggressions and effective communication channels to report and remedy these workplace ills. While implicit biases may be part of the human experience, this does not mean that they should be tolerated.

Chapter 9:

Accountability Driven through

Authenticity

The greatest need is for individuals in higher power positions to improve how they engage in identity conversations…everyone has baskets of advantage and disadvantage [sic] everyone is in the ally position at times, and everyone benefits from the allyship of others. —Kenji Yoshino and David Glasgow

The terms "accountability" and "responsibility" are often used synonymously, but when it comes to DEI in the workplace, these terms are quite different. "Responsibility" is more task-oriented and usually occurs during a situation: For instance, every team member has the responsibility to complete their individual tasks for a major team project. "Accountability," however, occurs before, during, and after the situation has ended or the project has been completed, and, here, the team leader and members take ownership of their individual and group work. Accountability is a salient part of an innovative, creative, and profitable organization that wants to achieve all its DEI goals. The DEI process requires organization leaders and employees to be transparent, honest, and clear in their DEI efforts, and if or when DEI goals are not achieved, the organization will be able to identify where things went wrong. Indeed, accountability in the workplace allows us to trace our steps, identify our mistakes, and work toward improving our DEI processes.

Embedding Accountability in DEI

In the context of the workplace, the term "accountability" refers to making or having clear agreements on what is expected and what the consequences of the actions leaders or employees take or do not take. Diversity, equity, and inclusion requires a commitment and alignment on how to challenge the status quo and confront systemic inequalities in the workplace. Everyone who enters a workplace brings with them different levels of knowledge, awareness, exposure, and comfort regarding cultural differences, so it is the responsibility of the organization and its leaders to provide employees with the tools, skills, and resources to build their cultural competence. When employees are aware of the importance of DEI in the workplace, they can be held accountable for any future discriminatory behaviors or biases.

There are three salient levels of accountability. The personal level describes the thoughts and actions of individuals, while the organizational level refers to what people think and do as part of a group, community, society, or organization. The third level, the systemic level, includes coordinated action over time that creates institutional and structural change. On a personal level, accountability means recognizing and dismantling our own biases and prejudices toward ourselves and others, whereas, on an organizational level, accountability focuses on how we treat other groups of people in our professional and personal lives. Accountability on a systemic level is often far more complex, as it entails dismantling existing systems to build new, diverse, equitable, and inclusive systems instead of bringing underrepresented people into our existing systems. The systemic level of accountability, including policy, process, and practice also involves a more authentic bond and sharing of power and leadership among individuals or communities.

Of course, this often requires the dominant culture or group in an organization or society to understand, leverage and wield some of their privilege in allyship and advocacy of organizational DEI efforts. Indeed, the dominant group may not have been the generation to build such unequal systems, but they can be held accountable for maintaining the systems that seek to oppress and marginalize certain groups of people. Thus, DEI policies and strategies cannot be successfully developed and implemented in the workplace without accountability. An organization may have good intentions with its DEI strategies, but these intentions are meaningless unless the organization's leaders are held accountable for any lack of support or unsuccessful implementation of DEI in the workplace. According to Rice (2022), accountability is vital as it "creates a sense of importance needed for DEI efforts to succeed… [and on] a foundational level, if no one is accountable for results, there is little to no incentive for things to get done." Indeed, accountability can be seen as a grounding framework that ensures organizations follow through on their DEI commitments so that they can actively and holistically foster a healthy and productive working environment for all. So, how can organizations ensure accountability when it comes to DEI policies and strategies?

Strategy One: Quantitative and Qualitative Data through Reporting and Goal Setting

Any effort toward DEI needs to have established benchmarks and results for organizations to determine whether they are successes or misses. The results or data from the measuring of DEI commitments and goals are often quantitative: The organization hired X number of employees who were racial minorities or promoted X number of neurodivergent employees to leadership positions. Yet, this data also needs to be qualitative to highlight employee performance and well-being, access to resources and opportunities, and skill-development investment. Quantitative data, for instance, demonstrates the diversity of an organization's workforce, but qualitative data shows whether or not employees from marginalized groups feel accepted, included, and have a sense of belonging in the workplace. Data that focuses on inclusion in the workplace, for example, rely on both quantitative and qualitative data to analyze how these two types of data interact with each other and identify any possible inclusion gaps in the data. When it comes to data, however, organizations should be transparent in their communication of DEI data to their leaders, employees, and the general public. Transparency not only helps build credibility and integrity but also demonstrates that accountability is at the core of DEI progress.

Setting public, measurable, and monitorable goals is particularly crucial for organizations and companies that are committed to advancing diversity, equity, and inclusion internally and externally. Public DEI goals communicate the organization's commitment to creating an inclusive workplace culture that values and respects differences among its employees, customers, and other stakeholders. It demonstrates the organization's willingness to be held accountable for achieving its DEI objectives, which can help build trust and credibility with stakeholders. Measurable DEI goals allow the organization to track progress toward achieving its DEI objectives, identify areas that require improvement, and celebrate successes. For instance, an organization that aims to increase the representation of underrepresented groups in its leadership positions can set a specific goal of having 30% of leadership positions filled by individuals from underrepresented groups within five years. By tracking progress toward this goal, the organization can determine whether its DEI strategies are effective and make necessary adjustments to achieve its objectives.

Monitoring progress toward DEI goals is essential to fostering accountability in the organization's efforts. By regularly checking in on progress toward its DEI objectives, the organization can identify any barriers that hinder progress and determine the best course of action to overcome them. It can also hold itself accountable for any setbacks and demonstrate its commitment to creating a diverse, equitable, and inclusive workplace culture.

In addition to fostering accountability, setting public and measurable DEI goals can also increase employee engagement and retention. Employees are more likely to be engaged and committed to an organization that values their differences and promotes a culture of inclusion. When employees see that the organization is making progress toward its DEI goals, they feel a sense of pride in their workplace and are more likely to stay with the organization long-term. Public and measurable DEI goals can also improve the organization's reputation and attractiveness to potential employees, customers, and investors. In today's increasingly diverse and socially conscious society, many stakeholders consider a company's commitment to DEI when making decisions about where to work, shop, or invest. By setting and achieving public and measurable DEI goals, the organization demonstrates its commitment to creating a diverse and inclusive workplace culture, which can enhance its reputation and appeal to a broader range of stakeholders.

Strategy Two: Empower Leaders as DEI Ambassadors

DEI commitments and accountability begin at the higher echelons of an organization, where those in leadership or senior management positions have the power, resources, and authority to incite structural change and weave DEI into the fabric of the organization. As such, the leaders of an organization must be held accountable for any missteps or continued gaps in the development and implementation of DEI strategies in the workplace. Leadership accountability is all the more important as DEI gaps have real consequences for the organization's employees from marginalized backgrounds. Diversity teams (such as DEI officers or ERGs) and HR play an active role in DEI advancement and advocacy, but ultimately, it is the executive leadership's responsibility to ensure the successful implementation of DEI in the organization. Besides, when leadership is not held accountable for DEI, it sends a message to the entire organization (and the public) that diversity, equity, and inclusion are not a priority for the organization. Moreover, the lack of accountability in leadership can trickle down to the various departments of the organization and result in these departments stagnating in their DEI efforts.

One way to hold leaders accountable is to empower them as DEI ambassadors. Here, the CEO and other senior leaders need to endorse diversity, equity, and inclusion deliberately, intentionally, and publicly in their organizations by providing written DEI commitments and developing a policy statement to serve as the organization's guide for its DEI commitments. In doing so, leaders pave the way for deeper, more meaningful internal and external conversations on DEI and its potential impacts, boost openness and engagement among employees, and reduce explicit and implicit bias and prejudice in the workplace. When leaders become DEI ambassadors, others will be more likely to follow suit, and this can result in more inclusive workplace environments in which all employees are heard, validated, and valued. Certainly, a more inclusive working environment can attract a greater talent pool, boost creativity and innovation, and give the organization a competitive advantage.

Strategy Three: Accountability Support Systems

When the accountability for DEI progress is in the hands of the leaders, these leaders need to have a strong support system to ensure that an adequate amount of the organization's resources and budgets are allocated to supporting the leaders' organization-wide implementation of DEI. Without such support, it is usually the Chief Diversity Officer (CDO) who must single-handedly drive systemic and cultural change within the organization. This is no easy feat and requires support from departments across the organization. However, larger organizations—and especially those that operate in several countries—may need to establish a DEI task force or action council of important stakeholders to help with the execution of DEI strategies across the organization's branches.

The task force can outline the organization's DEI goals and strategies according to the needs of the underrepresented communities in every country in which the organization operates. For example, the Indian branch of a particular organization may have unique DEI needs and goals in comparison to its Canadian branch. It will therefore be less challenging for the DEI task force to align the DEI strategies with the business practices and working norms and cultures of the organization's various branches. In addition to overseeing the implementation of DEI across branches and countries, the task force will also be able to provide clear insight into the current state of DEI to the organization's leader(s), employees, and clients or customers. This may seem like the organization is shifting accountability to the DEI task force, but ultimately, the task force can serve as an extension of the organization's leadership.

Advocacy and Allyship

Creating a culture of accountability entails being allies with and advocating for marginalized individuals and communities. Doud et al. (2022) define an ally as "someone who is not a member of an underrepresented group and who is active and purposeful in supporting, promoting, and advancing real change for a marginalized group through a focus on inclusion, equity, and diversity." For example, able-bodied employees can help advocate for reasonable accommodations for disabled persons, and men can help promote pay equity in the workplace for women, transgender, and non-binary communities. While an ally may not understand what it feels like to be part of a marginalized group, they can still support members of the group and encourage meaningful, systemic change in the workplace and beyond. Allies "lend" their power, privilege, or access to individuals who may or may not have the same privileges as them. Using an intersectional lens, allies, too, can be from marginalized backgrounds but use some of their privileges to uplift others. For example, heterosexual women can be allies to queer women, Asian Americans can be allies to African Americans, and so on.

Workplace allyship can be formal (offering support through mentorships, sponsorships, and advocacy) or informal (raising awareness on social issues or simply lending an empathetic ear), but it is usually an ongoing process that prioritizes resource sharing and long-term career advancements. As a dynamic exchange of resources and interests, allyship is often a life-long process that involves unlearning and learning, active listening, and dismantling one's own prejudices or biases. For instance, allies should not let discriminatory remarks slide in the workplace but also should not try to speak for or over those who are at the receiving end of such remarks. Instead, allies can focus on supporting their marginalized coworkers and peers while also advocating for greater diversity, equity, and inclusion in the workplace.

Allies usually hold more power in the workplace, and this power comes with the ability *and* responsibility to help foster an inclusive corporate culture. Those who occupy leadership, supervisory, or management positions have a unique platform that allows them to spark meaningful, systemic change to the benefit of marginalized employees and the organization as a whole. Leaders who are allies should make DEI a priority and inspire their employees to want to learn more about different cultures, social issues, and perspectives. Moreover, allies in the workplace can practice amplification by using their privilege to validate and empower those whose voices have been ignored or silenced. For example, if an employee's idea is ignored (perhaps due to implicit bias), then their ally coworker can raise their hand, acknowledge the employee's idea, and show their support for the employee's idea (if they truly like the idea, of course). Having strong allies in the workplace helps employees from marginalized groups feel more comfortable expressing their true selves and fosters a workplace culture underpinned by trust and empathy.

This should come from the top down, with leaders being visible about their allegiance and advocacy so that middle management and the employees are inspired to follow suit. There is no clear blueprint for allyship, but here are a few examples of allyship in the workplace: Advocating for private, clean rooms for new mothers to pump breast milk; inviting a coworker to work with you on an important project so that they can be noticed by the organization's leaders; publicly acknowledging the achievements of a mentee to boost their reputation and demonstrate their potential for promotion; advocating for interpreters and captioning in all virtual meetings; or asking people who are not the same race, gender, or age as you to help you with a job interview; the development of prayer rooms for individuals from religious identities that necessitate it; or ensuring that acknowledgment and recognition of pronouns are common practice in the organization. Of course, there is always the risk of there being a gap between intent and action, so it is incredibly important for individuals to practice mindful and impactful allyship in the workplace and beyond.

In addition, the responsibility for systemic changes falls to the organizations rather than the individuals, but we must also remember that organizations (and systems) are composed of individuals. As such, a key part of impactful allyship is to incite individuals to collectively prioritize belonging, inclusion, and advocacy in the workplace. Because allyship is an action, there is bound to be trial and error in the process of becoming an effective ally. In this case, organizations can develop workshops and training programs to equip employees with the knowledge on how they can use their power and privilege to advocate for those with fewer privileges than them. As with most DEI topics and elements, leaders should be at the forefront of promoting allyship in the workplace, but employees, too, must put in the effort if they want to drive social change. So, let us look at how leaders and employees can become allies in the workplace and in broader society.

Strategy One: Educate Yourself

Whether this involves reading books on systemic inequality or diversifying one's professional and personal networks, immersing themselves in the stories of those with different experiences, perspectives, and backgrounds helps leaders and employees develop their cultural competence and intelligence and practice empathy. Education is only the first step in the process, and individuals need to be able to translate the knowledge gained from books and other people into their own realities and contexts. It is also beneficial for individuals to diversify their reading material, as the books, articles, academic texts, and blog posts written by those from marginalized groups do not represent all there is to know about the said groups. For example, the books on racism written by an African author may differ from the books on racism written by an African American author. Similarly, feminist texts by African American women may include experiences and perspectives that cannot be found in feminist texts written by white American women.

Strategy Two: Practice Active Listening

This is a fantastic skill for any situation, but it is especially advantageous in allyship. Active listening involves not only being conscious and intentional when listening to others but also listening to others without forming judgments or thinking about how to respond. It is through active listening that individuals can form an understanding of and empathize with the experiences and perspectives of those from diverse backgrounds. For authentic allyship, it may not be enough to identify as "not racist," "not homophobic," or "not sexist," but rather, allies need to be actively anti-racist, anti-sexist, anti-homophobic, and so on to truly help dismantle systemic inequality and discrimination. A key benefit of practicing active listening is being able to identify the exact advocacy and support needed to drive DEI goals in the workplace. What one individual needs from allies may differ from what another individual needs from allies, so it is vital that allies practice active listening instead of assuming the needs of others.

This is also how allies can bridge the gap between intent and action, as some allies (who have good intentions) can still run the risk of undermining the agency of marginalized individuals by assuming the type of support or advocacy the marginalized individuals need. For instance, an individual who experiences race-based discrimination in the workplace may feel uncomfortable with a white ally publicly calling out the perpetrators of such discrimination. Or, an ally reporting a case of sexual harassment in the workplace without consulting the victim can add to the anxiety and trauma of the victim. An authentic and effective ally knows when and how to support marginalized individuals without centering themselves in the situation and without causing further (albeit unintentional) harm.

Strategy Three: Avoid Putting People Into Boxes and Sweeping Generalizations

As humans, we make sense of the world by categorizing experiences, people, and things, and while this works in some cases, we need to refrain from categorizing individuals as one thing or one identity. Everyone has multiple identities: A woman can be queer, a millennial, and a first-generation immigrant, while another woman can be Muslim, neurodivergent, and a Gen Zer. Authentic allyship provides individuals with the opportunity to share their identities and experiences with each other so that everyone can feel connected to and have a sense of belonging in a broader community. While marginalization can play a minor or major role in the individual's life, it may not encompass their entire life and identity, which is why it is incredibly important for allies to avoid seeing individuals only through the lens of their marginalization. Humans are complex beings who, owing to their unique histories, experiences, and perspectives, can face various forms of privilege and marginalization throughout their lives. So, it is best for allies to avoid making assumptions about others and putting them in a single box.

Strategy Four: Understand How Privilege Equates to Power

The term "privilege" is not simply a social justice buzzword, and while it can be rather polarizing, we must be able to identify privileges as a result and continuation of power dynamics that exist in our political, social, cultural, and economic spheres. Being privileged does not mean that an individual has not worked hard in their life, nor does it suggest that the individual has not faced any hardships. Instead, privilege refers to the power an individual has because of the invisible benefits that help them exist and succeed in the world. Indeed, an individual can experience multiple privileges and/or multiple points of marginalization, but the more privileges an individual has, the easier it may be for them to access resources, opportunities, and power. Privilege is often invisible to those who have it, yet it is hypervisible to those who do not, and as a result, it can be a significant divider among individuals and communities. When it comes to allyship, privileges must be acknowledged in a constrictive, intersectional, and honest manner so that leaders and employees can have open conversations on privilege and how it impacts the power dynamics in the workplace.

Embracing Consequential Accountability in Leadership

To support DEI progress, an organization can adopt a system of consequential accountability in which its senior leader(s) and managers make significant progress in terms of their DEI goals so that they may advance their careers within the organization. Simply put, if a leader's career advancement is directly influenced by their achievement of DEI goals or successful implementation of DEI strategies, then the leader is more likely to be committed to the organization's short- and long-term DEI goals.

Hasan & Adeleye (2021) write the following:

> Using compensation to achieve DE&I strategic alignment is particularly promising since organizations extensively use incentives for other financial and business goals. Executives understand incentives, which

apparently help align their individual goals to their firm's strategic priorities. Why reinvent the wheel? (paragraph 3)

Indeed, connecting DEI goals to executive pay makes it easier to cascade DEI goals to the middle managers and then to the rest of the organization. Pay is a powerful motivator of performance, and when leaders have a stake in the matter, they are more motivated to find creative ways to advance and advocate for DEI policies and strategies. Companies such as Microsoft, Uber, and Salesforce have recently announced their plans to boost representation at their leadership levels, with executives being compensated if they deliver results.

Strategy One: Prioritizing DEI Goals on an Executive Level

Consequential accountability encourages leaders to make better-informed decisions when it comes to new talent and succession. Because leaders will be held accountable for eliminating bias and advancing underrepresented talent in a sustainable yet accelerated way, achieving DEI goals becomes a more personal and relevant activity for them. Of course, this also means that there needs to be standardized mechanisms in place to track the leaders' progress in achieving individual or personal DEI goals, to promote transparency among leaders, and to integrate the leaders' personal achievement of DEI goals into their performance reviews to ensure that they can advance in their organizations. In a post-COVID-19 world, there are several external priorities competing for executive attention, such as environmental sustainability, social issues, and political factors. Organizations must adjust to the "new normal" following the pandemic, and there is mounting pressure for organizations to not only take a stand against discrimination and prejudice but also to actively contribute to positive social change.

In an ideal world, leaders should not have to be compensated for developing and implementing DEI policies and strategies in their organizations, but with the countless internal and external concerns, leaders or executives need the extra motivation to prioritize and pursue measured commitments in this space. Of course, DEI is inextricably linked to environmentalism and socio-economic issues, so it should not be viewed as a separate part of the organization's external social justice initiatives. But inciting systemic and social change within the organization and in broader society is no easy feat. DEI efforts also need to be extensive, intersectional, and radical, as far too many organizations engage in "woke-washing" rather than driving actual change. The public tends to take notice of DEI efforts that pander to social justice issues while doing very little for marginalized employees and their communities. Organizations, therefore, need to demonstrate to clients, consumers, activists, various stakeholders, and the media that DEI is a top priority for the organizations, and there is no better way to communicate this message than by connecting consequential accountability (that is, executive pay) to the achievement of DEI goals.

However, this also means being cognizant of both the business and moral case for connecting executive pay to DEI goals. As more and more organizations have started tying their executives' pay to DEI goals—with 27% of S&P 500 companies implementing this strategy in 2021 and over 38% in 2022—the more issues are arising (Carlos, 2021; Farient Advisors, 2022). Financial incentives tend to undermine the intrinsic value or interest in DEI because such incentives lead us to believe that executives or leaders are mainly or only working toward achieving DEI goals for the financial benefits. The ethics (and optics) of connecting executive pay to achieving DEI goals become even more problematic when we look at the demographics of senior leaders and executives. Those in the senior management, decision-making, and leadership echelons of many organizations are typically part of a privileged and powerful demographic (that is, white men), and yet they are being compensated for hiring and treating marginalized people in a fairly and equitably. This also contrasts with the fact that most formal and informal DEI work is performed by marginalized individuals and communities who receive little to no compensation.

Financial compensation being linked to DEI goals can also undermine efforts toward boosting DEI in the workplace. A recent study (Leslie et al., 2016) found that in companies with aggressive DEI goals, the women hired to meet diversity targets receive a paid premium (that is, they earn more than their male counterparts), whereas the rest of the organizations' women employees still experience a pay inequity. Simply put, the employees with "diversity value" are prioritized and compensated at the expense of the rest of the workforce—a workforce that includes employees from marginalized backgrounds. As such, the organization "achieves" its DEI goals without having actually increased representation or a sense of belonging in the workplace.

Strategy Two: Distinguish Between Short-Term and Long-Term DEI Goals

DEI efforts are an ongoing process that can take multiple years to implement in organizations, yet financial compensation is usually included in the organizations' annual plans. As such, this creates a significant gap between long-term DEI efforts and the annual financial compensation for achieving DEI goals. For example, if a particular DEI goal takes three years to implement in an organization, will the organization's leaders still be financially rewarded in the first year (when there are little to no significant results)? Or, what if the leaders are financially compensated for all three years, but by the third year, the DEI goal is still not achieved? In some cases, leaders may feel compelled to engage in unethical behavior, such as falsifying DEI data, because they want to receive financial compensation without having to do the DEI work. Connecting executive pay to DEI goals can certainly motivate leaders to prioritize DEI, but, like almost all forms of financial incentives, it can also encourage them to participate in corruption. Indeed, achieving DEI goals requires a strong sense of trust and transparency between the leaders of the organizations and the relevant stakeholders (employees, consumers or clients, the media, and the general public).

Strategy Three: Creating Conditions for Consequential Accountability

Connecting executive pay to DEI goals varies from sector to sector, with two-thirds of utility companies and over half of financial services companies in the S&P 500 mentioning DEI in their incentive processes. These relatively higher statistics may be because these companies tend to be highly regulated and are closely linked to the local communities in which they operate (Farient Advisors, 2022). The information technology and industrial sectors, however, have low rates of connecting executive pay to DEI goals: Only 25% of IT and industrial companies use DEI in their executive incentive plans.

Semler Brossy Consulting has identified six salient conditions needed to optimize DEI metrics in compensation programs:

1. There needs to be an extensive, clear strategy on how DEI success will be defined.

2. The organization understands that elevating DEI may have unintended consequences.

3. DEI metrics are part of a balanced, comprehensive assessment rather than being narrowly defined.

4. The organization is willing to maintain the connection between DEI and pay over an extended period of time.

5. The organization is willing to set realistic stretch goals that are strong enough to withstand changes in strategy.

6. If the DEI goals are not achieved, the leaders of an organization are willing to publicly disclose the reasons for such failures.

If all six of these conditions are met, then organizations can choose one of three potential paths to prioritize DEI goals. Firstly, if the organization is not ready or willing to connect DEI goals to compensation or pay, it can instead publish a detailed DEI report that explores the organization's commitments, progress, and metrics of the main DEI strategic priorities. This report can also be tied to the organization's corporate social responsibility (CSR) report. Secondly, if the organization wishes to tie DEI goals to an incentive program, it can use a scorecard to boost individual accountability. The scorecard allows the executives, board members, and/or leaders to choose multiple metrics to create a more balanced assessment of DEI within the organization or specific functions. This potential pathway also enables leaders to exercise discretion regarding how the DEI goals are achieved while still providing them with the flexibility to assess DEI in a holistically. Thirdly, the organization can select one or two DEI metrics and assign clear weightings to these metrics as part of its long-term or annual incentive plan. Unlike the previous pathway, the organization focuses on only one or two metrics (such as people of color and women), and in the case of the latter, the two metrics are equally weighted or prioritized.

Connecting Accountability to Authenticity

Authenticity and psychological safety in the workplace is apparent when employees sense that leaders are open and transparent about the organization and about themselves. That is, when a company culture is seen as authentic, the employees will feel as though their leaders are being "real" with them and that they lead with good intentions. Authentic corporate culture and leadership often include self-awareness (of their values, limitations, and strengths), transparency, a tendency to consistently "do the right thing," high levels of emotional intelligence and empathy, and open-mindedness. For example, an authentic leader can admit when they have made a mistake and will take the necessary steps to remedy the mistake. An authentic corporate culture is open to differing opinions, ideas, and perspectives and in which employees can ask questions and voice their concerns without fearing any repercussions. Authenticity in the workplace can be demonstrated in several ways. Firstly, an organization should clearly define its values and culture to determine what type of organization it should be and how its people will treat each other. Perhaps the company or business aims for technological innovation or wants to help serve its community by creating jobs and developing the professional skills of its people. Or, a company may want to establish a collaborative corporate culture in which its employees work well with each other and various stakeholders to achieve common goals. Defining its goals, values, and culture boosts the organization's authenticity and ensures that it does not stray too far from its higher purpose.

Secondly, an authentic workplace practices vulnerability to create genuine, meaningful connections with others. Leaders and employees alike should feel free to be their true selves in the workplace and be open about their limitations, strengths, and passions. Of course, this may be challenging for some, but it is still beneficial to at least try to share your feelings and thoughts every so often. This also highlights the importance of open communication in the workplace. An authentic corporate culture encourages employees to speak up about their concerns and engage in open dialogues on both professional and personal levels. Whether this involves formal staff meetings or idle chatter by the water cooler, open communication helps employees challenge unhealthy working norms and express their differing opinions and thoughts constructively. Open communication is also underpinned by mutual respect, which helps to build rapport between leaders and their employees.

The third aspect of authenticity is constructive feedback, as employees need to know what they are doing right and what needs further improvement. Organizations can help nurture the skills and knowledge of their employees, and as such, employees should be praised when there are instances of success and provided with feedback when they make a mistake or cause issues in the organization. Ideally, praise should be genuinely encouraging and should inspire the employee(s), but it also should not be too lavish or superficial. Indeed, the purpose of praise is to show the employee(s) that they are valued in the organization. Feedback should never be unkind; instead, it should help the employee(s) develop on both professional and personal levels while also nudging them in the right direction. Besides, if praise is superficial and feedback is not constructive, the employees may feel like they are being micromanaged, or they may feel insecure about their position in or value to the organization.

Fourthly, authentic workplaces also know when it is time to assess and change their organizational structure and culture. Because people evolve over time, organizations, too, need to adapt, and while organizational change can bring about confusion and uncertainty, an authentic workplace knows how to reassure its employees during the transition period. Organizational change can entail creating new departments or task forces, or it can involve evaluating how the organization's values and aims link to broader society and culture. Whatever the reason for the change, organizations must ensure that any changes are clearly communicated to their employees. If not, the employees may become distrustful of the organization. Better yet, organizations can include their employees in the organizational change by letting their employees cultivate and influence the new status quo (that is, the new working norms and corporate culture). Besides, an organization's culture is largely affected by its employees, so they should have a say when it comes to change. For example, organizations can establish an employee advisory committee or council to identify ways in which the organization's working norms, and culture can be improved.

Finally, the fifth aspect of authenticity is transparency at all levels and in all practices. This includes self-awareness, accountability, and openness among the organization's leaders and employees, and in relation to DEI strategies, authenticity means creating and maintaining a work environment that is inclusive, fair, and equitable. Practicing authentic DEI, for example, means that organizations should not limit their workforce diversification to only women and racial minorities, but instead, they should strive to attract every dimension of difference. Authentic inclusion, too, encourages organizations to prioritize perspectives, experiences, and ideas that challenge the status quo, not to create conflict but to include a wide array of perspectives before making important decisions. Authentic equity focuses on recognizing and accepting that some employees require more resources and support to succeed at their jobs. Altogether, practicing authentic diversity, equity, and inclusion can dismantle the systemic barriers that have marginalized many employees for centuries.

Accountability and authenticity are essential parts of DEI in the workplace, as these qualities help ensure leaders use their positions of power and authority in a transparent, healthy, and non-exploitative manner. Since DEI efforts are usually a top-down process, leaders are responsible for developing, implementing, and reviewing all DEI commitments and goals so that they may serve marginalized employees rather than mainly (or only) line the pockets of those in the higher echelons. Accountability is part and parcel of authentic leadership, as leaders must be willing to be held responsible for DEI failures, power inequities, or gaslighting that may occur during organizational change. Indeed, leadership is not simply focused on moving the organization forward but also ensuring that all employees advance with the organization.

Chapter 10:

Lead and Leverage with a Growth

Mindset

We need to give each other the space to grow, to be ourselves, to exercise our diversity. We need to give each other space so that we may both give and receive such beautiful things as ideas, openness, dignity, joy, healing, and inclusion. –Max de Pree

Leading Inclusively: The Makings of an Inclusive DEI Leader

Inclusive leaders are those who take charge of an organization's DEI policies and strategies, and similar to other effective leaders, they must be self-aware, self-confident, and committed to achieving those DEI objectives. These leaders prioritize inclusion and, therefore, are not afraid to challenge the status quo and influence and motivate others to follow suit. Inclusive leaders should treat their employees based on their unique skills and traits rather than on stereotypes to ensure fairness and equity in the workplace. Indeed, inclusive leaders recognize and celebrate the uniqueness of employees from marginalized groups without tokenizing them or expecting them to perform much of the (unpaid) labor of DEI.

Deloitte's Six Signature Traits of Inclusive Leadership

When I started my career at DEI, I worked as a strategy and operations consultant at Deloitte Consulting in Houston, Texas, where I was further inspired to focus on social policy. It was here that I learned that the leadership of the future not only prioritizes transformation, inclusion, and curiosity but also embraces and leverages individual differences to stay ahead of the curve. Indeed, inclusive leadership helps leaders thrive in ever-changing and increasingly diverse workplaces while also empowering all employees to step outside of their creative comfort zones. Deloitte's six traits of inclusive leadership are a framework that boosts the diversity of talent, ideas, customers, and markets in organizations for better business performance and profits.

Commitment

Inclusive leaders are committed to DEI efforts as these objectives align with their personal and business values. DEI is an ongoing, energy- and time-consuming process, so leaders must understand the commercial advantages and moral reasons for DEI in the workplace to stay committed to their goals and to inspire others to do the same. The intellectual commitment (that is, commercial advantages) and emotional commitment (a strong sense of fairness and caring for people as humans rather than as "resources") of inclusive leaders must be balanced for DEI efforts to be successful for all employees within the organization.

Courage

Courage is an important trait in inclusive leadership, as leaders must be willing to speak up about socio-economic issues and be willing to challenge the status quo. This includes confronting one's own unconscious biases, acknowledging one's mistakes, and inciting systemic change in the organization—all acts of bravery. Inclusive leaders can spark uncomfortable conversations on marginalization and privilege and teach others how they, too, can communicate openly and constructively about their own identities. For inclusive leaders, these acts of bravery do not constitute a single action but instead must be performed daily for DEI policies and strategies to be successfully developed and implemented within the organization. There is also an element of vulnerability in courage, as challenging the status quo will most likely be met with criticism and/or hesitation from various stakeholders. Yet, understanding the risks of systemic change and knowing that mistakes will most likely occur is also part of good, inclusive leadership. These leaders must be able to support their arguments for change and remedy any confusion or hesitation that will come with systemic change.

Curiosity

Inclusive leaders are lifelong learners who have an open-minded yet respectful curiosity about different people, cultures, and beliefs. As stated by Gupta (2021), an inclusive leader's "desire is to understand other people's points of view and to empathize with them, and they like to imagine the world from these other perspectives," and to do this, the leader must "actively listen—without judgment—from a desire to empathize, improve decision-making, and ensure the people around them feel valued." A curious leader is proactive instead of reactive and will seek different ways to help employees understand and value each other. Life-long learning requires time and energy, but the result is worth it, as curious leaders gain loyalty by making others feel valued and secure in their work.

Cultural Intelligence

Inclusive leaders are those who are able to function effectively in a wide array of cultural settings and frameworks while also recognizing that their own culture will impact their personal worldview. This goes hand-in-hand with curiosity, as inclusive leaders are motivated to deepen their understanding of different people and cultures and identify how employees' unique circumstances and overlapping identities play out in the workplace and impact their professional careers. Being culturally intelligent requires a strong level of self-awareness, as inclusive leaders must be willing to recognize and address their own unconscious biases and be open to anything or anyone who challenges their perspectives. It is human nature to become defensive when we perceive something as a threat, but an inclusive leader must overcome their own defensiveness and know how to reduce it in others. Self-awareness also helps leaders have empathy for the experiences and hardships of others, and, in turn, these leaders can develop meaningful and genuine relationships with employees from marginalized backgrounds.

Cognizance of Bias

When it comes to inclusive leadership, leaders must be mindful of personal (and organizational) blind spots and should be able to self-regulate their own thoughts, opinions, and perspectives to ensure fairness in the workplace. On a larger scale, inclusive leaders acknowledge that their organization has an unconscious bias—in its corporate culture and/or its structures—and are committed to developing or updating policies, processes, and strategies to eradicate such bias. Mitigating implicit (and explicit) bias in the workplace includes three key aspects: Ensuring that all processes are transparent, bias-free, inclusive of all individuals, and applied consistently; all communication is clear and respectful; and the outcomes (such as performance evaluations, pay, and promotion opportunities) are unbiased and based on skills, effort, and capability.

Collaboration

Inclusive leaders seek to empower their employees and leverage the creativity and innovation of diverse groups. Nowadays, it is not so much about how smart a leader is but, rather, how smart they make their team, and under the guidance and encouragement of the inclusive leader, the team members work together, build on each other's ideas, and create something new or solve a problem. Moreover, collaboration efforts can be extended to customers, clients, and other stakeholders. In all cases of collaboration, the inclusive leader highlights the importance of diverse thinking and perspectives and ensures that all employees feel valued for their contributions; here, the inclusive leader focuses on empowering and encouraging the team instead of dictating to them. These leaders are also acutely aware of how groupthink, confirmation bias, and in-group favoritism can hinder collaboration, and as a result, they should know how to reduce these process biases.

Inclusive Leadership for a Global Workforce

Changing workplace landscapes mean that inclusive leadership, too, must adapt to managing and empowering a global workforce. Managing a large workforce is challenging enough, but managing team members who are from various countries and/or who work from different locations can lead to misunderstandings, distrust, or decreased cooperation among employees. The key difference between global teams that work well and those that struggle lies not in social distance but rather in the degree of emotional connection and community among team members. Neeley (2015) explains that even if team members "come from different backgrounds, people can interact formally and informally, align, and build trust" to arrive at a common understanding of their work and their role and purpose in the organization. For example, there often exist structural power imbalances among global teams: If most team members are located in Germany, and only a few are situated in Nigeria, there may be a sense that the German team members have more power. Besides, we cannot dismiss the Global North and Global South divide in this example.

Empathy is a fantastic way to reduce the social distance between team members or employees, as it often fosters mutual respect and understanding among diverse groups of people. However, empathy can only be truly beneficial if organizations help balance the participation of all employees, bridge language and fluency gaps, eradicate stigmas and stereotypes, and ensure transparent and honest communication in the virtual and physical workplace. Inclusive leaders do not necessarily have to address and remedy all the issues that arise from managing global teams all at once, but leaders should acknowledge that these issues exist: Workplace norms, management styles, and productivity expectations vary from culture to culture; language barriers and time zone differences may impede communication efficacy; and countries across the globe have different labor and employment laws and regulations. To provide a more specific example, the contract negotiations, union rules, leave policies, and employment customs in the US may be vastly different from those of Sweden, New Zealand, or Ghana. As such, inclusive leaders will need to have a keen understanding of the employment laws, regulations, and customs of the countries in which their organizations operate. One possible way to boost inclusivity across global teams is for organizations and their leaders to adopt a growth mindset.

Overcoming DEI Barriers: The Growth Mindset

There are many barriers to the successful implementation of DEI in the workplace, such as DEI fatigue, a lack of employee buy-in, various stakeholders being resistant to systemic change, a non-intersectional approach to marginalization and privilege, and DEI efforts prioritizing certain marginalized groups over others. These challenges are to be expected, as DEI is an ongoing process that requires a multi-pronged approach and consistent action. However, one major way to overcome DEI challenges is to adopt a growth mindset in the workplace. Stanford University psychologist and mindset expert Carol Dweck coined the term "growth mindset" to describe why some individuals were successful in achieving their goals while others struggled. Dweck (2016) states that success is based on the individual's mindset: "With a growth mindset, people believe that their most basic abilities can be developed through dedication and hard work, [and this] view creates a love of learning and a resilience that are essential for great accomplishment."

The growth mindset suggests that individuals can change their intelligence, talents, and abilities and can find value in what they do regardless of the outcome. In contrast, the "fixed mindset" refers to the belief that an individual's abilities are innate, and that talents, intelligence, and traits are inherited rather than developed. The fixed mindset also suggests that because these qualities are fixed from birth, they stay stable throughout the individual's life. Of course, a fixed mindset can be rather limiting and may hinder individuals from developing and improving certain skills and abilities. On an individual level, the growth mindset helps people excel, and on an organization-wide level, the growth mindset can boost DEI efforts. This is because employees with a growth mindset are less likely to judge others based on stereotypes or mutable traits, and instead, they attribute stereotypes to extrinsic factors such as systemic barriers and social norms.

The growth mindset also allows employees to gather more information and context before drawing conclusions about other people or situations. Interestingly, the growth mindset helps employees from marginalized groups reach their full potential as the idea of intelligence, skills, and abilities changing over time counteracts the fixed, negative stereotypes assigned to marginalized groups. For example, an African American employee may perform poorly on a project because they have internalized the stereotype that African Americans cannot excel in the workplace. With a growth mindset, the employee recognizes that stereotypes are baseless and not innate and that skills, abilities, and intelligence can be improved over time. Moreover, the growth mindset encourages employees to not only learn from their mistakes but also to re-engage after they have made a mistake. Employees with a growth mindset are able to "bounce back" after failure, and they will most likely be armed with the knowledge or awareness needed to prevent the failure from reoccurring.

Connecting the Growth Mindset to Inclusive Leadership

Making the growth mindset part of the foundation of an organization helps its leaders buy into DEI efforts, recognize their own personal and professional shortcomings, develop themselves, and drive systemic and social change within their organization. Those who lead by example can inspire a growth mindset in the employees and motivate them to challenge their own biases and assumptions, celebrate diversity in all of its forms, and find long-term, meaningful solutions to issues in the workplace. The growth mindset focuses on continuous improvement, which makes it especially appropriate for DEI efforts. To embed a growth mindset in an organization's culture, leaders can practice self-awareness and inspire others to do so. This involves linking the growth mindset to the employees' personal and professional values and goals and showing the employees how DEI efforts are beneficial for everyone (and not just employees from marginalized backgrounds). Connecting the growth mindset to DEI not only helps the organization establish an inclusive and equitable culture, but it also answers the question often asked by employees: What's in it for me? Indeed, employees are more likely to embrace the growth mindset if it is connected to the betterment of their career progress and overall employee well-being.

Encouraging a growth mindset in employees also entails asking employees to change or adapt how they think, feel, or act so that they know that it is okay to take risks, have difficult conversations, and make mistakes. There are bound to be multiple setbacks in the implementation of DEI, so leaders may need to reiterate the importance of progress, not perfection. This is where good leadership is tested: Inclusive, competent leaders understand the prioritization of progress takes time, resources, and continued commitment, even in the face of setbacks. These leaders need to first invest time in assessing and reflecting on their own implicit biases and problematic thinking before they can examine any discrimination, bias, or exclusion in their organizations. Dweck's growth mindset serves as an important tool in identifying such issues, and leaders, in particular, can use this mindset to drive and stay committed to DEI in the workplace.

Inclusive leaders who employ the growth mindset acknowledge that intelligence is learned (rather than being innate), challenges and setbacks are part of the process, success is achievable regardless of the circumstances, and employees and coworkers should be rewarded for their hard work and commitment to DEI. Once leaders gain a nuanced understanding of this mindset, they can lead by example and help shape the growth mindset for others. While there is no single action a leader can take to demonstrate their allyship and commitment to DEI, instilling the growth mindset in others is a good place to start challenging the status quo. Indeed, it is the intentional and consistent actions of an inclusive leader that will inspire others to follow suit, which, in turn, can lead to a positive, powerful change in the workplace.

Leaders can demonstrate a growth mindset in numerous ways. Firstly, leaders should start with what they know: their culture, their personal and professional experiences, their perspectives, and their relationships with others and their community. Every individual comes from unique circumstances that have informed their thoughts and actions throughout their lives, and to understand other people, individuals should first seek to understand themselves. Simply put, leaders can start in their comfort zone and then branch out from there. This branching out allows leaders to absorb information from others without making education the responsibility of their marginalized employees. Secondly, leaders should learn to become comfortable with being uncomfortable, as it is impossible to grow (as a person and a working professional) by staying in one's comfort zone. This may entail being part of uncomfortable conversations, calling out problematic behaviors, navigating instances of discrimination, bias, and prejudice in the workplace, and understanding how their power and authority as a leader provide them with a platform to initiate significant change.

Thirdly, leaders recognize that intelligence and skills can be developed and are therefore willing to invest time and resources into training and skills-development sessions, workshops, conferences, and seminars, as well as education programs for their employees. Employees enter the workforce with varying levels of education, work experience, and skills—job requirements that many individuals have limited or no access to due to systemic barriers—and inclusive leaders recognize these systemic barriers and seek to level the playing field among employees. Leaders can also benefit from listening to their employees to understand their specific needs and professional goals. In doing so, leaders have a better understanding of their employees' unique circumstances and, subsequently, of the specific workshops or training sessions that their employees need. Here, leaders can also build rapport with their employees by making them feel valued and that their opinions matter. Fourthly, inclusive leaders can promote the growth mindset by framing it as a shift in thinking rather than a complete overhaul of one's thinking. The growth mindset acknowledges that minor and major barriers and setbacks are to be expected in times of change, and instead of being overwhelmed, inclusive leaders see such setbacks as ways to learn. For example, if a leader notices the lack of women employees in their department, they will be motivated to rectify this lack of representation instead of avoiding it or shifting the responsibility to others.

The Growth Mindset on a Global Scale

The notion that we have the ability to learn, change, and improve seems to be universal and perhaps a key part of human action and nature. As workplaces are becoming more global and multicultural, organizations should encourage the adoption of a growth mindset among all employees. Here, the growth mindset can help employers and employees adapt to different cultural contexts, embrace various forms of diversity, and boost their global partnerships or collaborations. The fixed mindset, for example, is seen in employees and leaders who believe that they would not be much help in globally connected workplaces or who think they are unable to learn a new language or understand a new culture. However, employees and leaders who have a growth mindset will embrace any and all opportunities to learn about a new culture, build networks with people from other countries, work in a globally connected environment, or even relocate abroad to help achieve the organization's objectives. The growth mindset means that our brains are malleable, and this helps us become more welcoming toward varying people, cultures, ideas, or beliefs and minimizes the chances of interpersonal or intergroup conflicts.

Leading Strategically and Operationally: The DEI Action Plan

An organization can have extensive DEI policies and frameworks, but these are futile unless they are appropriately and adequately translated into long-term action and change. This is one of the many reasons action plans are an essential part of DEI: A DEI action plan turns diversity, equity, and inclusion efforts into business imperatives that positively impact the organization at all levels. A DEI action plan is usually a multi-year framework that includes developing the infrastructure for DEI policies, strategies, and actions, modeling inclusive behavior aligned with core values and principles, and establishing a transparent and engaging communication strategy to scaffold the organization's DEI commitments. DEI action plans can (and should) be developed and implemented across organizations and industries that seek to incite organizational and social change, but such action plans are dependent on the organization or industry's specific needs, goals, and business imperatives.

As such, below is a universal DEI action plan framework that aligns the key aspects of DEI and is beneficial for all employees of an organization:

1. Create a DEI Baseline

The first step is for an organization to perform an assessment of its current workforce and the demographics of the employees. Demographics should extend beyond race and gender to also include data on age, neurodiversity, ethnicity, nationality, ability, religion, socio-economic status, sexuality, gender identity, and other factors of identity. This data is invaluable when it comes to mapping out where the organization is succeeding and continues to experience gaps and opportunities in terms of representation and the facilitation of an inclusive culture.

Here, organizations should also ask the following questions:

- Do our employees believe that our senior leaders or executives are promoting an inclusive culture in the workplace?

- Are the senior leaders concerned about the lack of diversity, equity, and/or inclusion?

- Is the workplace environment accepting and welcoming of all individuals?

- Are our employees comfortable enough to be their authentic selves in professional settings?

- Have our employees from marginalized or underrepresented backgrounds reported any instances of discrimination, harassment, bias, or prejudice in the workplace?

Organizations should have this data on hand when they start developing their DEI action plan but must also be mindful of their employee's right to privacy and voluntary self-identification. For example, employees may not feel comfortable or may not want to disclose their sexuality to their employers. Considering the stigmas surrounding sexuality, disability, neurodiversity, gender identity, and so on, it is understandable why some employees withhold such information, but this should not deter organizations' DEI efforts.

2. Identify the Key Areas of Opportunity

Once the demographics and other related data have been mapped out, the organization can identify the main areas of DEI opportunities: Which demographic(s) are severely underrepresented in the organization? Is there diversity at the senior leadership and management levels? Is the organization's approach to identity intersectional? Are there employees with the same job who earn different compensation? For example, a company may have a female-majority workforce, but its senior leadership positions are disproportionately occupied by men. Or, a company has a female-majority workforce, but this workforce is also overwhelmingly white and able-bodied. These are just a few of the questions to help the organization gain a better and more nuanced understanding of its workforce.

This also provides an organization with the opportunity to listen to what its workforce believes or feels about the organization's corporate culture, representation, diversity (or lack thereof), and general atmosphere. The combination of quantitative data and employee feedback paints a clearer picture of the areas that need immediate and long-term improvement. Of course, there is always room for improvement, but the organization needs to carefully choose a starting point, such as increasing racial diversity at the management level or renovating the office space to be more accessible for disabled employees. Because various DEI efforts and improvements require different approaches, the organization cannot (and should not) use one action plan or strategy for all of the improvements.

3. Outline the Metrics for DEI Success

A DEI action plan must have clear, realistic goals and key performance indicators (KPIs) for the organization to track and measure its DEI efforts from the beginning. For example, the organization must have a clear definition of "increased racial diversity," as this may refer to hiring more African American employees and/or recruiting more Asian Americans. Moreover, the action plan should indicate if the goal of increased racial diversity refers to the lower levels and/or the senior leadership levels of the organization. Does the action plan also include goals for retaining racially-diverse employees, and does it outline clear pathways for promotion for such employees? Does the organization want to hire more racially-diverse candidates, or does it want to hire candidates according to the demographics of its consumer or client base? DEI is rather complex, so these questions and concerns are important in the initial stages of systemic and social change in the organization.

4. Start the DEI Process

Armed with data on the workforce, the main areas of opportunity, and clear metrics for success, the organization is now ready to create actionable steps to meet its DEI goals. For instance, should the organization wish to hire more Black candidates, then it can partner with Historically Black Colleges and Universities (HBCUs) to recruit recent graduates. Should the organization want to increase its representation of neurodiversity, it can partner with neurodiversity education programs to recruit neurodivergent candidates and make their workplaces more accessible. Depending on the DEI goals and the size of the workforce, some organizations may need to hire DEI professionals or a Chief Diversity Officer (CDO) to oversee and manage DEI efforts. It is also important for the organization to communicate its DEI action plan to its workforce, as employees should be aware of the timelines, expectations, goals, and progress of DEI efforts. This not only shows the organization's commitment to its DEI efforts, but it also holds the organization accountable.

5. Review and Iterate

DEI efforts take time and resources to produce results, and some DEI goals can even take years to achieve. Nevertheless, an organization should measure and track the chosen DEI metrics and review any goals or targets that miss the mark. For example, if the organization has not reached one or two short-term DEI goals in the first or second year since starting the process, it may need to review the related DEI strategy to see where it failed to garner traction. Perhaps the organization struggled with employee buy-in, or the commitments were abandoned halfway through. Whatever the reason, the organization must be committed to reviewing the specific goal or initiative and finding ways to improve it so that the second attempt will be successful. The review process of the DEI action plan should be periodic and should also include feedback from employees to gain a greater understanding of whether or not the DEI approaches and actions have truly benefited the employees.

For instance, an organization may have succeeded in its goal of hiring more neurodivergent employees, but these employees may be struggling in the workplace due to systemic barriers and social stigmas. Through employee feedback, the organization will realize the need for more reasonable accommodations (such as noise-canceling headphones) and neurodiversity education and sensitivity training. The results of the organization's DEI efforts should also be accessible to its entire workforce. Transparency is a significant part of DEI, and every employee at every level should be able to stay updated on the organization's DEI progress. The organization's clients or consumer base should also be able to view the DEI data and progress. This can also help the organization expand its professional networks, as many clients and consumers want to work with and/or support organizations that are transparent about their DEI commitments.

6. Adapt to Address New Concerns

Our political and socio-economic landscapes are ever-changing, and this means that certain issues are now at the forefront of social justice discourses, debates, and conversations. On June 24, 2022, the US Supreme Court overturned Roe v. Wade—the change in legal policy that made access to an abortion a federal right in the country—and subsequently allowed individual states to limit or completely ban abortion rights. While some companies voiced their concern about the overturning of the case on their social media accounts, others have taken it a step further by adjusting their employee benefits packages to help their employees who live in states where reproductive rights are limited. Companies across industries, such as JPMorgan Chase, Snap, Inc., Discord, and eBay, have pledged to do what they can to help their employees who need access to reproductive healthcare. Many of these companies had already established a rubric framework to improve their employees' access to reproductive healthcare services before the Supreme Court's decision. In most cases, these frameworks have been translated into actions that include covering the travel costs for employees who need to leave their state to access reproductive healthcare services, expanding on their employee benefits packages, donating to pro-choice causes, and placing pressure on Congress to codify Roe v. Wade into the law. This is just one example of how organizations have had to adapt their DEI or DEI-related plans, policies, and strategies to address current social issues and concerns.

Leading an organization is not easy, and leading an organization during times of social and political polarization can be even more challenging. But meaningful change must come from the top, and any organization that wants to advance its DEI efforts and social justice objectives must have strong leaders. These are leaders who are ethical, transparent, and intentional in their work, and most importantly, they lead by example. Indeed, a fantastic, fool-proof way for a leader to incite systemic and social change in the workplace is to show others how it is done.

A growth mindset is essential for leaders who want to develop the capabilities to lead in the DEI space and create a culture of inclusion that attracts and retains the best talent. Leaders who fail to embrace a growth mindset risk being left behind as their competitors build more innovative and engaged teams. In contrast, leaders who lead with a growth mindset are better equipped to navigate the complexities of the DEI space and create an environment where all employees can thrive. To truly thrive in the DEI space, leaders must commit to developing their capabilities as inclusive leaders. This requires a willingness to learn, grow, and evolve as a leader. Leaders who take this approach are better equipped to ensure success in today's rapidly changing business environment and cultural climate. By leading with a growth mindset, leaders can create a better world for themselves, their employees, and their customers.

Conclusion

Diversity in the world is a basic characteristic of human society, and also the key condition for a lively and dynamic world as we see today. —Jintao Hu

When we think about diversity, equity, and inclusion, we must turn away from what we consider "normal" in the workplace and in broader society. The COVID-19 pandemic forced many of us to adapt to a "new normal" where remote and hybrid work replaces the traditional nine-to-five job, where equity is seen as a pathway to equality, where inclusion and collaboration are prioritized over exclusion and individualism, and where diversity must be approached through an intersectional lens. DEI is more than policies, strategies, and initiatives; it is a catalyst for systemic change and social justice. DEI efforts look to the past to create a more sustainable, progressive, and fair future—a future in which all people are provided with the education, skills, and resources to thrive in their professional and personal lives. Indeed, DEI forms part of an organizational ecosystem that promotes a healthy, highly productive, and creative work environment where diversity (in all of its forms and iterations) is celebrated for its intrinsic and extrinsic value. In this ecosystem, the vast array of experiences, perspectives, and ideas from individuals are celebrated and become part of the organization's corporate culture.

DEI is not simply a once-off action, as many of its challenges are rooted in systemic power imbalances. DEI is a complex and intersectional framework for organizations that involves establishing a culture of community and belonging, increasing representation and developing inclusive talent processes and practices, boosting empathy through education and efforts toward decolonization and neurodiversity, prioritizing equity, mitigating implicit bias, instilling a sense of authenticity and accountability, and leveraging a growth mindset in the workplace. DEI is an ongoing process that requires regular reviewing, measuring, and adapting to ensure that its policies, strategies, and initiatives truly serve those who are marginalized by and in the workplace. Organizations—whether they are small businesses or multinational corporations—provide marginalized or underrepresented individuals with the resources and socio-economic mobility to improve their own well-being and empower their families and communities. Indeed, DEI efforts in workplaces cannot be separated from social justice efforts; instead, they need to work hand-in-hand to ensure that all people are empowered in all aspects of their lives.

Likewise, we cannot separate the moral responsibility of DEI from its business objectives. DEI sees cultural differences as an asset rather than a divisive force that pits individuals against each other and sees marginalized individuals as their authentic and whole selves—all while boosting creativity, innovation, profits, and employee well-being in the workplace. When approached through a decolonized, intersectional, and empathetic lens, DEI policies, strategies, and initiatives have the power to dismantle the systemic barriers that render so many as "the "Other." Marginalized individuals should never have to assimilate to succeed: African Americans should never have to change their hair to get a job, queer individuals should never have to pass as "straight" to be accepted, disabled individuals should never have to wonder whether their workplaces have accommodations, and women should never have to police their own tone for fear of being seen as too aggressive, bossy, or angry.

While I could wax lyrical about what should not happen in the workplace, the reality is that marginalized individuals will face varying and overlapping degrees of exclusion and discrimination. As more and more organizations promote solidarity and embed DEI into their structures and corporate cultures, they empower their employees from marginalized backgrounds, and their DEI efforts have a ripple effect and uplift entire communities. As we delve into the recent histories and current legacies of countries around the world, it is striking to see how important solidarity is in our DEI efforts. It is through this solidarity that we can form meaningful connections with not only other people but also other struggles so that we all can work to dismantle the intertwined oppressions that plague our workplaces and societies. Greater diversity, equity, and inclusion in our government structures, social institutions, and workplaces is only the first step toward developing and maintaining equitable human relationships and sustainable ways of being. From the #BlackLivesMatter and #MeToo movements to the fight for LGBTQIA2+ and reproductive rights to global wars and outright assaults on women's rights globally, we are witnessing a time of immense social change and injustice that necessitates immediate attention and action. It is only right that our organizations keep up and lead the change!

Glossary

Ableism: Discrimination against individuals with disabilities. Ableism can manifest in various forms, such as inaccessible spaces, exclusion from social or professional opportunities, and negative stereotypes and attitudes toward individuals with disabilities.

Acculturation: The process of adapting to a new culture or environment. Acculturation can occur through various means, such as immersion in the new culture, exposure to new ideas and customs, and language acquisition.

Ageism: Discrimination or prejudice against individuals based on their age, whether they are perceived as too old or too young. Ageism can lead to unequal treatment in the workplace, healthcare, and social settings.

Allyship: The practice of actively supporting and advocating for individuals from marginalized groups. Allyship involves acknowledging and challenging one's own biases and privileges, actively listening and learning from individuals from marginalized groups, and taking action to create a more inclusive and equitable society.

Antiracism: The active practice of challenging and dismantling racism. Antiracism involves acknowledging and challenging systemic racism and discrimination, actively promoting equity and justice, and taking action to create a more equitable society.

Bias: A preference or inclination for or against a particular group, often based on stereotypes or limited understanding of different perspectives. Bias can manifest consciously or unconsciously and can have negative impacts on individuals from marginalized groups.

BIPOC: An acronym used to refer to Black, Indigenous, and People of Color, highlighting the shared experiences of systemic oppression and marginalization faced by these groups.

Colorism: Discrimination or prejudice against individuals based on their skin color or shade, often perpetuated through social and cultural norms. Colorism can manifest in various forms, such as lighter-skinned individuals being favored for social and professional opportunities, while darker-skinned individuals are excluded.

Cultural competence: The ability to interact effectively with individuals from diverse backgrounds and understand and respect their unique perspectives and experiences. Cultural competence involves developing awareness of one's own cultural background and biases, acquiring knowledge and skills to interact with individuals from diverse backgrounds, and adapting one's behavior and communication style to be more inclusive and respectful.

Diversity: The representation of different backgrounds, experiences, and identities in a group or organization. Diversity can encompass various aspects, such as race, ethnicity, gender, sexual orientation, religion, ability, and socio-economic status.

Equity: The principle of fairness and justice in providing equal access to opportunities and resources, regardless of differences in background or identity. Equity involves addressing systemic barriers and creating conditions where everyone has a fair and equal chance to succeed.

Gender identity: An individual's personal sense of their gender, which may or may not align with their assigned sex at birth. Gender identity can be fluid and can encompass a wide range of identities beyond the binary male-female construct.

Homophobia: Discrimination or prejudice against individuals who are perceived to be or are LGBTQIA2+ (Lesbian, Gay, Bisexual, Transgender, Queer/Questioning, Intersex, Asexual or Ally). Homophobia can manifest in various forms, such as negative attitudes and beliefs, exclusion from social or professional opportunities, and physical or verbal harassment.

Inclusion: The active effort to create a sense of belonging and community within an organization or group that values and respects individuals' differences. Inclusion involves creating a safe and supportive environment where individuals from diverse backgrounds can thrive and contribute to their fullest potential.

Intersectionality: The interconnectedness of different aspects of an individual's identity, such as race, gender, sexual orientation, ability, and socio-economic status, which can compound and exacerbate experiences of discrimination and marginalization. Intersectionality recognizes that individuals' experiences are shaped by multiple factors and that a single-axis approach to diversity and inclusion is insufficient.

Islamophobia: Discrimination or prejudice against individuals who are perceived to be or are Muslim. Islamophobia can manifest in various forms, such as negative attitudes and beliefs, exclusion from social or professional opportunities, and physical or verbal harassment.

Microaggressions: Small, often unconscious actions or comments that are perceived as discriminatory or offensive by individuals from marginalized groups. Microaggressions can be intentional or unintentional and can have negative impacts on individuals' sense of belonging and well-being.

Non-binary: An umbrella term used to describe individuals whose gender identity does not exclusively align with the male-female binary. Non-binary individuals may identify as a combination of genders, or as no gender at all.

Oppression: The systemic and institutionalized mistreatment and marginalization of individuals from marginalized groups, often rooted in historical and social power imbalances. Oppression can take many forms, such as discrimination, exclusion, and violence.

Privilege: Unearned advantages and benefits that individuals from dominant groups receive based on their identity, such as race, gender, sexual orientation, and socio-economic status. Privilege can manifest in various ways, such as access to opportunities, resources, and social capital.

Queer: An umbrella term used to describe individuals who identify as LGBTQIA2+ (Lesbian, Gay, Bisexual, Transgender, Queer/Questioning, Intersex, Asexual or Ally). Queer can be used as a reclaimed term by individuals who identify as non-heterosexual or non-cisgender.

Racism: The systemic and institutionalized mistreatment and marginalization of individuals based on their race or ethnicity. Racism can take many forms, such as discrimination, exclusion, and violence.

Sexism: Discrimination or prejudice against individuals based on their sex or gender, often perpetuated through social and cultural norms. Sexism can manifest in various forms, such as gender-based violence, unequal pay, and exclusion from leadership and decision-making roles.

Social justice: The principle of promoting fairness and equality in access to resources and opportunities for individuals from diverse backgrounds. Social justice involves addressing systemic barriers and promoting equity and inclusion for all.

Stereotype: A generalized and oversimplified belief about individuals from a particular group, often based on limited or biased information. Stereotypes can perpetuate negative attitudes and biases toward individuals from marginalized groups.

Tokenism: The practice of including individuals from marginalized groups solely to fulfill a diversity quota or to appear more inclusive, without addressing systemic barriers and promoting equity and inclusion for all individuals.

Transgender: An umbrella term used to describe individuals whose gender identity does not exclusively align with their assigned sex at birth. Transgender individuals may identify as male, female, non-binary, or a combination of genders.

Unconscious bias: Biases and preferences that individuals hold without conscious awareness or intention, often based on social and cultural conditioning. Unconscious biases can manifest in various forms, such as assumptions, stereotypes, and microaggressions.

White fragility: The defensiveness and discomfort that many white individuals feel when their racial identity is challenged or when discussions of racism and privilege arise. White fragility can impede progress toward equity and inclusion by avoiding uncomfortable conversations and dismissing the experiences of individuals from marginalized groups.

Xenophobia: Discrimination or prejudice against individuals based on their national origin or perceived foreignness. Xenophobia can manifest in various forms, such as negative attitudes and beliefs, exclusion from social or professional opportunities, and physical or verbal harassment.

Notable Global DEI Holidays

1. World Braille Day (January 4): A global holiday celebrating the birth of Louis Braille, the inventor of the Braille language for the visually impaired.

2. World Religion Day (Third Sunday in January): A global holiday promoting the unity, diversity, and harmony of world religions and raising awareness of their common values and teachings.

3. Martin Luther King Jr. Day (Third Monday in January): An American holiday honoring the legacy and values of Martin Luther King Jr., the civil rights leader and advocate of nonviolent social change, and promoting community service and activism.

4. International Day of Acceptance (January 20): A global holiday celebrating acceptance of diversity and differences.

5. Australia Day (January 26): An Australian holiday celebrating the arrival of the First Fleet in Sydney Cove and promoting national pride and identity.

6. International Holocaust Remembrance Day (January 27): A global holiday honoring the victims of the Holocaust and promoting education and awareness about genocide and human rights.

7. National Freedom Day (February 1): An American holiday commemorating the signing of the 13th Amendment, which abolished slavery and involuntary servitude, and promoting liberty, justice, and equality.

8. World Interfaith Harmony Week (First week of February): A global holiday promoting interfaith dialogue, cooperation, and

understanding, and raising awareness of the role of religion in promoting peace and social justice.

9. Chinese New Year (date varies, usually in late January or early February): A Chinese holiday celebrating the beginning of a new lunar year and promoting family gatherings, feasting, and gift-giving.

10. World Hijab Day (February 1): A global holiday celebrating the headscarf worn by some Muslim women as a symbol of religious identity and modesty.

11. International Day of Zero Tolerance for Female Genital Mutilation (February 6): A global holiday promoting the elimination of female genital mutilation, a practice that affects millions of girls and women around the world.

12. International Mother Language Day (February 21): A global holiday celebrating linguistic and cultural diversity and promoting multilingualism.

13. Ash Wednesday (date varies, usually in February or March): A Christian holiday marking the beginning of Lent, the 40-day period of fasting, prayer, and reflection before Easter.

14. Holi (date varies, usually in February or March): A Hindu holiday celebrating the arrival of spring and the victory of good over evil, and promoting the throwing of colored powder and water, singing, and dancing.

15. Mardi Gras (Date varies, usually in February or March): A French holiday celebrating the last day before Lent and promoting parades, masks, and carnival festivities.

16. Women's History Month (March): An American holiday celebrating the contributions and achievements of women throughout history and promoting gender equality and empowerment.

17. International Women's Day (March 8): A global holiday celebrating the social, economic, cultural, and political achievements of women.

18. St. Patrick's Day (March 17): An Irish holiday celebrating the patron saint of Ireland and promoting the wearing of green, the drinking of beer, and the singing of songs.

19. World Down Syndrome Day (March 21): A global holiday celebrating the lives and accomplishments of people with Down syndrome and promoting inclusion and acceptance.

20. International Day of Nowruz (March 21): A global holiday celebrating the Persian New Year and promoting family gatherings, feasting, and cultural exchange.

21. International Day for the Elimination of Racial Discrimination (March 21): A global holiday promoting the elimination of racial discrimination and intolerance.

22. International Day of Remembrance of the Victims of Slavery and the Transatlantic Slave Trade (March 25): A global holiday honoring the memory of millions of enslaved Africans and promoting the recognition of slavery as a crime against humanity.

23. International Transgender Day of Visibility (March 31): A global holiday celebrating transgender people and raising awareness of the discrimination they face.

24. Passover (date varies, usually in March or April): A Jewish holiday celebrating the liberation of the Israelites from slavery in Egypt, and promoting family gatherings, feasting, and the retelling of the Exodus story.

25. Memorial of Christ's Death (varies, but typically between March and April): This is the most important holiday for Jehovah's Witnesses, held on the anniversary of the death of Jesus Christ according to the Gregorian calendar. It is

celebrated with a solemn commemoration service, usually held after sunset on the 14th day of Nisan.

26. International Romani Day (April 8): A global holiday celebrating Romani culture and raising awareness of the discrimination and persecution that Roma people have faced throughout history.

27. Yom HaShoah (Holocaust Remembrance Day) (April 11): A Jewish holiday honoring the victims of the Holocaust and promoting education and awareness about genocide and human rights.

28. Earth Day (April 22): A global holiday promoting environmental awareness and action to protect the planet.

29. International Day of Multilateralism and Diplomacy for Peace (April 24): A global holiday promoting international cooperation and diplomacy as key to achieving peace and security.

30. International Workers' Day (May 1): A global holiday celebrating the achievements of workers and promoting their rights and well-being.

31. Cinco de Mayo (May 5): A Mexican holiday celebrating the victory of Mexican forces over French forces at the Battle of Puebla and promoting the wearing of traditional costumes, the eating of Mexican food, and the singing and dancing of folk music.

32. International Day Against Homophobia, Transphobia and Biphobia (May 17): A global holiday promoting the elimination of discrimination and violence against LGBTQ+ people.

33. World Day for Cultural Diversity for Dialogue and Development (May 21): A global holiday promoting the value and importance of cultural diversity and raising awareness of the role of culture in promoting peace, understanding, and sustainable development.

34. Africa Day (May 25): A holiday celebrating the formation of the Organization of African Unity (now the African Union) and promoting African unity, culture, and development.

35. International Day of UN Peacekeepers (May 29): A global holiday honoring the sacrifices and contributions of UN peacekeepers in promoting peace and security around the world.

36. Eid al-Fitr (date varies, usually in May or June): A Muslim holiday celebrating the end of the month of Ramadan, the holy month of fasting and spiritual reflection, and promoting family gatherings, feasting, and charitable acts.

37. LGBT Pride Month (June): A global holiday promoting the visibility and rights of lesbian, gay, bisexual, and transgender people and raising awareness of their contributions and challenges.

38. Juneteenth (June 19): An American holiday commemorating the end of slavery in the United States.

39. World Refugee Day (June 20): A global holiday raising awareness of the plight of refugees and promoting their protection and support.

40. International Day of Yoga (June 21): A global holiday celebrating the physical, mental, and spiritual benefits of yoga.

41. Pride Month (June): A global celebration of LGBTQ+ rights, culture, and visibility.

42. Canada Day (July 1): A Canadian holiday celebrating the formation of the country and promoting Canadian culture and identity.

43. Independence Day (July 4): An American holiday celebrating the formation of the country and promoting American culture and identity.

44. International Nelson Mandela Day (July 18): A global holiday honoring the life and legacy of Nelson Mandela, the South African anti-apartheid revolutionary and statesman, and promoting his values of justice, equality, and reconciliation.

45. World Day Against Trafficking in Persons (July 30): A global holiday raising awareness of human trafficking and promoting prevention and prosecution efforts.

46. Eid al-Adha (date varies, usually in July or August): A Muslim holiday commemorating the willingness of Ibrahim (Abraham) to sacrifice his son as an act of obedience to Allah (God), and promoting family gatherings, feasting, and charitable acts.

47. International Day of the World's Indigenous Peoples (August 9): A global holiday celebrating the cultural and linguistic diversity of indigenous peoples and promoting their rights and well-being.

48. International Youth Day (August 12): A global holiday celebrating the contributions and potential of young people and promoting their empowerment and participation in society.

49. National Hispanic Heritage Month (September 15-October 15): An American holiday celebrating the history, culture, and contributions of Hispanic and Latino Americans.

50. International Day of Peace (September 21): A global holiday promoting peace, nonviolence, and cooperation among nations and peoples.

51. Rosh Hashanah (date varies, usually in September or October): A Jewish holiday celebrating the Jewish New Year and promoting family gatherings, repentance, and reflection.

52. Yom Kippur (date varies, usually in September or October): A Jewish holiday commemorating the Day of Atonement and promoting repentance, prayer, and fasting.

53. National Coming Out Day (October 11): An American holiday promoting the visibility and acceptance of LGBTQ+ people.

54. International Day of the Girl Child (October 11): A global holiday promoting the empowerment and well-being of girls and young women and raising awareness of their rights, challenges, and potential.

55. International Day for the Eradication of Poverty (October 17): A global holiday promoting the elimination of poverty as a human rights and development priority and raising awareness of the causes and consequences of poverty.

56. Diwali (November 4): A Hindu holiday celebrating the victory of light over darkness and knowledge over ignorance, and promoting family gatherings, feasting, and gift-giving.

57. Veterans Day (November 11): An American holiday honoring military veteran who have served in the U.S. Armed Forces and promoting their well-being and support.

58. International Day for the Elimination of Violence Against Women (November 25): A global holiday promoting the elimination of all forms of violence against women and girls.

59. International Day of Persons with Disabilities (December 3): A global holiday promoting the rights and well-being of persons with disabilities and raising awareness of their challenges and contributions.

60. International Volunteer Day (December 5): A global holiday celebrating the power and potential of volunteerism to create positive social and environmental change.

61. Human Rights Week (December 10-17): A global holiday marking the anniversary of the Universal Declaration of Human Rights and promoting human rights education, activism, and advocacy.

62. Human Rights Day (December 10): A global holiday honoring the adoption of the Universal Declaration of Human Rights by the United Nations General Assembly and promoting human rights education, awareness, and action.

63. Hanukkah (December 10-18): A Jewish holiday celebrating the miracle of the oil that lasted for eight days in the Temple, and promoting family gatherings, gift-giving, and the lighting of the menorah.

64. Las Posadas (December 16-24): A Mexican holiday celebrating the journey of Mary and Joseph to Bethlehem and promoting community gatherings, processions, and reenactments.

65. Christmas (December 25): A Christian holiday celebrating the birth of Jesus Christ and promoting family gatherings, gift-giving, and charitable acts.

66. Boxing Day (December 26): A British holiday traditionally associated with the giving of gifts to tradespeople and service workers and promoting charity and generosity.

67. Kwanzaa (December 26-January 1): An African American holiday celebrating the values of unity, self-determination, collective work and responsibility, cooperative economics, purpose, creativity, and faith, and promoting family gatherings, cultural awareness, and community building.

68. Omisoka (December 31): A Japanese holiday celebrating the end of the old year and the beginning of the new year and promoting cleaning, cooking, and ritual practices to welcome good fortune and ward off evil spirits.

References

Ajayi-Hackworth, F. (2020, April 30). *A Point of View: Gaslighting in Diversity and Inclusion.* The Inclusion Solution. http://www.theinclusionsolution.me/a-point-of-view-gaslighting-in-diversity-and-inclusion/

Alyn, J. (2016, June 22). *From Inclusion to Accountability.* Alyn Consulting. https://www.alynconsulting.com/diversity-blog/key-concepts-conversations/from-inclusion-to-accountability/

Archer, V. (2022). *Moving your talent acquisition strategy beyond diverse candidate slates.* Mercer. https://www.mercer.com/our-thinking/moving-your-talent-acquisition-strategy-beyond-diverse-candidate-slates.html

Armstrong, T. (2011). *The Power of Neurodiversity: Unleashing the Advantages of Your Differently Wired Brain.* Da Capo Lifelong.

Anderson, M. (2018, January 10). *Black STEM employees perceive a range of race-related slights and inequities at work.* Pew Research Center. https://www.pewresearch.org/fact-tank/2018/01/10/black-stem-employees-perceive-a-range-of-race-related-slights-and-inequities-at-work/

Angel, T. (2011, July 29). *Everything You Need to Know About ADHD.* Healthline. https://www.healthline.com/health/adhd#symptoms

Asare, J. G. (2020, February 20). *Are Job Candidates Still Being Penalized for Having "Ghetto" Names?* Forbes. https://www.forbes.com/sites/janicegassam/2020/02/20/are-job-candidates-still-being-penalized-for-having-ghetto-names/?sh=4bc4552b50ed

Asare, J. G. (2022, May 1). *4 Ways Companies Tokenize Underrepresented Employees.* Forbes. https://www.forbes.com/sites/janicegassam/2022/05/01/4-ways-companies-tokenize-underrepresented-employees/

Austin, R., & Pisano, G. (2017, July 18). *Neurodiversity Is a Competitive Advantage.* Harvard Business Review. https://hbr.org/2017/05/neurodiversity-as-a-competitive-advantage

Baboolall, D., Greenberg, S., Obeid, M., & Zucker, J. (2021, November 10). *Being transgender at work.* McKinsey. https://www.mckinsey.com/featured-insights/diversity-and-inclusion/being-transgender-at-work

Bagalini, A. (2020, July 22). *5 ways intersectionality affects diversity and inclusion at work.* World Economic Forum. https://www.weforum.org/agenda/2020/07/diversity-inclusion-equality-intersectionality/

Bailin, A. (2019, June 6). *Clearing up some misconceptions about neurodiversity.* Scientific American Blog Network. https://blogs.scientificamerican.com/observations/clearing-up-some-misconceptions-about-neurodiversity/

Barnes, S. (2020, August 5). *Debunking Myths About Neurodiversity in the Workplace.* Medium. https://stephanie-barnes.medium.com/debunking-myths-about-neurodiversity-in-the-workplace-76f1a82fa0ec

Barron, B. (2021, February 1). *Why Representation and Diversity Matter for Your Company.* Business Envato. https://business.tutsplus.com/tutorials/representation-and-diversity-matter--cms-36492

Bartelds, H., Savenije, G. M., & van Boxtel, C. (2020). Students' and teachers' beliefs about historical empathy in secondary history education. *Theory & Research in Social Education, 48*(4), 529–551. https://doi.org/10.1080/00933104.2020.1808131

Baumer, N., & Frueh, J. (2021, November 23). *What is neurodiversity?* Harvard Health. https://www.health.harvard.edu/blog/what-is-neurodiversity-202111232645

Bedayn, J. (2022, February 3). Targeted universalism: A solution for inequality? *CBS8 News.* https://www.cbs8.com/article/news/local/california/targeted-universalism/509-2127090b-7f50-4a91-91e7-04c47acf3309

Belfi, E. & Sandiford, N. (2021). *Decolonization Series Part 1: Exploring Decolonization.* In S. Brandauer and E. Hartman (Eds.). Interdependence: Global Solidarity and Local Actions. The Community-based Global Learning Collaborative. Retrieved from: http://globalsolidaritylocalaction.sites.haverford.edu/what-is-decolonization-why-is-it-important/

Bittker, B. M. (2020, September 7). *Racial and Ethnic Disparities in Employer-Sponsored Health Coverage.* American Bar. https://www.americanbar.org/groups/crsj/publications/human_rights_magazine_home/health-matters-in-elections/racial-and-ethnic-disparities-in-employer-sponsored-health-coverage/

Blackburn, S.-S. (2019, March 21). *What Is the Model Minority Myth?* Learning for Justice; Southern Poverty Law Center. https://www.learningforjustice.org/magazine/what-is-the-model-minority-myth

Blakemore, E. (2018, September). *How Dolls Helped Win Brown v. Board of Education.* History.com. https://www.history.com/news/brown-v-board-of-education-doll-experiment

Bloom, S. G. (2022, February 25). *A second look at the blue-eyes, brown-eyes experiment that taught third-graders about racism.* The Conversation. https://theconversation.com/a-second-look-at-the-blue-eyes-brown-eyes-experiment-that-taught-third-graders-about-racism-177430

Bourke, J. (2016, April 14). *The six signature traits of inclusive leadership.* Deloitte Insights. https://www2.deloitte.com/us/en/insights/topics/talent/six-signature-traits-of-inclusive-leadership.html

Buckley, T. (2015, August 20). *5 Tips for Building a Global Workforce.* Fast Company. https://www.fastcompany.com/3050069/5-tips-for-building-a-global-workforce

Callister, L. (2022, February 21). *How to Reduce Unconscious Bias at Work.* Skill Cast. https://www.skillcast.com/blog/reduce-workplace-unconscious-bias

Cannon, K. (2016, March 23). *Respect Political Diversity in the Workplace.* LinkedIn. https://www.linkedin.com/pulse/respect-political-diversity-workplace-kim-cannon/

Carlos, I. (2021, July 29). *DEI is now a factor in executive pay. But there's one big disconnect.* Bizjournal. https://www.bizjournals.com/bizjournals/news/2021/07/29/dei-is-not-in-long-term-incentive-programs.html

Carter, M., Davis, L. R., Filosa, M., Alqaseer, F., Carlock, S., & Quinn, S. (2022, January 18). *For Good Measure: Current Best Practices in Tying Diversity, Equity and Inclusion Metrics to Executive Compensation.* Teneo. https://www.teneo.com/for-good-measure-current-best-practices-in-tying-diversity-equity-and-inclusion-metrics-to-executive-compensation/

Carter-Rogers, K., Smith, S., & Tabvuma, V. (2022, November 27). *Diversity in the workplace isn't enough: Businesses need to work toward inclusion.* The Conversation. https://theconversation.com/diversity-in-the-workplace-isnt-enough-businesses-need-to-work-toward-inclusion-194136

Cassino, D., & Besen-Cassino, Y. (2019). Race, threat and workplace sexual harassment: The dynamics of harassment in the United States, 1997–2016. *Gender, Work & Organization*, 26(9). https://doi.org/10.1111/gwao.12394

Catalino, N., Gardner, N., Goldstein, D., & Wong, J. (2022, December 7). *Effective employee resource groups are key to inclusion at work. Here's how to get them right.* McKinsey. https://www.mckinsey.com/capabilities/people-and-organizational-performance/our-insights/effective-employee-resource-groups-are-key-to-inclusion-at-work-heres-how-to-get-them-right

Charisma, T. (2021, June 30). *Cultural appropriation vs cultural appreciation: what's the difference?* Harper's BAZAAR. https://www.harpersbazaar.com/uk/culture/a36798089/cultural-appropriation-vs-cultural-appreciation/

Chamorro-Premuzic, T. (2022, March 2). *The Business Case for Women in Leadership.* Forbes. https://www.forbes.com/sites/tomaspremuzic/2022/03/02/the-business-case-for-women-in-leadership/?sh=7e8ca62b9cbb

Chmura, A. (2022, June 28). *How to Improve Employee Experience - 8 Proven Ways in 2022.* Workhuman. https://www.workhuman.com/blog/how-to-improve-employee-experience/

Choi-Allum, Lona. (2022). *Age Discrimination Among Workers Age 50-Plus.* Washington, DC: AARP Research. https://doi.org/10.26419/res.00545.001

Ciaramicoli, Arthur; Ketchum, Katherine, (2016). *The Power of Empathy*, Penguin Publishing Group, New York, N.Y.

Clark, S. (2021, March 2). *What Is Inclusion and Why Is it Important to Companies?* Reworked. https://www.reworked.co/leadership/5-reasons-why-your-company-should-be-more-inclusive/

Cletus, H. E., Mahmood, N. A., Umar, A., & Ibrahim, A. D. (2018). Prospects and challenges of workplace diversity in modern day organizations: A critical review. *Journal of Business and Public Administration*, *9*(2), 35–52. https://doi.org/10.2478/hjbpa-2018-0011

Cohn, T. (2022, January 5). *Decolonising the workplace – 14 ideas on how to get started.* EW Group. https://theewgroup.com/blog/decolonisation-the-workplace/

Conor, L. (2017, October 10). *Dove, real beauty and the racist history of skin whitening.* The Conversation. https://theconversation.com/dove-real-beauty-and-the-racist-history-of-skin-whitening-85446

Cooks-Campbell, A. (2022, June 24). *Neurodiversity in the Workplace: Creativity, Innovation, and Inclusion.* Better Up. https://www.betterup.com/blog/neurodiversity-in-the-workplace

Corbett, H. (2022, January 24). *6 Ways to Be an Authentic Ally at Work.* Forbes. https://www.forbes.com/sites/hollycorbett/2022/01/24/6-ways-to-be-an-authentic-ally-at-work/?sh=7a5d767e70dd

Cramer, J. (2022, August 12). *This is what Boomers, Gen X, Millennials, and Gen Z can learn from each other at work.* Fast Company. https://www.fastcompany.com/90820025/boomers-gen-x-millennials-gen-z-at-work

Deloitte Global. (2021, July 1). *Deloitte BrandVoice: Why Women Are Leaving the Workforce After the Pandemic—And How to Win Them Back.* Forbes. https://www.forbes.com/sites/deloitte/2021/07/01/why-women-are-leaving-the-workforce-after-the-pandemic-and-how-to-win-them-back/?sh=30d51447796e

Desmond-Harris, J. (2015, February 16). *What exactly is a microaggression?* Vox. https://www.vox.com/2015/2/16/8031073/what-are-microaggressions

Doyle, N. (2020). Neurodiversity at work: a biopsychosocial model and the impact on working adults. *British Medical Bulletin, 135*(1), 108–125. https://doi.org/10.1093/bmb/ldaa021

Doud, K. J., Miller, K., & Lewis, C. (2022). *Allyship: An Important Part of the Inclusion, Equity, and Diversity Conversation.* Association of Corporate Counsel (ACC). https://www.acc.com/allyship-important-part-inclusion-equity-and-diversity-conversation

Driving a strong culture of belonging at work. (2021, November 5). Achievers Workforce Institute. https://www.achievers.com/resources/white-papers/workforce-institute-culture-of-belonging/

Dublino, J. (2022, August 20). *7 Things about Competition in the Workplace.* Business.com. https://www.business.com/articles/gal-rimon-workplace-competition/

Dupree, W., & Robison, J. (2022, June 28). *LGBT Employee Experiences: Here's What We Know.* Gallup. https://www.gallup.com/workplace/393983/lgbt-employee-experiences-know.aspx

Durden, M. (2013). *Fifty Key Writers on Photography.* Routledge.

Dweck, C. (2016, January 13). *What Having a "Growth Mindset" Actually Means.* Harvard Business Review. https://hbr.org/2016/01/what-having-a-growth-mindset-actually-means

Education Without Authority? Quote of the Week. (2016, May 25). The Hannah Arendt Center. Medium. https://medium.com/quote-of-the-week/education-without-authority-da3b9e1798db

Eisenmenger, A. (2019, December 12). *Ableism 101 - What is Ableism? What Does it Look Like?* Access Living. https://www.accessliving.org/newsroom/blog/ableism-101/

Elder, A. (2021, November 8). *10 Inclusive Employee Benefits That Can Help Create a More Supportive Workplace.* LinkedIn. https://www.linkedin.com/business/talent/blog/talent-engagement/inclusive-employee-benefits-to-create-more-supportive-workplace

Empathy Executive Summary White Paper. (2021). Business Solver. https://resources.businesssolver.com/c/2021-empathy-exec-summ?x=OE03jO

Equity Vs. Equality in The Workplace (with Examples). (2022). Coach Diversity Institute. https://coachdiversity.com/blog/equity-vs-equality-in-the-workplace-understanding-the-difference/

Estelle, I. (2021, October 25). *A Max de Pree quote.* The CP Diary. https://www.thecpdiary.com/a-max-de-pree-quote/

Examples of Equality and Equity in the Workplace. (2021, March 6). Human Rights Careers. https://www.humanrightscareers.com/issues/examples-of-equality-and-equity-in-the-workplace/

Executive Pay Increasingly Tied to DEI Goals. (2022). Farient Advisors. (pp. 1–5). https://farient.com/2022/10/10/executive-pay-increasingly-tied-to-dei-goals/

Farrell, J. (2020, August 10). *Racial microaggressions: definition, examples, and practical actions.* EW Group. https://theewgroup.com/blog/racial-microaggressions-definition-examples-actions/

Fernandez, C. (2019, January 8). *12 Audre Lorde Quotes That'll Spark Conversation.* Oprahdaily. https://www.oprahdaily.com/life/relationships-love/g25776736/audre-lorde-quotes/

Five Fundamentals of Equitable Employee Resource Groups. (2019, December 10). The Feminuity Team. https://www.feminuity.org/post/five-fundamentals-of-equitable-ergs-employee-resource-groups

Forty+ Stats for Companies to Keep in Mind for 2021. (2020). Glassdoor for Employers. https://www.glassdoor.com/employers/resources/hr-and-recruiting-stats/#diversity-inclusion-and-belonging

Friesen, N. (2022, February 10). *6 Tips to Create an Authentic Workplace Culture*. ION Future. https://www.ionfuture.org/building-an-authentic-workplace-culture/

Gardner, R. (2021, December 8). *What is a Total Rewards Strategy? A Practical Guide*. AIHR. https://www.aihr.com/blog/total-rewards-strategy/

Gardner, W. L., & McCauley, K. D. (2022). The gaslighting of authentic leadership. *Leadership*, *18*(6), 801–813. https://doi.org/10.1177/17427150221111056

Gartner Says HR Leaders Must Establish Consequential Accountability to Achieve Diverse Leadership Benches. (2021, June 22). Gartner, Inc. https://www.gartner.com/en/newsroom/press-releases/2021-06-21-gartner-says-hr-leaders-must-establish-consequential-accountability-to-achieve-diverse-leadership-benches

Gattuso, R. (2021, June 1). *The risks of coming out at work*. BBC News. https://www.bbc.com/worklife/article/20210526-the-risks-of-coming-out-at-work

Giaccardi, S., Cooper, R., Heldman, C., Cooper-Jones, N., McTaggart, N., Juliano, L., Phillips, H., Esparza, P., & Conroy, M. (2019). *Bias and inclusion in advertising: An analysis of 2018 Cannes Lions Film Craft ads*. The Geena Davis Institute on Gender in Media at Mount Saint Mary's University.

Gill, G. (2022, April 5). *Breaking the Chains of Tokenism in the Workplace*. LinkedIn. https://www.linkedin.com/pulse/breaking-chains-tokenism-workplace-gobinder-gill/

Global Report on Ageism (2021). United Nations Department of Economic and Social Affairs. (pp. 1–202). https://www.un.org/development/desa/dspd/wp-content/uploads/sites/22/2021/03/9789240016866-eng.pdf

Gomez, K., Mawhinney, T., & Betts, K. (2018). *Welcome to Generation Z*. Deloitte.

https://www2.deloitte.com/content/dam/Deloitte/us/Docu ments/consumer-business/welcome-to-gen-z.pdf

Gonzalez, J. A., & Simpson, J. (2020). The workplace integration of veterans: Applying diversity and fit perspectives. *Human Resource Management Review*, 100775. https://doi.org/10.1016/j.hrmr.2020.100775

Green, B. (2021, June 22). *Gen Z in the Workplace: Transforming the Workforce.* Corporate Training. https://corporatetraining.usf.edu/blog/gen-z-in-the-workplace-transforming-the-workforce

Griffin, C. (2019, July 3). *How Natural Black Hair at Work Became a Civil Rights Issue.* JSTOR Daily. https://daily.jstor.org/how-natural-black-hair-at-work-became-a-civil-rights-issue/

Grisard, D. (2021, December 24). *Art on My Mind: Ten Reasons to Revisit bell hooks.* The Art of Intervention. https://theartofintervention.blog/2021/12/24/art-on-my-mind-ten-reasons-to-revisit-bell-hooks/

Grissom, J. A., Rodriguez, L. A., & Kern, E. C. (2017). Teacher and Principal Diversity and the Representation of Students of Color in Gifted Programs: Evidence from National Data. *The Elementary School Journal*, *117*(3), 396–422. https://doi.org/10.1086/690274

Gupta, S. (2021, August 19). *Council Post: Three Characteristics of Effective DEI Leadership.* Forbes. https://www.forbes.com/sites/forbescoachescouncil/2021/08 /19/three-characteristics-of-effective-dei-leadership/?sh=671217ef10dc

Halcrow, N. (2021, March 9). *5 Different Types of Implicit Bias.* Culture Wizard: Global Inclusion Experts. https://www.rw-3.com/blog/5-different-types-of-implicit-bias

Hasan, E., & Adeleye, I. (2021, May 25). *Should Employers Tie Executive Compensation to DE&I Goals?* SHRM.

https://www.shrm.org/hr-today/news/hr-magazine/summer2021/pages/should-employers-tie-executive-compensation-to-diversity-goals.aspx

Hastwell, C. (2021, August 21). *How to Build and Support Neurodiversity in the Workplace.* Great Place to Work®. https://www.greatplacetowork.com/resources/blog/how-to-build-and-support-neurodiversity-in-the-workplace

Hayes, M., Chumney, F., Wright, C., & Buckingham, M. (2018). *The Global Study of Engagement.* ADP Research Institute. https://www.adpri.org/assets/the-global-study-of-engagement/?referrer=%7b95522E03-C5DD-4626-8BE8-7D223D961259%7d

Haynes, A. (2022). *Neurodiversity: the little-known superpower.* Korn Ferry. https://www.kornferry.com/institute/neurodiversity-the-little-known-superpower

Horne, C., Rodriguez, J. K., & Twumasi, R. (2020, July 17). *How to start decolonising your business.* The Conversation. https://theconversation.com/how-to-start-decolonising-your-business-141750

How Diversity, Equity and Inclusion Impact the Culture of the Entire Workplace. (2021, July 23). Virgin Pulse. https://www.virginpulse.com/blog-post/how-diversity-equity-and-inclusion-impact-the-culture-of-the-entire-workplace/

How To Manage a Global Workforce Effectively: 6 Tips. (2022, February 25). Indeed Career Guide. https://www.indeed.com/career-advice/career-development/managing-global-workforce

Huang, G. (2017, November 13). *90% Of Fortune 500 Companies Already Have a Solution to Gender Equality but Aren't Utilizing It.* Forbes. https://www.forbes.com/sites/georgenehuang/2017/11/13/90-of-fortune-500-companies-already-have-a-solution-to-gender-equality-but-arent-utilizing-it/?sh=4d15da081c34

Humber, N. (2022, March 22). *Five neurodiversity myths that must be challenged.* The HR Director. https://www.thehrdirector.com/features/diversity-and-equality/neurodiversity-celebration-week-five-neurodiversity-myths-every-employer-must-challenge/

Hunt, D. V., Layton, D., & Prince, S. (2015, January 1). *Why diversity matters.* McKinsey & Company. https://www.mckinsey.com/capabilities/people-and-organizational-performance/our-insights/why-diversity-matters

Inclusive leaders have a growth mindset - Tools to Develop Diverse & Inclusive Workplace Cultures. (2021, September 15). Next Pivot Point. https://nextpivotpoint.com/inclusive-leaders-have-a-growth-mindset/

Inclusive Mobility: How Mobilizing a Diverse Workforce Can Drive Business Performance (2018). Deloitte. (pp. 1–18). https://www2.deloitte.com/content/dam/Deloitte/us/Documents/Tax/us-tax-inclusive-mobility-mobilize-diverse-workforce-drive-business-performance.pdf

Jeffries, T., West, K., & Swift, M. (2022). *How employee benefits and DEI initiatives affect Black employees.* Mercer. https://www.mercer.com/our-thinking/career/how-employee-benefits-and-dei-initiatives-affect-black-employees.html

Johnson, S. K., Hekman, D. R., & Chan, E. T. (2016, October 5). *If There's Only One Woman in Your Candidate Pool, There's Statistically No Chance She'll Be Hired.* Harvard Business Review. https://hbr.org/2016/04/if-theres-only-one-woman-in-your-candidate-pool-theres-statistically-no-chance-shell-be-hired

Kurt, D. (2021, July 21). *Corporate Leadership by Race.* Investopedia. https://www.investopedia.com/corporate-leadership-by-race-5114494

Lagace, M. (2008, April 14). *The Surprising Right Fit for Software Testing.* HBS Working Knowledge. https://hbswk.hbs.edu/item/the-surprising-right-fit-for-software-testing

Laldin, M. (2016, February 11). *The Psychology of Belonging (and Why it Matters)* https://www.learningandthebrain.com/blog/psychology-of-belonging/

Lee, S. (2022). *Culture fit: What you need to know.* Culture Amp. https://www.cultureamp.com/blog/culture-fit

Lee, S. (2022). *Diversity in the workplace.* Culture Amp. https://www.cultureamp.com/blog/benefits-diversity-in-workplace

Legal Scholar Khaled Beydoun Says It's Time to Finally Define Islamophobia (2018, April 2). Religion News. Aysha Khan. https://religionnews.com/2018/04/02/legal-scholar-khaled-beydoun-says-its-time-to-finally-define-islamophobia/

Leslie, L. M., Manchester, C. F., & Dahm, P. C. (2016). Why and When Does the Gender Gap Reverse? Diversity Goals and the Pay Premium for High Potential Women. *Academy of Management Journal, 60*(2), 402–432. https://doi.org/10.5465/amj.2015.0195

Letterman White, S. (2022, October 5). *Five Steps to Create a Growth Mindset Culture.* ABA Law Practice Today. https://www.lawpracticetoday.org/article/five-steps-to-create-a-growth-mindset-culture/

Lloyd, C. (2020, July 15). *Black Adults Disproportionately Experience Microaggressions.* Gallup. https://news.gallup.com/poll/315695/black-adults-disproportionately-experience-microaggressions.aspx

Lloyd, C. (2021, January 12). *One in Four Black Workers Report Discrimination at Work.* Gallup. https://news.gallup.com/poll/328394/one-four-black-workers-report-discrimination-work.aspx

Limbong, A. (2020, June 9). *Microaggressions Are a Big Deal: How to Talk Them Out and When to Walk Away.* NPR.

https://www.npr.org/2020/06/08/872371063/microaggressio
ns-are-a-big-deal-how-to-talk-them-out-and-when-to-walk-away

Lin, L. (2022). *15 Examples of Implicit Bias in the Workplace.* Manage
Better. https://managebetter.com/blog/examples-of-implicit-
bias-at-work

Lorenzo, R., Voigt, N., Tsusaka, M., Krentz, M., & Abouzahr, K.
(2020, July 17). *How diverse leadership teams boost innovation.* BCG
Global. https://www.bcg.com/publications/2018/how-
diverse-leadership-teams-boost-innovation

Luc, K. (2022). *Microaggressions at work: Recognizing & overcoming our biases.*
Culture Amp.
https://www.cultureamp.com/blog/microaggressions-at-work

Mahto, M., Hogan, S. K., Hatfield, S., & Sniderman, B. (2022, January
18). *Creating support for neurodiversity in the workplace.* Deloitte
Insights.
https://www2.deloitte.com/us/en/insights/topics/talent/neur
odiversity-in-the-workplace.html

McGovern, M. (2021, December 14). *8 ways to improve the employee
experience in 2022.* HR Morning.
https://www.hrmorning.com/articles/employee-experience-
2022/

Men or Women: Who's the Better Leader? (2008, August 25). Pew Research
Center's Social & Demographic Trends Project.
https://www.pewresearch.org/social-
trends/2008/08/25/men-or-women-whos-the-better-leader/

Miles, M. (2022, March 24). *Why Cultural Fit is Being Replaced by Culture
Add.* Better Up. https://www.betterup.com/blog/cultural-fit

Milman, O. (2022, September 21). *Indigenous leaders urge businesses and
banks to stop supporting deforestation.* The Guardian.
https://www.theguardian.com/environment/2022/sep/21/ind
igenous-leaders-amazon-rainforest-businesses-banks

Minow, M. (2021). Equality vs. Equity. *American Journal of Law and Equality*, 1, 167–193. https://doi.org/10.1162/ajle_a_00019

Mobilio, L. (2016, March 10). *Why Talent Management Matters More than You Think*. LSA Global. https://lsaglobal.com/blog/talent-management-matters-think

Mohanty, C. T. (2007). *Feminism without borders: decolonizing theory, practicing solidarity*. Point Par Point.

Moksha, J. (2018, January 19). *Multicultural Marketing: How to Avoid Cultural Appropriation and Not Market Like Someone's Racist Grandmother.* Medium. https://medium.com/@jasminemoksha/multicultural-marketing-how-to-avoid-cultural-appropriation-and-not-market-like-someones-racist-7d8e2ddc2514

Mondal, S. (2021, April 14). *What are the 4 Types of Diversity in the Workplace?* Ideal. https://ideal.com/types-of-diversity-in-the-workplace/

Montvelisky, J. (2021, August 13). *Council Post: Neurodiversity as A Strengthening Point for Your Team and Our Society.* Forbes. https://www.forbes.com/sites/forbestechcouncil/2021/08/13/neurodiversity-as-a-strengthening-point-for-your-team-and-our-society/?sh=170bef2428f9

Moss, R. (2015, March 18). *"Gang Rape" Dolce & Gabbana Advert Brings Yet More Controversy for Brand After "Synthetic" IVF Comments.* HuffPost UK. https://www.huffingtonpost.co.uk/2015/03/18/dolce-and-gabbana0gang-rape-advert_n_6893044.html

Nadal, K. L. Y. (2021, December 27). *Why Representation Matters and Why It's Still Not Enough.* Psychology Today. https://www.psychologytoday.com/us/blog/psychology-the-people/202112/why-representation-matters-and-why-it-s-still-not-enough

Nasheed, J. (2019, August 9). *A Brief History of Black Hair, Politics, and Discrimination.* Teen Vogue. https://www.teenvogue.com/story/a-brief-history-of-black-hair-politics-and-discrimination

Neeley, T. (2015). *Global Teams That Work.* Harvard Business Review. https://hbr.org/2015/10/global-teams-that-work

Neurodivergent: What It Is, Symptoms & Types. (2022, June 2). Cleveland Clinic. https://my.clevelandclinic.org/health/symptoms/23154-neurodivergent

Nisenson, L. (2021, January 12). *Caregiver benefits gaining popularity among employers.* HR Morning. https://www.hrmorning.com/articles/caregiver-benefits/

OCD (obsessive-compulsive disorder): Symptoms & Treatment. (2022, December 14) Cleveland Clinic. https://my.clevelandclinic.org/health/diseases/9490-ocd-obsessive-compulsive-disorder

Okonkwo, J. (2022). *Implicit Bias in the Workplace. Association for Financial Professionals.* AFP Online. https://www.afponline.org/career-hub/management-resources/diversity-equity-and-inclusion-resources/implicit-bias-in-the-workplace

Pub chain and insurance hub "sorry" for slave links. (2020, June 18). BBC News. https://www.bbc.com/news/business-53087790

Paradiso, A. (2020, June 15). *The Importance of Inclusion in the Workplace.* Engage Blog. https://www.achievers.com/blog/the-importance-of-inclusion-in-the-workplace

Patel, M. (2021, June 7). *Does Diverse Slate Hiring Work?* Lattice. https://lattice.com/library/does-diverse-slate-hiring-work

Paul, M. (2016, February 27). *Moving from Blame to Accountability.* The Systems Thinker. https://thesystemsthinker.com/moving-from-blame-to-accountability/

Payne, A., & Duster, C. R. (2017, April 25). *"We really f-ed this one up": Shea Moisture apologizes for ad.* NBC News. https://www.nbcnews.com/news/nbcblk/shea-moisture-ad-falls-flat-after-backlash-n750421

Peakon. (2019). *The 9-Month Warning: Understanding Why People Quit— Before It's Too Late* (pp. 1–27). https://drive.google.com/file/d/1iixtl16U4lXUcKOM4Ml-0X_pwQR9H3Ux/view

Pendell, R. (2022, September 26). *Workplace Equity: The "E" in DEI and Why It Matters.* Gallup. https://www.gallup.com/workplace/401573/workplace-equity-dei-why-matters

Percil-Mercieca, K. (2018, February 21). *Study Shows Impact of Emotional Tax on Well-Being & Productivity of Women of Color in The Workplace.* https://www.linkedin.com/pulse/study-shows-impact-emotional-tax-well-being-women-color-karlyn-percil/

Peterson, M. (2022, June 24). *Companies vow to help employees access abortion after Roe vs. Wade is overturned.* Los Angeles Times. https://www.latimes.com/business/story/2022-06-24/companies-vow-to-help-employees-access-abortion-after-roe-v-wade-is-overturned

Petrova, J. (2022). *The Many Strengths of Dyslexics.* Dyslexia Help. http://dyslexiahelp.umich.edu/dyslexics/learn-about-dyslexia/what-is-dyslexia/the-many-strengths-of-dyslexics

Poushter, J., & Kent, N. (2020, June 25). *The global divide on homosexuality persists.* Pew Research Center. https://www.pewresearch.org/global/2020/06/25/global-divide-on-homosexuality-persists/

Powell, J. A., Menendian, S., & Ake, W. (2019, May). *Targeted Universalism. Belonging.* Berkeley Othering & Belonging Institute. https://belonging.berkeley.edu/targeted-universalism

Pulrang, A. (2019, November 4). *How To Make Workplaces More Welcoming for Employees with Disabilities.* Forbes. https://www.forbes.com/sites/andrewpulrang/2019/11/04/how-to-make-workplaces-more-welcoming-for-employees-with-disabilities/?sh=54110d853d8f

Quinn, R. E., & Thakor, A. V. (2018, July). *How to Help Your Team Find Their Higher Purpose.* Harvard Business Review. https://hbr.org/2018/07/creating-a-purpose-driven-organization

Racial/Ethnic Enrollment in Public Schools. (2022). National Center for Education Statistics. https://nces.ed.gov/programs/coe/indicator/cge.

Ray, J., Weller, C., & Derler, A. (2019, January 3). *Why Growth Mindset Is Crucial to Inclusion.* NeuroLeadership Institute. https://neuroleadership.com/your-brain-at-work/growth-mindset-crucial-inclusion/

Raypole, C. (2020, September 16). *The Difference Between Cultural Appreciation and Appropriation Matters.* Healthline. https://www.healthline.com/health/cultural-appreciation

Raz, I. (2021, September 9). *5 Steps to Create a Diversity and Inclusion Action Plan.* Staffing Hub. https://staffinghub.com/diversity/5-steps-to-create-a-diversity-and-inclusion-action-plan/

Reasonable Accommodations in the Workplace. (2018). ADA National Network. https://adata.org/factsheet/reasonable-accommodations-workplace

Reiche, S. (2018, September 27). *Growth Mindset in Global Work: The Impact of the Belief of Malleability.* IESE Business School. https://blog.iese.edu/expatriatus/2018/09/27/growth-mindset-in-global-work-the-impact-of-the-belief-of-malleability/

Rekow, V. (2021, September 25). *Implementing Diversity & Inclusion Programs: How A Growth Mindset Can Help You Overcome Challenges and Win at D&I.* Neuralshifts. https://neuralshifts.com/2021/09/25/implementing-diversity-inclusion-programs-how-a-growth-mindset-can-help-you-overcome-challenges-and-win-at-di/

Resnick, A. (2022, September 12). *What Is Neurodiversity?* Verywell Mind. https://www.verywellmind.com/what-is-neurodiversity-5193463#toc-what-is-neurodiversity

Rice, D. (2022, February 3). *How To Embed Accountability in Your DEI Efforts and Why It's Critical for Long-Term Sustainability.* DiversityInc Best Practices. https://www.diversityincbestpractices.com/how-to-embed-accountability-in-your-dei-efforts-and-why-its-critical-for-long-term-sustainability/

Romansky, L., Garrod, M., Brown, K., & Deo, K. (2021, May 27). *How to Measure Inclusion in the Workplace.* Harvard Business Review. https://hbr.org/2021/05/how-to-measure-inclusion-in-the-workplace

Roy, B. (2020, February 20). 100 *Powerful Diversity and Inclusion Quotes for a Stronger Company Culture.* Vantage Circle HR Blog. https://blog.vantagecircle.com/diversity-and-inclusion-quotes/

Roy, K. (2020, July 20). *How Effective Is the Diverse Slate Approach to Hiring?* Katicaroy. https://www.katicaroy.com/post/how-effective-is-the-diverse-slate-approach-to-hiring

Ruhl, D. (2022). *Workplace Culture and Conflict.* Sscctu. https://www.sscctu.com/blog/workplacecc

Runyan, A. S. (2018, November 1). *What Is Intersectionality and Why Is It Important?* AAUP. https://www.aaup.org/article/what-intersectionality-and-why-it-important

Sackeyfio, C. (2020, February 3). *Empathy: A key ingredient in effective diversity, equity and inclusion.* Charity Village. https://charityvillage.com/empathy-a-key-ingredient-in-effective-diversity-equity-and-inclusion/

Sample, G. (2021, April 13). *How do you define authentic diversity, equity, and inclusion, and why does authenticity relating to them matter?* Cleveland Fed Digest. https://www.clevelandfed.org/publications/ask-the-expert/2021/ate-20210413-sample

Schmidt, C. (2022, March 11). *Five Ways Business Leaders Can Address Workplace Discrimination In 2022.* Forbes. https://www.forbes.com/sites/forbeshumanresourcescouncil/2022/03/11/five-ways-business-leaders-can-address-workplace-discrimination-in-2022/?sh=33b6586838ed

Schoenhoff, B. (2021, July 6). *Building a Culture of Diversity, Equity & Inclusion (DEI) at Work.* GoCo.io. https://www.goco.io/blog/building-culture-of-dei-at-work/

Semler Brossy Consulting. (2021, March 17). *Using Compensation to Promote Diversity, Equity, and Inclusion.* Semlerbrossy. https://semlerbrossy.com/insights/using-compensation-to-promote-diversity-equity-and-inclusion/

Seven exceptional examples of equity in the workplace. (2021, May 6). InStride. https://www.instride.com/insights/examples-equity-in-the-workplace/

Signs & Symptoms: Autism Spectrum Disorder (ASD). (2022, March 28). Center for Disease Control and Prevention. https://www.cdc.gov/ncbddd/autism/signs

Simms, K. (2022, February 27). *Microaggressions in the Workplace: How to Identify & Respond to Them.* Great Place to Work®. https://www.greatplacetowork.com/resources/blog/microaggressions-in-the-workplace-how-to-identify-respond-to-them

Son, H. (2019, June 21). *JP Morgan is expanding fertility benefits to help LGBTQ employees have families.* CNBC. https://www.cnbc.com/2019/06/21/jp-morgan-is-expanding-fertility-benefits-to-help-lgbtq-employees.html

Spencer, A. (2021, June 16). *Understanding Implicit Bias in the Workplace.* BizLibrary. https://www.bizlibrary.com/blog/employee-development/understanding-implicit-bias-in-the-workplace/

Stacey, C. L. (2020, October 20). *Empathy is Hard. What We Need is (Sociological) Imagination.* Contexts. https://contexts.org/blog/empathy-is-hard-sociological-imagination/

Stay Interviews. (2022). Bamboo HR. https://www.bamboohr.com/resources/hr-glossary/stay-interviews

Stern, L. (2017). Post 9/11 veterans with service-connected disabilities and their transition to the civilian workforce: A review of the literature. *Advances in Developing Human Resources, 19*(1), 66-77.

Stille, G., & Simon, T. (2022, August 31). *Make Employee Benefits Part of Your DEI Strategy.* Segalco. https://www.segalco.com/consulting-insights/make-employee-benefits-part-of-your-dei-strategy

Tapp, J. (2019, February 28). *7,500 African Americans with Disabilities Lost Jobs.* Respect Ability. https://www.respectability.org/2019/02/african-americans-jobs-2018/

Taylor, T. A. (2019, March 29). *Gaslighting in the workplace.* Medium. https://medium.com/@c0d3rgirl/gaslighting-in-the-workplace-5f44d439ca21

Taylor, T. C. (2021, March 29). *12 Inclusive Hiring Practices You Should Implement.* AIHR. https://www.aihr.com/blog/inclusive-hiring/

The Crucial Impact of Workplace Diversity and Inclusion on Engagement and Retention. (2019, July 12). The Dreamer Group. https://thedeamergroup.com/workplace-diversity-inclusion-employee-retention

The Difference Between Empathy and Sympathy. (2022, October 11). Psychiatric Medical Care Communications Team. https://www.psychmc.com/blogs/empathy-vs-sympathy

The Importance of Inclusion in the Workplace. (2022). Korn Ferry. https://www.kornferry.com/insights/featured-topics/diversity-equity-inclusion/the-importance-of-inclusion-in-the-workplace

The Survey is in: Gen Z Demands Diversity and Inclusion Strategy. (2020, October 21). Tallo. https://tallo.com/blog/genz-demands-diversity-inclusion-strategy/

Theisen, A. (2019, March 8). *Is a sense of belonging important?* Mayo Clinic Health System. https://www.mayoclinichealthsystem.org/hometown-health/speaking-of-health/is-having-a-sense-of-belonging-important

Thompson, D. (2022). What We Do Matters: Fostering Inclusion and Belonging in the Workplace. *Revista Mexicana de Astronomía Y Astrofísica Serie de Conferencias, 54,* 9–15. https://doi.org/10.22201/ia.14052059p.2022.54.02

Thompson, E. (2021, February 16). *10 tips for inclusive talent management.* Diversity and Ability. https://diversityandability.com/blog/10-tips-for-inclusive-talent-management/

Todd, S. (2022). *What is Workplace Inclusion and Why Inclusion Matters in The Workplace.* Open-Sourced Workplace. https://opensourcedworkplace.com/news/what-is-workplace-inclusion-and-why-inclusion-matters-in-the-workplace

Travis, D. J., Thorpe-Moscon, J., & McCluney, C. (2016). *Emotional Tax: How Black Women and Men Pay More at Work and How Leaders Can Take Action* (pp. 1–12). Catalyst.org. https://www.catalyst.org/research/emotional-tax-how-black-women-and-men-pay-more-at-work-and-how-leaders-can-take-action/

Tregold, G. (2016, June 1). *49 Quotes That Will Help Boost Your Accountability*. Inc Africa. https://incafrica.com/library/gordon-tredgold-49-quotes-that-will-help-you-avoid-the-blame-game

Understanding the emotional tax on Black professionals in the workplace. (2022). Bloomberg. https://www.bloomberg.com/company/stories/understanding-the-emotional-tax-on-black-professionals-in-the-workplace/

Urwin, M. (2019). *The Cold, Hard Truth About Ageism in The Workplace*. Built In. https://builtin.com/diversity-inclusion/ageism-in-the-workplace.

Valerio, A. M. (2020, January 7). *Operationalizing Inclusion: Where Strategy, Tactics, and Values Intersect*. SHRM. https://www.shrm.org/executive/resources/people-strategy-journal/winter2020/pages/valerio-feature.aspx

Wagle, K. (2017, May 6). *Equity Vs Equality: 20 differences between Equity and Equality*. Public Health Notes. https://www.publichealthnotes.com/equity-vs-equality/

Wa Ngugi, M. W. N. (2018, March 23). *What Decolonizing the Mind Means Today*. Literary Hub. https://lithub.com/mukoma-wa-ngugi-what-decolonizing-the-mind-means-today/

Waters, S. (2022, January 12). *Understanding the difference between sympathy and empathy*. Better Up. https://www.betterup.com/blog/empathy-vs-sympathy

Westfall, C. (2021, January 15). *Understanding Empathy: How EQ Can Improve Your Career Impact*. Forbes. https://www.forbes.com/sites/chriswestfall/2021/01/15/understanding-empathy-how-eq-can-improve-your-career-impact/?sh=36f26a2f400b

What Is Inclusion? (2022). Inclusive Employers. https://www.inclusiveemployers.co.uk/about/what-is-workplace-inclusion/

What Is Tourette Syndrome (Tourette's)? (2015) Cleveland Clinic. https://my.clevelandclinic.org/health/diseases/5554-tourette-syndrome

White, H. A., & Shah, P. (2011). Creative style and achievement in adults with attention-deficit/hyperactivity disorder. *Personality and Individual Differences*, *50*(5), 673–677. https://doi.org/10.1016/j.paid.2010.12.015

Whitfield, C. T. (2019, January 29). *Only two percent of teachers are black men, yet research confirms they matter.* Andscape. https://andscape.com/features/only-two-percent-of-teachers-are-black-men-yet-research-confirms-they-matter/

Williams, J. C., Phillips, K. W., & Hall, E. V. (2014). *Gender Bias Against Women in Science* (pp. 1–60). UC Hastings College of Law. https://worklifelaw.org/publications/Double-Jeopardy-Report_v6_full_web-sm.pdf

Wooll, M. (2021, July 23). *Mentor vs. Sponsor: Why Having Both Is Key for Your Career.* Betterup. https://www.betterup.com/blog/mentor-vs-sponsor

Workplace learning: Everything you need to know. (2021, June 16). InStride. https://www.instride.com/insights/workplace-learning/

Wronski, L. (2021). *Workforce Happiness Index.* Survey Monkey. https://www.surveymonkey.com/curiosity/cnbc-workforce-survey-april-2021/

Young, H. (2022, July 25). *Why sensitivity readers matter–and should be paid properly.* The Conversation. https://theconversation.com/why-sensitivity-readers-matter-and-should-be-paid-properly-183531

Zeuch, T. (2020, October 15). *Build Diversity in Leadership in These 3 Ways.* Gartner. https://www.gartner.com/smarterwithgartner/3-ways-to-build-diversity-on-the-leadership-bench

Zinn, M. B., & Dill, B. T. (1996). Theorizing Difference from Multiracial Feminism. *Feminist Studies*, *22*(2), 321. https://doi.org/10.2307/3178416

Printed in the USA
CPSIA information can be obtained
at www.ICGtesting.com
JSHW021933260923
49033JS00005B/18